MW00980539

Tales from the Gringa

¡Hola Pat and Joe!

Remembering the good times and the dominoes —

Ruth Siler

Tales from the Gringa

Ruth Tolerton

iUniverse, Inc.
New York Lincoln Shanghai

Tales from the Gringa

Copyright © 2007 by Ruth Tolerton

All rights reserved. No part of this book may be used or reproduced by any means, graphic, electronic, or mechanical, including photocopying, recording, taping or by any information storage retrieval system without the written permission of the publisher except in the case of brief quotations embodied in critical articles and reviews.

iUniverse, Inc.

iUniverse books may be ordered through booksellers or by contacting:

iUniverse
2021 Pine Lake Road, Suite 100
Lincoln, NE 68512
www.iuniverse.com
1-800-Authors (1-800-288-4677)

The views expressed in this work are solely those of the author and do not necessarily reflect the views of the publisher, and the publisher hereby disclaims any responsibility for them.

ISBN: 978-0-595-44274-4 (pbk)
ISBN: 978-0-595-68596-7 (cloth)
ISBN: 978-0-595-88604-3 (ebk)

Printed in the United States of America

To my husband Nick with love and eternal thanks for the journey and for our life together. I am truly blessed.

Contents

The Dog Days of Mexico

Juanita and the Wander Home

Preface

Welcome to *Tales from the Gringa*! This book is the true story of our adventures travelling through the western United States and Mexico in 2001 and 2002.

The journey is conveyed in four parts and from different points of view. *In October of his Sixty-First Year* is told from the Man's viewpoint; I took a chance on articulating my husband's thoughts and feelings during the first month of this epic voyage!

Tales from the Gringa continues our path into the interior of Mexico, including an unbelievable Christmas in the beautiful Patzcuaro region of Michoacan State. "Gringa" is the not so flattering term for a North American woman travelling in Latin America and I, have always considering the term in a humorous light, took it on as a description of me.

Dog Days of Mexico is the third part of the trip and invites you to experience what living in a small Mexican town is like—only this time you view it through the eyes of our dog.

Finally, in *Juanita and the Wander Home* the journey back to Canada is detailed from all of our points of view, including that of our 1984 VW Westfalia, nicknamed Juanita.

Many of us dream of abandoning our often predictable lifestyles and deep within most of us is the soul of an adventurer. We took the leap and changed our lives. I hope you enjoy the true tales that resulted.

In October of His Sixty First Year

It Began ...

In October of his sixty-first year, he decided to weigh anchor and chart his life in a new direction. The choice of words seemed appropriate given he'd spent the last forty-three years toiling in the shipping industry. Not that he had felt himself chained in any way. To the contrary—he had for the most part enjoyed the challenges and diversity of ships and cargo, seafarers and those bound to serve from shore. He would miss the fraternity. He would not miss the mid-night climbing of gangways, the interminable wait for lines tied, the telephone jangling him from deep sleep to apprise of some foul up.

The decision for change had come some months past. In a time of almost overwhelming stress, his wife had suggested that running away to Mexico could be considered a viable option. Mexico brought to mind glorious stress-free vacations and perpetual sunny skies. Perhaps he had been subconsciously mulling this over for to his surprise, he agreed. In fact, to his wife's surprise he countered her flippant suggestion with "Why not?" Sober reflection and the morning light had not provided any logical deterrent either so the wheels were quickly set in motion. The house was sold and their belongings stored. Events succeeded with dizzying speed, culminating in this moment. He found himself snuggled with his wife on a sofa bed in a friend's apartment. It was the first day of October and their second full day of homelessness.

By the second of October a twitchiness had set in; an impatience to set the adventure in motion. The endless errands were completed, friends had been said goodbye to innumerable times, and there seemed no further reason for delay. In fact his friends were beginning to laughingly question whether he was indeed going ... saying that their livers were suffering in the parting. The Man and his wife set out for their old neighbourhood to pick up the dog boarding at the vet's.

Enroute they stopped in at the local police station so that his wife could pick up the sweatshirt she had weaselled out of one of the sergeants as a perk from her City Hall job. They chatted there for a while, enjoyed a tour of the facilities and a glimpse at the undesirable living conditions for those caught opposing the law. Even at the police station they were quizzed about their delayed departure. They explained about the anticipated difficulties in crossing the border. The recent 9/

11 terrorist attacks in the United States had the further unfortunate result of snarling officialdom at all border crossings. There were reports of waits up to six hours long, and with a camper full of household goods they anticipated lengthy slow downs while the vehicle was searched and studied. The Police Chief offered to smooth their way across the border with a phone call, and the Man's wife laughingly declined the honour of so much attention and the attendant jail cell for accommodation.

They stopped in, as well, at his brother and sister-in-law's home. There too there wasn't much more to be said and they chatted about the state of the camper, the route to be taken. His sister-in-law became teary as the hugs were exchanged. It seemed an era had ended and both couples wondered what they would find in each other in six months or more.

At the vet's the pup was overjoyed to see her masters. This six month old could barely tolerate separation for a few hours, let alone days. The Man accepted her welcoming licks and continued to wonder at this, his wife's chief folly of the last year. He knew that he had often talked of taking their beloved lab/shepherd to Mexico, but this hyper, northern breed, sled dog, puppy was not in the same league at all. He couldn't help feeling that she would be a major impediment on this trip, and wondered for the thousandth time if they would not have been better off giving her away.

The dog raced, as much as possible in the confined space of the camper, between backseat and front, constantly vying for attention and to assure herself that she would not be left behind again. He snapped angrily at her to sit still, and he could feel his wife tense up in effort to keep the dog from irritating him. The wife chattered at him all through the drive to his son's place in Burnaby, as if the chatter would distract him completely from the presence of the dog. Once there, his wife loaded herself down with all the last minute paraphernalia to be left at his son's place and hightailed it for the front door. It irritated him that she always insisted on carrying so much. She did it, not to irritate him, but in an attempt to say "see how easy everything is?"

Once in the apartment, the dog ran around and again refused to settle—her puppy exuberance at freedom too much to contain. The pup had disdained the suggestion that the front lawn might prove inviting for a good long relieve, and in the midst of their drinks, decided that the rug in the living room was much more appropriate. He looked on in disgust as wife and son hastened to clean the spot—this lack of dog training was yet one more reason his heart was hardened to the dog. Yet he had agreed with his wife in the decision to keep the dog and the joint decision was meant to ensure no further complaints.

He repeated last minute instructions about bank accounts to his son, and about mail and all the paid-off bills. His wife listened and irritably commented that they had already covered this information several times. She wondered if the son would feel cast adrift or emancipated from responsibility with his father away. In any case, the telltale silence by the son spoke volumes that he would miss his father. And finally they were on the front sidewalk, saying the last good-byes and "see you soon".

The drive to the border was mostly silent, punctuated only by non-informative radio reports about traffic. They opted for the truck crossing and silently contemplated the ordeal ahead. They were experiencing that all-Canadian anxiousness of border questioning even when all was in complete order. Just prior to the border they stopped at the duty free store where his wife scurried off to build her stash of Colts Mild cigarillos for the long months ahead. And then they were in the line up to the crossing with only a few cars ahead of them. The reported long line-ups were non-existent.

As they approached the border guard, a guttural sound came from the back of the camper. The dog, out of nervousness, motion sickness or some canine flu, was heaving her guts onto the camper backseat and the floor. His wife grabbed a proffered rag and slung open the side door to clean out the vehicle as much as possible. She hobbled along side, trying to sweep out puke and retain the dog while he moved the camper along. "Lucky dog puke doesn't smell!" she called to him. Disgusting evidence somewhat stowed, she joined him in the front cab just as it was their turn.

He, for the first time in his life, handed the US border guard their Canadian passports. Inside were criminal record checks that should further prove their innocent and non-threatening ways. The guard cast a cursory glance at the documents and moved back to peak into the windows of the camper. Perhaps the task of inspection seemed daunting to him, or perhaps he was just tired after a long day. The passports were returned and they were waved through. This was the last thing they had expected, and the Man motioned toward the dog. "We have papers for the dog too." The border guard looked as if he could not care less.

They kept looking over their shoulders as if expecting a summons back as they crossed onto the highway to Bellingham. Both shook their heads and exclaimed over their luck at the easy crossing, laughing now at the dog's upset stomach. At the same time, they tsk'd over the sloppy interrogation by the border guard. It seemed no wonder there were reports that terrorists had managed to infiltrate the United States through Canada

Forty-five minutes down the highway, they turned off into a Motel 6 parking lot. He blinked at the $40 US cost and did the calculations into Canadian dollars. Certainly this was not cheap and $40 US per night for accommodation would not fit their budget. However dogs were allowed in the room, and the stress of the day had caught up. It was time to stop. His wife disappeared in search of food and came back some time later carrying Burger King bags and a cold beer. She said with disgust that Burger King's so called flame broiled burgers had been microwaved, and expensive by Canadian standards; but on the other hand, wasn't America wonderful because you could purchase a cold beer at the gas station.

The following morning he was awakened pre-dawn by the dog and they stepped out into the dim light in search of the particular spot the dog would perform her morning ablutions. On unfamiliar territory, the dog chose to spend its time sniffing rather than anything productive. This was another familiar frustration.

Washington

They stopped for breakfast in Mount Vernon, leaving the dog yapping in the camper. The Man felt better if they could sit where the dog could see them, feeling instinctively that this would help calm her. They had their Yankee sized portion breakfasts and grew accustomed to the "Uh huh" that was the American equivalent of "you're welcome".

On the road another hour later, sounds came from the back indicating the dog being sick. His wife suggested he stop by the roadside, which seemed easier said than done at one hundred kilometers per hour. They pulled off and let the dog out on the leash. The dog just seemed bewildered by the traffic and became even more so when his wife forced a Gravol tablet down her throat. "It will settle her stomach and make her drowsy," his wife claimed as they set off again.

They passed Seattle's bedroom communities and began the climb into the Snoquolmie Mountains. This, at last, was new territory for both of them. As they climbed from west to east, the typical west coast cloudy skies began to lighten with bigger and bigger patches of blue. At the Pass, they pulled into the ski village for a look and to exercise the dog. The Gravol wore off in less than an hour and she was heaving again. While he felt an innate sympathy for the distressed animal, he was at the same time again wondering just how much more this animal would impede them on their travels. He didn't know that his wife was thinking similar thoughts and wondering what could be done with the dog now … a home on some ranch?

They drove on, winding down through the Cascade Mountains. The drive up from the east side seemed much steeper than their own ascent had been. The camper showed no strain. They passed a fenced area on the right hillside and wondered whether the deer on the other side were farmed or wild.

In the valley below signs pointed toward a Roman sounding town, Cle Elum. The dog was making familiar noises and they turned into the town to find green space. Instead they wound up in a dusty parking lot on the edge of railway tracks. As soon as the side door was open, the dog was out and heaving lemon coloured bile. By this stage annoyance had turned to worry, and his wife suggested they find a vet. He had noticed one on the road into town. His wife hadn't, which wasn't surprising because when driving he noticed far more details than the average person. He grunted his exasperation at his wife questioning his sense of direction and drove them directly to the vet. A female technologist listened to their woes and telephoned the vet. A prescription was issued for some pills that the techonologist said would calm the dog's nerves and stomach, but could also result in the dog looking doped. The dog was fed two tablets and they were advised to give the pills a chance to work. They found a green spot near the river and he set off for a walk with the dog. A half hour later they motored back toward the highway only to find themselves westbound instead of east. At this rate of progress, they would be fortunate to see Mexico by Christmas. Luckily there was a turn-around a mile away and the problem was quickly rectified.

They drove the plains of Washington in the later afternoon, watching the never-ending fields. In places it spoke of rich farm country; most of the time it was dry scrub broken by occasional pine forests. They dropped through barren canyons into the hot, arid valley and the town of Yakima. They had reached their destination for the day, although it had taken twice as long as anticipated. They drove through Yakima searching out an appropriate place to stay. As he drove down the main street, his wife commented on the number of Mexican restaurants and untypical so far north, taco stands. He reminded her that this was prime fruit growing country with likely a large influx of Mexican fruit pickers. They returned to the north end of town and settled at a motel, not a Motel 6, albeit this one seemed a modicum less expensive. It was also dingier and boasted vast expanses of asphalt rather than green. But then their earlier tour of the town hadn't offered much hope of green anywhere. The dog would have to learn to use asphalt, and for the morning walk there was a scrub lot a half block away.

He paid at the office and reported to his wife that there was a laundry behind the saloon across the street. Both operations had the same owner. His wife bundled up the dog's soiled blanket and set off to do her wifely duty. He took the dog for a walk. He caught up to his wife sitting outside the Laundromat a half hour later. She offered the news that they had settled in the poor Mexican portion of town and that there was more Spanish than English spoken in the Laundromat. She tried to get some cold beers from the saloon, but because they sold liquor, they could not have offsales. She wondered at that logic: you could buy beer in a gas station but not in a bar. Of course the owners declined customers with dogs, so they sat thirsty outside in the hot late afternoon, waiting for the dog's laundry to dry.

That task accomplished, his wife suggested checking out Happy Hour at Espinoza's Restaurant next door to their motel. It seemed a Mexican kind of place and they savoured the thought of chilled margaritas. The reality was a dark and dreary bar, narrow and gloomy with desultory service, uh huh. They had a drink each then waited an eternity before being served with a second watery concoction. They wondered what was happy about the hour. The television was on in the background talking only of the aftermath of the September 11 attack and showing the same pictures over and over again. Some of the clientele were engaged in playing crib with plenty of advice from onlookers. A group of four cowboys, dressed more like railroad workers, discussed the traits of a half blind horse. A couple of middle-aged 'babes' staked out seats at the end of the bar, looking ready to cast their hooks for the night. The place was too narrow of space to engage in any kind of observations without being eavesdropped, and instead his wife told him the story of the Laundromat manageress.

The manageress was American and a newcomer to the area. Though she looked blousy and fly-blown enough to belong in this poor end of town managing a Laundromat, she claimed higher origins. She had left behind a profitable business in California, married and moved north when her husband was transferred only a few months ago. He apparently, was god and manager of a number of radio stations. She explained that her hometown offered enough heat in summer to melt pavement, but that it could not compete with the hellishness of Yakima in summer. And hell here in the north had been compounded when her new husband found himself and abandoned the marriage for the lures of his own sex. She was temporarily stuck, but in the meantime had recommended a good Mexican restaurant at the other end of town.

The dog welcomed them back to the vehicle. She didn't appreciate being left alone but was getting used to the idea that her masters always came back. Barking at the windows didn't seem to hurry the process. She settled back on the rear seat as if wondering if this ride was going to be a long one.

The Man drove through town following his wife's directions. They turned a corner, went across some railroad tracks and she pointed to the sign for the restaurant. Yakima had decided to spruce up this area in the hopes of enticing tourism. Old rail cars had been converted to shops and restaurants, with a boardwalk guiding the visitor from one to the other. Although most of the restaurants were open, there was a still deserted feel to the place. Their restaurant of choice had outdoor seating, and although the air was getting cooler, his wife suggested they eat outside. "That way the dog can sit with us," she postulated. He sincerely doubted that a dog would be allowed anywhere within the vicinity of a restaurant, but couldn't dissuade her from taking the leash and bounding up the steps. The Mexican waiter seemed to have no objection to the presence of the dog. His wife beamed at him. "See? No rules! It's just like Mexico." The dog was tethered to a chair and leapt up happily to greet everyone who passed. He and his wife grinned at each other over the way the Mexicans moved in large circles, showing fear, around the harmless dog.

He listened as his wife practiced her Spanish on the waiter. The waiter, though polite, was more interested in getting on with their drink and dinner order. They ordered margaritas and food, and a *Negro Modelo* to accompany it. "The first of the trip!" his wife exclaimed. "This truly is Mexico north." Despite his usual distaste for Mexican food, and the North American versions in particular, he found the dishes were quite tasty. He noticed that his wife ate barely one third of hers, but then that wasn't unusual, as she tended to order big and eat small. Despite knowing the predictable answer, he found himself asking, "Is that all you're going to eat?" She shrugged off his boarding school rules about cleaning one's plate and replied that she was full. She didn't feel nearly as guilty about leaving food when she was paying the bill.

They decided to find a Walmart to pick up some cleanser and deodorizer for the camper to reduce the after effects of the dog's troubled travelling. Driving through downtown they discovered that Yakima did have a nicer and more modern side. As they approached the shopping centre, the camper's coolant light came flashing on. He was a little surprised considering that the vehicle had sat cooling while they were at dinner. He dropped his wife at the store's door and urged her to be quick. After some twenty minutes of driving around looking, without success, for a place to walk the dog, he parked and waited impatiently for his wife to return. He grumbled to himself about letting her loose in a store on her own, knowing her penchant for shopping. The coolant light continued to flash, worrying him. At last she made an appearance, laughing that only in America would hunting rifles be on prominent display at the end of the toy section.

Sleep that night was fitful. Sounds penetrated of people partying, coming and going at all hours. When it seemed that he had only just fallen asleep, he felt the wet nose of the dog urging him out for the morning toilet. It was cold outside, and he tugged the dog to complete her business in the vacant lot. Back in the room he managed to fall again into a fitful sleep and didn't hear his wife leave with the dog. She returned bearing coffee. "I couldn't sleep and so decided to take the dog out so that you could. We went to the vacant lot and I was going to let her run but the place was full of burrs—watch where you step because they're stuck in my shoes. Then we went to Wendy's to get coffee and because I had the dog with me and couldn't go in, we walked through the drive-thru. Would you believe I had to argue with the girl to sell me coffee because we weren't in a car?"

They packed up and decided to head down the road before stopping for breakfast. They came to Richland, a town that seemed to live up to its name. It was everything that Yakima was not, and had an endless park that ran along the river. They found a Denny's and a cheap, large breakfast with decent coffee. The breakfast put them in a more optimistic mood.

While his wife took the dog across the street to run in the park, he pulled into the gas station and set about ensuring the vehicle was at proper levels. He pumped gas, poured oil, and checked the tire pressure. He worried still about only having one spare tire, and thought that an extra battery would be a sensible precaution as well. He mentioned his thoughts to his wife and became annoyed again when she waved off his worries. She looked at him with exasperation and asked where he proposed to put these extras when they were already so loaded down. He flashed his own exasperation at her not understanding the need to prepare for the rough roads ahead. She mollifyingly suggested that he could still make those purchases along the way.

They set out on the highway, admiring the tidy, large, green tracts of land. Richland must have gotten its name from its bountiful soil. Unfortunately they were not very far along the highway when the familiar heaving sounds started up. "I gave her a pill but I guess it hasn't taken effect yet. I'll give her another—the vet said she could handle quite a number." He held dog firmly and opened its jaws so that his wife could stuff the medication down the dog's throat. "It certainly doesn't appear to make her at all groggy," he commented. With nothing else to be done, they pulled back on to the highway and hoped for the best. Glancing frequently over their shoulders, they noticed that the dog soon succumbed to sleep. With a sigh of relief, he turned his attention to the highway, the scenery, and the buffeting from the big tractor-trailers passing them.

They climbed high onto the plateau and stopped at an overlook to see the road and land behind them. The cameras came out for the first time in the journey. It seemed as if the true holiday was beginning.

Oregon and Idaho

In the early afternoon, and just outside Baker City, the Man was alarmed by the temperature gauge a way over to one side and the coolant light flashing again. He pulled onto the shoulder and shut the engine off. "We'll have to give the engine a chance to cool off," he explained. After sitting for five minutes. buffeted by the trucks passing them, he started the motor. To his dismay the coolant light remained flashing. "We're going to have to stop," he said, and took the next exit off.

Cooling off Juanita

They found themselves on a small side road with signposts indicating Pleasant Valley. He drove on for a bit in the hopes of coming to a town and a gas station, but it seemed that the ten miles indicated might be too much for the VW. He pulled over on a wide gravel shoulder. Hoping to cool the engine down faster, he popped up the canopy and moved the luggage to the upper berth above the rear passenger bench. That done, he lifted the mattress and propped open the engine cover to allow more air to access the engine.

His wife took the leashed dog and set off for a walk. She came back about ten minutes later laughing about the burrs in the brush making it dangerous for both her and the dog to squat. He asked her if she had seen the passing train, and told her about the engineer blowing the whistle and waving at him. She hoped it wasn't during her squat.

They pulled cool drinks out of the cooler and settled down to wait. After a little while, his restlessness took over and he and the dog set off for a stroll. They had gone about a quarter of a mile when the dog started pulling at the leash, trying to get at something by the fence. He went closer to investigate and found the fence twined through a skeleton, or at least through the ribcage portion of something that might once have been human. On returning to the vehicle he offered to show it to his wife. She looked at him with mild alarm and declined. He could tell that horror was battling with curiosity. "Maybe he was murdered for trespassing," she offered. "That would make a great book."

They set off again. The camper was cooled off and her front bra-less in the hopes of letting more air at the engine. He fretted about why the fan didn't appear to be working. It was another worry to add to the list in his mind.

Around four o'clock they approached Ontario, Oregon. They cruised through the town scouting out possible accommodations and a place to have dinner. They drove to the end of town, and turned back towards the highway. It was another town without much visible character. Further along the highway they came to the hub—the great American mall complex. They spotted the Denny's first and surmised that there must be a Motel 6 nearby. They had noticed that one usually accompanied the other, much as in British Columbia if you found a Safeway, you could find the liquor store.

He tied the dog's lead to the VW bumper and humped in the luggage, and the cooler. His wife pulled a chair outside and then poured them cocktails. They sat outside sniffing the pulp mill scented air and watched the twilight colour the sky pink. His wife eventually commented that the receptionist had mentioned a good restaurant just a couple of miles away. "It's in the next state, but apparently that's just over the bridge." They reminisced about the great birthday dinner they had

had in Kellogg, Idaho (their only other previous trip to the state) celebrating his fiftieth birthday with a twenty dollar steak meal complete with wine and tumbler size martinis. This recommended restaurant, "Nick's", had the same hopeful ring to it.

When it got dark, they set off. His wife had a tourist map in hand and provided directions. When they had driven through Fruitland and were approaching the highway, she shrugged and said "Sorry, it must have been to the left." He dutifully turned around and headed back in the opposite direction. "Turn here!" she cried urgently. He passed the street indicated and glowered at her. "I can't stop on a dime you know. There are cars behind me!" Her only response was a sigh, and a muttered "Sorry" under her breath. He swung around again and went back to the indicated intersection. This led them deep into a residential district. He was getting fed up, and beyond hungry. She noticed and suggested that maybe they should go back to the hotel and just get some chicken from the fast food outlet. He pulled over and took the map from her hand. After studying it briefly, he set out again wordlessly. "There it is!" she exclaimed. Nickel's Steakhouse. "Oh oh—they close at ten and it's quarter to" and she hurried to the door. After getting the dog settled with open windows, he followed her in. The place seemed empty.

"Smoking or non?" the hostess queried. He silently thanked his wife when she replied "Non" and followed. His wife halted abruptly and said, "Sorry, changed my mind. Can we sit at this one in the smoking section?" He was about to chastise his wife when he heard and saw the back section filled with many and noisy children. "I thought this might be preferable," she said and he smiled at her. He'd take smoke over screaming kids any day.

They ordered and to his surprise his wife said all she wanted was a baked potato and salad—astonishing from his carnivorous wife. The waitress brought the requested beer and wine, and they helped themselves to the salad bar. It consisted of small town fare—iceberg lettuce, coleslaw, and two kinds of potato salad, pickled beets, pickles, Jello salad and three kinds of bottled dressing poured into ceramic containers. His T-bone arrived bloody and sizzling on a cast iron plate. There was enough meat to feed him for a week. Well, if his wife didn't want any more than two mouthfuls, the dog would be happy. Amazingly, his wife made a second trip to the salad bar but came back only with a plate of carrots. "For the dog," she said and proceeded to slip them into her purse. Sated, they paid the bill and left. The food had been OK, but not as memorable as his birthday meal and certainly a lot more than the twenty dollars it had cost them then.

They breakfasted at Denny's. That, like staying at Motel 6, seemed to be the establishing pattern. They didn't even need menus anymore.

In the early afternoon they made a stop in Twin Falls, Idaho, a pretty town, with large tree lined streets. They parked conveniently opposite a VW repair shop. He strolled over to chat with the young, hippy-looking types working on an assortment of VWs, old and new. He asked what could account for the fan not working. The young fellow said it could be a fuse, or a relay switch, or any number of possibilities. "Probably the relay" and squatted down to show him where the switch was found. He wished that it was later in the day or that they were staying in this town. It would relieve his mind to get the switch fixed. But then, according to the mechanic, it was a simple operation and he was convinced he could fix it himself. He would check it out when they camped.

They walked back towards the town in search of an Internet Café. His wife was anxious to check her email. She was waiting for her replacement to be hired and was anticipating retro pay if the individual was hired at a rate higher than she had been compensated.

There was some kind of fair going on in town and there was an outdoor restaurant advertising beer. "Here, you can wait here," his wife said and vanished. He and the dog strolled further on. There were all kinds of activities. There were stands selling crafts and homemade preserves, sausages. There was a train made of metal barrels sawn in half, weaving through the street to the delight of the young passengers. There was a band, and another beer stand. He and the dog walked on and came to a petting zoo. The dog came to an alert standstill, watching the animals. The first to notice the dog was a pig, and it came snorting toward the fence. Then to his amazement, more animals followed: miniature goats, ducks and chickens all edged the fence to get a better look at the dog. All stood stock still for quite a number of moments, checking each other out.

He bought himself a beer and found a bench to watch the goings on. He wondered how much longer his wife was going to be. She seemed to have a habit of losing track of time. The dog attracted a lot of attention. Many people approached him asking if the dog was a wolf or coyote. Eventually his wife found him and they strolled back to the petting zoo. He wanted to show her the dramatic mutual attraction between the farm animals and their dog, but when they got there all creatures showed disinterest and he was disappointed. They listened to the band a while and watched the people and then headed back to the vehicle. He called out to the VW mechanics "If I had known we were going to be here so long you could have fixed my car!"

With The Mormons

They got back on the highway and decided that they would try to get as far as Ogden, Utah. The driving seemed reasonably easy across straight plains, though the altimeter showed that they were at 5,000 feet. The engine was staying cool, though he remarked to wife again about the strangeness of the gauge that moved in a direction opposite to logic when the engine was getting hot. "Why would it move from centre to the left?" he puzzled.

They concentrated on the scenery. There were occasionally huge farming tracts but for the most part, the land was scrubby and desert like. The mountains appeared in the distance and the whole plain showed a majesty as the sun dropped lower. "Not a cloud in the sky," he said. "Do you realize that we haven't seen any clouds since we crossed the Cascades?"

After miles of silence, he turned to his wife. "Talk to me. Don't you have anything to talk to me about?" She smiled at him and shrugged. "I thought you like peaceful and quiet driving."

They began a gradual climb and he watched the altimeter inching up. Now large farmed tracts were appearing. There would be a lone house surrounded by fields, with no other habitation in sight. "What a lonely life that must be," his wife commented. "Can you imagine what it's like in winter? Or can you imagine what it must have been like for the settlers?"

They stopped at a rest area to let the dog out. It was a nice rest area with large clean washrooms, a tourist centre and marked trails leading off into the desert. The area had obviously been planned by someone who wasn't a pet owner—dogs were prohibited anywhere off leash, and were relegated to a small square of gravel, with only a fake hydrant to entice them. Both he and his wife took turns with the dog, but the dog disapproved of such discrimination and refused to leave her signature.

The road passed between two mountain ranges, each at quite a distance. The approach had led them to think that they would be going close to, or even over, one. It was amazing how the wide expanse of land distorted perspective. Soon they found themselves heading down. The number of semis increased steadily indicating the approach to Ogden. The closer they came to the urban zone, the more frequent the semis passing. Each passing truck buffeted the camper making steering difficult, more so when the semis veered in front with little regard for room for the vehicle they passed. It had been a long, tiring day of driving and he was anxious to stop. His eyes stung from the wind, the sun and the concentration and he hoped that he had eye drops in the bathroom kit.

They turned into Ogden, marvelling at the beauty of the sun shining on the mountain the town nestled against. The familiar Motel 6 sign welcomed them. Again came the humping of luggage into the room. He thought about taking just what they needed for the night but knew that inevitably that would lead to repeated trips to the camper. The motel chain was consistent in its decorating and the room looked familiar.

His wife came back from walking the dog. She reported a nice grassy boulevard in back of the neighbouring church where the dog had made a deposit. "It was Baptist, though, I think," she said. He looked at her and wondered what the significance was in regard to the dog's toilet. She continued without explanation, "The dog had a good run playing ball with some boys on the side lawn."

They watched the news over cocktails and learned there was a large Mormon convention happening in Salt Lake City. Reportedly a handful of protesters took advantage of free speech and the presence of a good number of police officers to vent their opposition to this Church. A scuffle ensued despite the five thousand to ten odds, and was quickly subdued by officers. The reporters appeared delighted, but warned people to stay out of downtown Salt Lake over the weekend. "Great timing on our part" his wife commented.

Neither of them wanting a repeat of last night's tour in search of sustenance, he picked a nearby Chinese restaurant. They drove around the block and found a Chinese restaurant with a different name a half block away. The parking lot looked promisingly full. His wife pointed across the street. "Isn't that the one we were looking for?" His wife suggested they could walk over but he felt better with car, and more particularly, dog in sight so they drove. This parking lot was empty, as was the restaurant. Everyone knows you judge a restaurant by the number of clientele … but they were led to a table anyway. His wife scanned the menu and noticed the absence of any mention of alcohol. "No beer," she said, and suggested they return across the street. He pointed out that this was non-drinking Utah and the other restaurant would likely be dry as well. "Maybe" she replied, "but they have customers."

The other restaurant proved popular and large, and did in fact offer drinks including Chinese beer. They each ordered specials, with his wife pleading for a substitution to compensate for her seafood allergy. The plates arrived with each holding enough for a dinner for three. He asked for hot sauce and was rewarded with a smile for his "*Sze sze*" response. He explained that he didn't speak much Chinese but that he had been to China on many occasions. He complimented the server on the many expensive Chinese artefacts decorating the room.

He ate everything on his platter and a good portion of food remaining on his wife's plate. She commented on how hungry he must have been and he just shrugged. He really did hate to see food wasted.

They set off in the morning with the plan of exploring Salt Lake City, finding a VW garage, and looking up their friend Utah Bill. Despite it being Saturday, the truck traffic on the freeway was nerve-racking and horrendous. They followed the signs for city centre and found themselves on wide streets absolutely crammed with people. Despite their circling many blocks, parking spaces were totally unavailable. His wife suggested they park in a restaurant parking lot and have breakfast. They could leave the car there afterwards and explore on foot. During breakfast, they discussed how to contact their friend; they had left his phone number in Canada. His wife checked the telephone directory without success. She was equally unsuccessful in contacting any of their friends in Calgary and came back to the table frustrated. They set that problem aside for the moment and ventured out into Brigham Young's world.

Two blocks away was the massive Mormon Church compound. The church spires were imposingly visible over the wall. The gate stood open to a well-sculpted garden and walkways leading to several churches. There were a lot of people waiting patiently on line outside the compound to attend some session. They were dressed in their finest, whether that consisted of suit and tie, or prim dress, or dress-up clothes best reserved for weddings and evening functions. They all clutched bibles or leather portfolios and all looked equally serious. Everywhere couples walked hand in hand, and children walked decorously beside their parents.

Speakers set about at regular intervals relayed sounds of the famed Mormon Tabernacle Choir. His wife tugged him towards the enclosure but he pulled back saying the dog wouldn't be allowed in. She confirmed this with a hostess/nun type patrolling the entryway, so they agreed to take turns looking around. He perched himself on a nearby bench to wait. The dog tugged impatiently at its leash, wanting to greet everyone.

In minutes, he handed the leash over to his wife and entered the grounds. There were two large churches, a large modern visitors' centre, and the Tabernacle building that looked more sports arena than ecclesiastical. Inside people sat on folded metal chairs intent on the service being simultaneously broadcast on a large-screen television. He noted from nametags that attendees were from all over the world. Ironically the doors of the largest and oldest church were locked.

The Mormon Temple

He rejoined his wife and they strolled the streets towards the Salt Lake City visitors' centre. They marvelled at the number of Mormons, and at the wealth of the church. The Mormons own the largest part of downtown Salt Lake City. He came out of the visitors' centre armed with pamphlets and maps of the Four Corners area they planned to explore. Few things gave him the pleasure and satisfaction of maps. His wife frequently teased him about this passion. She didn't seem to understand the sense of knowing his position in the world these afforded him, or the comfort of good navigational bearings.

Despite its rest in the parking lot, the camper responded to the key's turn with coolant light blinking. The need to find a VW repair place took on urgency. They happened on a dealership but luck was against them as the service department was closed. The salesman offered the unfortunate news that this would be the case with all dealerships as prescribed by Utah ordinance. One could, perhaps, understand the strange rules pertaining to liquor consumption but the why a car couldn't be repaired on a Saturday seemed more mysterious than the bible.

They drove back to a Sears's depot where this information was borne out. He worried about tackling the mountains with the coolant problem unresolved. His wife suggested that they check the phone book for private garages and he wondered aloud, "why bother." Her impatience bubbled over and she snapped at him to just ask for a phone book. A number of calls later, they had in fact located a VW garage open for business despite the ordinance. Still impatient, his wife seemed bent on providing directions and not wanting an argument he turned here and there as directed. Soon they were lost, and he asserted his better navigational skills. Miles further they found the VW repair shop, and although the mechanic was unable to effect the repairs, he did sell them coolant (which seemed to clear the immediate problem) and a switch for the fan.

While he had been negotiating these, his wife had borrowed another telephone directory and came back smiling. She'd located Utah Bill's phone number and address. She suggested that although there was no answer, they drive to the house to see if he was still in Utah or on his annual migration to Mexico. It seemed like a good idea except that the directions were again unclear and after much driving and snapping at each other, they found themselves facing a vacant lot. "No wonder he doesn't answer his phone!" he quipped and was rewarded with a hearty chuckle from his wife. They decided to put the twists and wrong turns of the day behind them and to settle in neighbouring Provo for the night. Tomorrow they would head for Moab, Utah and the start of their exploration of the Four Corners. This was what they had been waiting for.

They anticipated a long hard climb through the mountains and so set out early to catch the cool of the day. His wife didn't even grumble about the lack of coffee—unlike her to be cheerful in the morning. Perhaps she was trying to atone for the irritability of the day before. Surprisingly the road was gradual and straight and they found themselves on the other side of the pass within the hour. The vehicle didn't exhibit any effects from the journey. They turned off into a small town to get coffee at a gas station and heard the first shocking news reports of bombing in Afghanistan. They took the coffees to go and followed directions to a field where the dog could get a run.

By noon they were at Green River and stopped for lunch. There wasn't much to the town but Ray's Tavern offered enticing smells. It also featured an outside patio where the waiter ok'd the dog to sit with them. It was really pleasant in the 70-degree sunshine. He ordered Indian Pale Ale to go with his hamburger. The beer was incredibly good and made him hopeful for the American brewery industry. Surprisingly it was brewed in Salt Lake City. The burgers were fat and juicy and both he and his wife agreed they were the best they had ever had. His wife shared hers with the dog, which seemed to enjoy it equally. They rested in the sun, pleasantly lulled.

Red Rocks and Granite Stone

The highway approached Moab and they got their first look at the red rock cliffs that were the highlight of the area. They turned into Arches National Park intent on setting up camp and finally relaxing for a few days. There weren't many cars about, but the sign indicated the campground was full. The ranger informed them that campsites were filled up by 8:30 am each morning and advised them to return early the next day.

They drove the final twenty miles to Moab in search of accommodation for the night. Moab proved to be the tourist Mecca described in their guidebook. It was mostly one road through a town full of promising looking restaurants, gift and t-shirt shops, and private campgrounds. He glanced at his wife, knowing that her feet would be itching to explore and shop all those stores. "We'll come back later or tomorrow," he promised, wanting to get settled first.

They retreated to the beginning of town and pulled into a private campground that also boasted chalets. It would be easier to rent one of these than to go to all the bother of setting up the camper because an early start the next day was vital. He pulled in line behind some rvs and his wife jumped out to make enquiries in the office. She came back shaking her head. "They want seventy American dollars for one of those cabins, and no dogs are allowed. Not only that, but the owner seems to be a regular Nazi. He's unfriendly and full of rules about no guests being allowed, noise restrictions, do this, don't do that, and that's just from my enquiring about vacancies. Definitely not the place for us—we're allergic to that type, not to mention the money he's asking!"

They drove to the next campground along the road, Slickrock. The dog leaned out the window and barked as he and his wife went in the office. Here they were met with a friendly man who rented them a cabin for a reasonable price, showed them the pool and laundry facilities, and waved at the dog. They instantly felt at home.

The cabin was tiny but quaint. It was a wooden, one-room structure with just enough space inside for two beds. There were plastic chairs on a small, railed, wooden porch, and a picnic table below. His wife expressed delight with the place. They brought the clothes bag in and checked out the clean washrooms/

showers across the lane. They smelled satisfyingly of bleach. That done, they changed into bathing suits and gathered up dirty laundry set out for a combination hot tub soak and laundry duty.

They drove to the entrance so that the dog would be able to see them from the car; she wasn't allowed in the pool enclosure. The dog protested for as long as they were in sight, and then settled down. They had their choice of three hot tubs, so he chose one in the sun and turned the jets on. His wife quickly called out for him to turn on a different one—this one was ice cold and probably reserved for truly hot days! They lounged and stared vacant eyed at the red rock mountains around them. He felt the tensions of the drive start to slip away. They collected their laundry. He stood guard while his wife slipped out of her wet bathing suit and threw it in the drier. She narrowly missed providing a peep show to some other tourists just coming through the door.

For the remainder of the evening they sat at their picnic table and poured over maps and pamphlets. They talked about the possibilities of horse back rides, or airplane tours. Dinner consisted of drinks and a large bag of barbecue chips. They were going to cook a proper dinner but the effort seemed too much for their small appetites, and instead they turned in early.

The cabin was totally devoid of light in the middle of the night. The dog was restless again and couldn't seem to settle down. He whispered at her to lie down, but she kept poking him with that cold, wet nose. He was getting accustomed to her waking him at six each morning, but this surely was still the middle of the night. He cursed the dog and the feeble light of the flashlight as he sought clothes for the foray into the dark campsite. When they returned the dog still seemed uneasy; and sleep for the rest of the night was fitful. They were awake and fully packed by seven, heading for the national park in the chill of first light.

At the park gates they were directed to the information lodge and told to wait for instructions at seven thirty. A number of other campers pulled in, and he joined the group waiting at the locked door. All were anxious to be among the first to be allocated the potentially few campsites. Exactly on time, the door opened and a ranger beckoned them in. He explained the system of happy face symbols on the campsite posts which indicated which spaces would be free, and instructed them on completing registration forms and payment. The ranger chuckled and said "Now just because the site you want might have a happy face doesn't mean you should hassle the people into leaving. They have until ten o'clock to vacate the site and just might want to have breakfast first. There's no sense in you standing there tapping your foot while the poor fellow tries to cook his eggs." The group shared smiles, although he wondered how many had actually had it mind to do just exactly that to get the site they wanted.

The Man returned to the VW and explained the system to his wife. She had been busy reading the park pamphlet and reported that pets were very restricted in their movements about the park. "I can understand about wanting to protect the ecology … but why wouldn't you be able to take your dog on a fenced and marked path?" She dreaded the forthcoming comments about how the dog (her purchase after all) was once again keeping them from their desired actions.

They started the drive toward the campsite some twenty kilometers away, and were quickly in awe of the rock formations all around them. The shapes were fantastic, and in some places the rocks were improbably balanced. The early morning sun cast amazing shadows, and they stopped to take pictures.

Window Arch

They arrived at the Devil's Playground—the name of the campground, and drove through scouting sites. Approximately half seemed available. They picked one that offered privacy and a level parking spot for the camper and, as it was already vacant, pulled in to set up camp. They walked through the campsite to the ledge and came to a stunning view of the valley surrounded by red rock cliffs. Turning the other way, they were presented with red rock formations and blue sky. Pinion pines, offering a sense of shade, punctuated the ground. It was, without doubt, the most beautiful spot they had ever camped.

Having partially settled and feeling relieved to have a site, they decided to drive back to Moab to pick up provisions for the next few days' stay. His wife also wanted to use the Internet, and he doubted that he would be able to dissuade her from trinket shopping. He just hoped that it wasn't going to take all day. He was anxious to explore the countryside here in the park.

1800s Women Going to Market?

He stopped along the way to video the scenery. His wife, single-minded, whined about the frequent stops. He barked at her that he had come to see this part of the country and that was what he was going to do. He slammed the car door and stalked away in irritation. He was damned if he was going to let her spoil this for him. He noticed that she sulked the rest of the way but made no further protests about stops. She, as well, couldn't resist the formations that teased the imagination and got busy with her cameras.

Herd of Elephants?

In Moab, his wife disappeared in short order, intent on sending and receiving emails. He barely had time to admonish her to not take too long. She came back, frustrated that no one seemed to be responding to her messages. He diverted her with the suggestion she buy herself a t-shirt. He and the dog strolled the street, trying to find shade in the hot sun. He mustered patience.

They left the dog in the car for a quick trip into the grocery store to buy provisions and stopped at the gas station to purchase ice and firewood. Unlike their BC campgrounds, wood was not provided here and foraging was forbidden. It cost $4 for a few measly chunks so their fires would be kept small. And finally, they were able to head back to the park. He stopped at a few viewpoints on the way to the campsite. They walked what little distance they could, but it was too hot to leave the dog in the car. His wife suggested that he hike up to the window arch while she returned to the dog. He thought she was probably secretly grateful not to have to walk any further. His wife wasn't one much for hiking. She suffered from calluses on the soles of her feet that sometimes clicked when she walked on a tile floor. She claimed it was the mark of Capricorn! They were painful when hardened and she used this as the reason for not wanting to go for long walks. He noticed, however, that it didn't seem to slow her up in a mall.

The walk to the arch wasn't far. He marvelled at Mother Nature's sculpting. The shape was so symmetrical, and spoke of the eons it took to carve. Places like this humbled a person. He looked back at the camper and wished his wife were next to him to share the moment.

They returned to the campsite and watched the shifting sun cast new colours and shadows on the stone walls around them. His wife wandered to the ridge edge and called to him to witness the panorama of clouds starting to billow. The clouds began to take on dark tones and he suggested they start dinner.

He fed the bag of briquettes into the barbecue built on a stand to prevent ground fires and lit it. Once the coals turned white, his wife laid seasoned steaks on the grill. Thunder rumbled occasionally, and in the distance lightening flashed. His wife started to count, to try and measure the distance of the impending storm. She waved the tongs at him. "I don't exactly feel safe standing on top of a mountain in a lightening storm, waving a piece of metal in my hands! I think it's going to be close whether the steaks are done or the storm hits." He set the table in the camper—they would eat indoors rather than risk having dinner interrupted. Placemats, napkins, cutlery, wine glasses, a candle: it looked quite cosy.

His wife dashed to the camper just as the first splotches of rain fell. She kicked off her runners and tucked them under the vehicle. He went out and folded their chairs against the bumper. He moved the firewood to a dry spot underneath and hustled to join his wife.

The steaks were perfectly done, although the potatoes could have cooked longer. They savoured the food, the wine and the cocoon of their living quarters. Outside the storm grew in intensity. "This is very romantic," his wife nodded appreciatively. "Imagine that—we're in the desert and it's raining. What are the odds!"

The rain was flowing in torrents now. The lightening forked the sky all around them, accompanied by jarring claps of thunder. Their position on top of the mountain gave them a 360-degree view, like surround-sight-and-sound at the planetarium. They oohed and ahhed at each spectacular flash. The ground outside had been so dry that the raindrops hitting the ground sent up little puffs of red dirt smoke.

More than an hour later, the lightening flickered off in the distance and the rain reduced itself to periodic splattering. They stepped out of the camper into the clean, ozone scented air and looked for stars amongst the scattered cloud. It seemed too late to build a fire, so they washed the dishes, leaving them to dry on the picnic table for the morning's breakfast. Flashlight in hand, dog on leash, they walked in the absolute quiet of the night down the road to the washrooms and then back up the hill to bed.

He woke in the middle of the night to the sound of more thunder. He lay back on the bed and watched the lightening through the windows. This storm was as fierce as the one earlier. He glanced at his wife to see if she was awake to enjoy the show, and thought twice about disturbing her sleep. But she was awake, and nodded appreciatively at the storm before rolling over and taking up snoring again.

The morning dawned with a brilliant blue sky dotted with puffy clouds. There was a strong wind blowing and the air was noticeably cooler. He pulled his wife's shoes out from under the camper and held up the sodden mess for her inspection. "Those will never dry" she exclaimed. "So much for an inch of rain all month!" He found her cowboy boots for her and announced his intention to go for a hike after breakfast.

He packed the video camera, still camera and water bottle into his backpack and set off. The dog yipped calling to him to take her along as he set off down the road. He would explore the Devil's Garden. Again he wished that his wife shared more of his passion for walking in the outdoors. For that matter, he wished his wife shared more of his passion in general.

The battery of the video camera spent itself early into his hike and he cursed himself for not having brought the spare along. He contented himself with the still camera, focusing on the numerous arches and rock formations. The air grew warm and he shed his jean jacket. The oxygen at this altitude was thin, and despite being in good shape, he found himself puffing. He followed the myriad of trails, letting his mind wander and his thoughts concentrate only on the beauty around him, the magnitude of the silence.

He returned to the campsite in the early afternoon, well content with the morning's exploration. He relayed what he had seen, and his frustration with the video camera. His wife reported that she had walked with the dog to the other end of the campground and discovered more sites. He reminded her that he had told her about those the previous day, and asked if she had walked into the amphitheatre. He suggested that they go listen to the talk that evening. His wife strolled off to view the amphitheatre and take pictures. He caught up on reading her journal and listing impressions in his own.

As the afternoon progressed the wind picked up in intensity. It was warm enough to sit and read a book provided you sheltered in a sunny spot out of the wind. They decided to cook and eat in the camper. By the time the sun was setting, it was bitterly cold and windy outside and they decided to forego sitting in the amphitheatre. He felt sorry for the female ranger who was scheduled for the slide show and wondered if she would have any audience.

In the morning, they fuelled themselves with coffee and set off for Moab for breakfast. He insisted that his wife drive. She had yet to drive the camper and he reminded her that he was not prepared to do all the driving to Mexico. "This is the perfect road for you to get used to her," he said. "There's no traffic and a low speed limit so you can just take your time." "Sure" she replied, "It's only got lots of curves and windy hills!" but grudgingly took the wheel, determined not to let on about her fears of driving such a big vehicle.

They stopped at the post office and the pharmacy and then, leaving the dog in the car, went for breakfast at a new-age, trendy restaurant. They had variations of Eggs Benedict served at an astronomical price and with fiery home-style hash browns.

"Did you notice how there are so many bike shops in town and this is supposed to be a biking Mecca? But I didn't see any cyclists anywhere!" his wife commented. He had seen a few but decided not to argue with his wife's lack of attention to details.

Leaving Arches, the next part of their exploration took them through Monument Valley and a visit to the national park featuring stone bridges. This park proved to be a circular drive of about fifteen miles, punctuated by lookout points for the stone bridges. Again there were the restrictions on pet access. The day was cloudless but a strong, cold, wind still blew, making dawdling at the lookouts unpleasant. The bridges were granite coloured and spanned canyons and riverbeds. There were trails available to take you closer, but these involved steep hikes down stone-cut steps and were at the very least a half hour in time. It was cold, and he didn't feel any more inclined to exert himself than his wife did. So they contented themselves with the drive, following and passing repeatedly the same groups of tourists. They said "Hi" to the same people over and over again, until the stupidity of this prompted them to shrug by in silence.

They returned to the park entrance and he studied the map. He would prefer to not retrace steps but the alternate route was indicated in a broken line. He wondered how rough the "rough" road would be and decided to chance it. For miles the paved blacktop meandered through wooded areas and he supposed that the road had been upgraded since the map was printed. Then all of a sudden they approached a wide outlook and a gravel road. He stopped at the incredible view. Monument Valley stretched for endless miles below them and the highway at the bottom looked as if a child playing with dinky toys had engineered it. His wife gasped at the tiny road some two thousand feet below them.

They declined the opportunity to purchase necklaces from a Native girl staked out at the lookout and left her to dicker with some other tourists. As he approached the first switchback curve carved into the mountain face, the term "rough road" took on fresh meaning. Back and forth they wended down, being startled occasionally by a semi-trailer swerving around them at great speed on the very narrow path. There was no margin for error here, and he hoped the VW could hug the gravel on the steeper pitches. They both heaved a sigh of relief when they reached bottom, and looked back with wonder at where they had come from.

Indian Land

They drove across the flat valley floor and then climbed again slightly into hills on the other side. Around the bend they came to the San Juan River. The rock balanced upside down like a sombrero on a pillar announced they were in Mexican Hat. They checked out a couple of motels, no Motel 6 here, and settled on a reasonably priced one that allowed dogs. Their room faced the San Juan River and they were able to enjoy a cold drink on the veranda. They had the place all to themselves. The dog quickly learned that the ground was littered with burrs shaped like Japanese Ninja death-stars that attached themselves painfully to any surface. The dog knew it wasn't safe to walk, but wasn't smart enough to keep from throwing her toys off the veranda.

He explored the grounds and reported back about the nice seating area overlooking the river. They thought maybe they would sit there later. They always had the best intentions of using all the amenities any place provided.

They peered at the menu in their room and decided to try out the restaurant associated with the hotel. It was next door in the General Store. But on entering, his wife wrinkled her nose and suggested they go elsewhere. He couldn't see anything wrong with the place—it was rustic but that seemed appropriate to the countryside. Nevertheless, acceding to his wife's wishes, they drove up the road to the other restaurant they had spotted coming into this one highway "town".

The sun had set and the air was taking on a chill when they parked the vehicle. The restaurant had an indoor room, but was mostly set up outside. There was a bar, and tables, but the centrepiece was the large barbecue. This was table high and four feet by three feet in measure. Two burning logs provided cooking heat, and suspended over the fire was a grill swinging on a pulley system. The cowboy in charge leaned against a counter and kept the grill swinging lazily over the fire. He was cooking enormous steaks. The rig was ingenious as the swinging motion kept the steaks from burning, despite the flames from the logs.

A look at the menu showed that steaks, and large ones of over a pound each at that, were the main offering. His wife said that she couldn't possibly eat something that size. He glanced at her in surprise and asked her if she was turning vegetarian on him. They decided to have a beer and think about dinner, and the lady owner obligingly popped open some Buds. They struck up conversation, and he wished he were wearing his cowboy boots and hat. He felt out of place in his "civvies" here amongst the cowboys. Still, he comforted himself that he was at least wearing jeans and a denim jacket and had on his silver buckle. After a while, he slipped back to the camper purportedly to calm the dog, and came back cowboy hat on head. He joined the rest of the cowboys in their slouched stances and took part in the conversation about ranching, the cost of keeping horses, life here in the southwest.

They had a long chat about the design of the barbecue and whether it could be built on a smaller, more economical scale for camping use. They talked about marketing it, and selling on order via Internet. They talked about mules and how they were smarter and more reliable than horses; that a mule will break ice or dig to find water. Having a goat amongst your herd of cows or cattle keeps distemper down.

His wife admired the footwear of JD, the barbecuer. He was wearing a hybrid of tennis shoes and cowboy boots. The bottom half was running shoe, the upper half red leather cowboy boots. "Tenny Lamas" he said, available on the Internet. Wearing those would certainly cause a stir at the Calgary Stampede!

The owner told the Man's wife all about Navajo art, and how the cost of rugs and Kachina dolls had skyrocketed. At his wife's request she led them into her house to show off some of the prizes in her collection. The living quarters had been joined into one large room, full of beams and wooden walls. Navajo rugs, pottery and Kachina dolls decorated the space. "You could start your own museum!" his wife breathed with awe. Back outside they met the Native dishwasher who had served at the restaurant for half of his twenty-eight years. He was a quiet, shy man-boy but his eyes lit up and he became animated when the baskets he had woven were admired. He had been taught by his grandmother, a recognized Navajo artist, and spoke of the time it takes to gather the right kind of willow, the natural dyes, and the two weeks weaving labour it takes to fashion one basket.

Finally, six beers later, the party broke up and everyone said their good nights. It had been a memorable evening, despite what he considered weak and tasteless beer. He had missed dinner, but decided the morning's breakfast would compensate.

In the morning, as he re-stowed the camper and his wife took a bath, the dog took advantage of their turned backs and set off to explore on her own. When they noticed her absence, she was out of sight and apparently out of earshot. He worried that she might have found her way to the dangers of the highway and set off to find her, calling and whistling. About ten minutes later his wife called out to him from the veranda. From the other side came the dog, grinning and well pleased with herself for her self-proclaimed freedom, limping though, with the burrs embedded in her paws. He and his wife breathed a sigh of relief. All safely in the camper, they set off for breakfast in Arizona on Navajo land.

They drove across dusty plains with mesas and points of rock heaved up millions of years ago to break the monotony of the landscape. Occasionally they spotted horses grazing amongst the cactus scrub and sparse grass, or the odd steer. It didn't look as if this land would provide much sustenance of any kind. Yet this was the tract of land the Navajo and other Indians had been herded onto—the Big Rez they called it.

Soon they came to the town of Kayenta. It was set in the plain but with some rocky hills not too far off. With few exceptions, the houses were all small box like shapes with only the colour of the outside walls to differentiate each from its neighbour. The bright blues, oranges and yellows had faded some in the repetition of harsh winters and sweltering summers. Wherever there was an open field, so too there was the shell of a car broken down and abandoned. This was apparently a trademark of reservations everywhere.

The Blue Coffeepot Coffee Shop stood along the highway on the edge of a substantial mall. The presence of the shopping emporium seemed in sharp contrast with the little the locals owned, but there were quite a number of cars in the parking lot. The Blue Coffeepot was doing a brisk business as well. Although it was after ten in the morning, the majority of the tables were full. The clientele were all Indian and of varying ages. The little girl with her mother at the next table could have been a poster child with her dark skin and blushed cheeks, the dark sombre eyes offset by the fountain like pony tail sprouting gaily from the top of her head.

The coffee shop itself was built round and domed, reminiscent of the traditional Navajo hogans. But where the hogans were dark and claustrophobic with the only light shining in from the roof vent and door, here were open beams set with a skylight at top. The menu informed that blue coffeepots were amongst the first items the whites had traded and became symbols of friendship.

Over breakfast they studied their map, planning the day's adventures. The map listed Fort Apache in the write up but they could not locate the marker on the map itself. He and his wife were both puzzled what Fort Apache would be doing here in Navajo territory and wondered if it wasn't some touristy kitsch dreamed up to drum up tourist dollars. His wife asked a passing Navajo waiter about it, and they learned that it was two hundred miles south towards Phoenix, in Apache land. They supposed it was listed on their map to lure them south, but unfortunately it was in the opposite direction of their proposed route.

They set off down the secondary highway to visit the Navajo Monument, and to get a first hand look at how the Indians of old had lived. They climbed into countryside of granite cliffs and pine, areas that reminded them of parts of British Columbia. Finally they arrived at the monument site. The ranger advised that normally one could hike to the settlements, but they were closed for the season. His wife expressed doubt that they would have hiked in any case: it was a considerable distance away, down and around cliffs, and typically dogs weren't allowed. Besides that, it was blustery and cold again. They contented themselves with looking at the artefacts in the visitors' centre; his wife bought a t-shirt and a book for her mother and they resumed their journey.

About mid-afternoon, and a half hour from their destination of Canyon de Chelly, he abruptly pulled to the side of the road. His back hurt so that sitting was uncomfortable, and he felt so bone weary that he thought he could fall instantly asleep. His wife looked at him in alarm, fearing an impending heart attack. He reassured her that it was only his back and too much driving, that he would rest a few minutes and be fine. She noted that he didn't appear to be pasty in colour or sweating, and let him be. She put the dog on the lead and walked back along the highway boulevard a ways, hoping to entice the dog into a good long pee. No luck there. She returned to the car and offered to drive, but he assured her he was fine for at least another half hour.

They reached the Canyon de Chelly Park and discovered that camping was free. They looked at more artefacts in the visitors' centre, and watched part of a movie on the settlement of the area. His wife dropped some money into the donation box in appreciation of free camping, but he couldn't see how much. He donated dollars of his own.

The Park was organized into two loops of road that took the visitor around the various viewpoints to see past and present settlements. They went past horses tethered under trees with signs advertising horseback tours. Neither of them mentioned them, both sensitive to the presence of the dog and that this would negate any riding. They scouted out the large, open campground and assured themselves that there were plenty of spaces available. They carried on and took the first loop of the park road. The first lookout provided a view of a farmed settlement below in the Canyon itself. Of more interest, at least to his wife, were the art goods set out for sale on the sidewalks. They admired some of the pottery, and thought about buying a vase. The artist was in the back of covered small pickup, glazing additional pieces. She freely answered questions about the pottery, made by her and her husband, and about the silver jewellery made by her and/or her nephew. His wife, unable to resist further, bought an earring cuff, and a pair of earrings shaped like howling coyotes. The cuff, she said, was a novelty. The coyotes reminded her of their dog.

He picked up a vase and asked whether his wife thought it would make a good purchase. "Go ahead" she said but seemed unenthusiastic. Having watched her mother painstakingly hand decorate pottery, she thought the slap-dash way this vendor was dabbing on glaze probably meant these pieces were mass-produced elsewhere.

They decided to postpone the rest of the tour until the next day and drove the few miles back into town for groceries for supper and breakfast. The grocery store was a hybrid of a large American grocery store, K-Mart and a Mexican super-*mercado*. You could buy virtually anything there—from steaks to hardware—with the exception of liquor. Liquor is prohibited on Indian Reservations, and the Canyon de Chelly, although in Arizona, is still part of the Big Rez.

They returned to the car, bags in hand, and looked at each other.

"Felt strange in a way, didn't it?" his wife enquired.

"Yes" he answered. "I noticed we were the only white people in the place!"

Back in the park, they picked out a site near one edge of the campground. Other campers were at a distance and there was a field where they hoped they could let the dog run. In the meantime, they put her on a long lead tethered to the bumper and busied themselves setting up home for the night. A trio of dogs, belonging to the ranchers in the area, approached bringing whines of delight and frustration from their pup. The dogs looked reasonably well fed and friendly. The local mutts simulated play and let their dog dance around and over them, while they circled in steadily. Finally, the leader of the pack pounced on their dog's bone and with his intended prize in mouth, ran off followed by the others. They kept coming back later, but the Man and his wife shooed them off realizing that they had no intention of playing with a camping dog and only wanted to distract her from her food so that they could grab and run.

His wife was tending the barbecue and noticed a grey housecat approaching. The cat seemed as fearless as the Indian dogs. It took a few moments for their dog to notice the cat, but as she approached the cat's back arched and the warning hisses were loud. His wife asked him to restrain the dog, as she offered the cat a piece of sausage. The cat rewarded her with a sharp claw to the hand, batting the offered meat. "Well aren't you just the most ungrateful puss," his wife snapped, but offered the feral cat another piece just the same. The cat was cautious, but fearless and they watched her jump into the camper to look for more food. Worrying about the dog getting a bloody nose, or worse, a scraped eye, they eventually chased the cat off as well. After dinner his wife took the dog to the open field and let her loose for a run. However, with all the stray dogs about, and not knowing how the pack might react to the stranger in their midst, she soon returned and retethered their dog on her long lead.

They woke in the middle of the night to a howling wind. The wind was so fierce that the camper rocked. He lay awake for quite a while listening to it and wondering what the morning would bring. If the wind didn't abate, they would have to spend another day here at the campsite because there was no way he would attempt to drive on a highway across the desert in such a gale.

The sun was out in the morning, and the gales had stopped. The wind was still brisk, but not enough to stop them from travelling on. It was cold once again, and after a hurried breakfast, they broke camp and were on their way.

Hubbell Trading Post, Arizona

Whether it was the fitful sleep, or the many days travelling, they were not of a mind to explore the area further. They turned back onto the highway and headed for Albuquerque. They were out of the scenic rock formations, and getting closer to the border. All of a sudden Mexico didn't seem so far away and they were growing more anxious to get there.

Their road took them past the Hubbell Trading Post, oldest continuously operating store in the west. His wife naturally insisted that they stop. "Anything for a shopping trip!" he teased her. She pointed out that she had been well behaved thus far and had in fact done extremely little shopping. "And remember that," he said. "There's no room for any more stuff in the camper."

The trading post didn't seem to have changed since its inception. The rooms were crowded with foodstuff, materials by the yard, bridles, guns, blankets, shoes, Indian baskets, and jewellery.

They marvelled at the artistry of the Navajo blankets, and marvelled more at the price tags. One "blanket," about the size of a placemat, commanded $600. Something that might actually be useful as a blanket ranged from $3,000 and up.

His wife picked up a belt made of silver disks. "I used to have one of these. I bought it a flea market for 50 cents. I don't have it anymore because it long since stopped fitting. This is priced at $300 US!"

Ever mindful of her sore feet, his wife turned her attention to finding a pair of moccasins. She tried on innumerable pairs, but sorrowfully had to put them back. They were all either just too big or just too small. Finally she gave up, and he was able to lead her out and back to the car.

Not long after crossing the Arizona-New Mexico border, they left behind the two lane highway and found themselves again on a divided highway with semis roaring past. The land was flat and scrubby, and the mountains faded away to their right. The licence plates read "Land of Enchantment" but there wasn't any truth to those words on this road.

For about the last fifteen miles he had noted the billboards advertising the largest store to buy Indian goods to be found this side of Albuquerque and he knew that he'd be making a stop soon. It turned out the "trading post" was smack on the Continental Divide, and the side road was historic Route 66. He told his wife to be quick about her shopping, and he and the dog wandered around. They examined the tourist attraction next door, and he straddled the Continental Divide.

She came back carrying a bag and beaming. "I found really great moccasins, and a belt.!" He was pleased for her, but happy to get away from shopping. His response was a shrug and a grunt.

They left the highway at the turn-off indicating downtown Albuquerque and found themselves again on Route 66. It lead through a poor side of town with back-to-back motels that had seen better days and better clientele. As they neared town, these gradually improved, and they noticed one that proclaimed to have been in business since the 1920s. It didn't look as if much redecorating had happened in the intervening years either. They decided to find a tourist office and soon he was enmeshed in rush hour. Somehow, just following the flow, they ended up downtown and he waited in the parking lot while his wife scouted out the tourist office.

"What a sour biddy they have working in that place! Why people like that work in the hospitality industry is a mystery." she exclaimed when she returned. "And guess what? The world famous International Balloon Festival is on this weekend and the biddy implied that we don't have a hope in hell of getting a hotel room. The Balloon Festival is up by the northeastern part of town. I asked her about the historic district and she didn't know anything about it. I've got a map anyway, and if everyone's at the Balloon Festival then maybe the historic district will be empty."

His wife called out directions from the map and they found themselves retracing their earlier route. They found the historic district and thought it would be a nice area to explore after dinner. He pulled into several motels and waited while his wife checked out rates and dog approval. She came out shaking her head each time—too expensive, no vacancy, and no dogs. After the last one, she suggested she try the original Route 66 motel; the sign now seemed more alluring, and the motel was kitty corner from where they were.

She came out of the office brandishing a key and directed him to room 11. He couldn't pull all the way into the carport because the camper roof wouldn't clear. They opened the door on a basic 1940s motel room—but it was clean and it was only for one night. "They don't allow dogs, but the young guy took pity on me," his wife reported. "The incense in the office, which is part of their living quarters, would choke a dying horse. But they seem to be veddy, veddy nice people" she went on in a poor imitation of an East Asian accent, wagging her head

After a quick and successful loo trip to the far end of the parking lot, they tethered the dog so that she could come and go through the open door. There wasn't much room left to navigate around the furniture. He settled on the bed, and his wife sat by the open window as they watched the news. They talked about diverting their trip to visit Santa Fe. The tourism magazine and all they had previously heard made it an appealing prospect and being so close, it seemed a shame to miss it. His wife waggled the tourism brochure and said she would organize the hotel. "This weekend will be my treat. We'll find a doggy day care for the pooch, and we'll live it up."

He listened to her on the phone. She hung up several times grumbling about the 1–800 numbers not working, and wound up using up her calling card. He kept asking her how much the hotels charged and balked at the prices. "No way we're spending $300 on a hotel," he exclaimed.

"No we're not, but just you never mind. We're going to Santa Fe and it's my treat, and I want to stay in a nice hotel. But I'm not rich nor stupid." In the end she reported that her hotel of choice advised that they could get the best rate just walking in. A couple of more phone calls, and the dog had a hotel to stay in as well.

It was getting to be around 8:00 pm so they drove the few blocks to the historic district to find a place to eat. The buildings were clustered around a leafy square, framed in by an old church. The shop windows held an appealing array of artwork, tourist junk, clothes and postcards. Though the windows were lit up, almost three quarters of the places were closed. "Strange, don't you think considering there's a big festival in town?" his wife expressed her disappointment.

"I guess everyone must be at the balloon sites, and it is late in the year," he responded with a note of relief in his voice. He could just imagine spending an hour or two marching in and out of stores that bored him beyond belief. Still, he allowed himself to be led around for a while and agreed that the vase his wife was purchasing was pretty and unique. It was fired with horsehair mixed in the glaze to provide an interesting pattern.

It was getting late and he suggested that they better eat while the two available restaurants were still open. He checked on the dog in the camper and was content to find her asleep.

Both restaurants offered southwest cooking and he grumbled. Except for the occasional taco, he didn't much care for Mexican food and he liked the Americanized versions of it even less. Still, there was fried chicken offered and his wife insisted that Southerners were famous for the way they prepared that. They were led through a series of rooms to a table. Next to them a tree was growing through the ceiling. The restaurant had once been someone's mansion, and the room they were in had formed a part of the courtyard before it was roofed in. Whatever the food might bring, at least the place had atmosphere.

He ordered a margarita from the waiter and waited while his wife dithered over what to drink. He convinced her to try the house special cocktail even though it was priced at ten dollars. The waiter insinuating that one would put her under the table was enough of a dare that his wife agreed. The drinks came and they ordered dinner. They waited a long time and heard a crash then the hoots of laughter from the other servers. Their young and earnest server came to them red-faced and explained that he had just dropped the platter with their dinners. The wait would be longer, and his wife suggested free drinks as compensation. The waiter obliged with a free beer for the Man, but didn't bring another drink for his wife. It must have been his dinner that had been dropped. The dinner, when it finally arrived, was delicious. Maybe he would become a fan of southwest cuisine after all.

He woke in the morning and found himself alone. He had just come out of the shower when his wife returned with the dog and coffee. "Oh my god, what happened to your face?" she exclaimed at the sight of his bloody eyebrow.

"The dog was getting sick in the middle of the night, probably from all the plaster she chewed," pointing at a corner. "I got her onto the tile bathroom floor in time, but cracked by head on the dresser straightening up. I bled like a stuck pig but it's OK now."

"Poor baby," she commiserated, "at least the cut is hidden by your eyebrow. You're lucky you didn't poke your eye."

They set off for Santa Fe. The traffic on the freeways was light, and they approached the turn-off to the boarding kennel within an hour. The girl at the desk didn't seem at all bothered by the cacophony of howling and barking behind her. She assured them that the dog would be quite happy to socialize through the pens with the other dogs, and they paid the extra for the exercise program. If they were going to have a first class hotel for the weekend, then the dog would get first class treatment as well. They handed over dog, leash, dishes and toys, and assured the dog they would be back tomorrow.

Their first impressions of Santa Fe delighted them. It displayed the distinctive rounded stucco architecture of the southwest and strung the buildings together through a series of winding streets and alleyways. The place bustled and they were anxious to explore. They found the La Fonda Hotel, immediately off the main square. His wife explained that she chose it because it was on the main square, had a pool and hot tub and first class service. Unfortunately, the first class service didn't start with the receptionist.

His wife enquired if they had a room available and was assured that they did. It could be had for Two hundred eight dollars a night. His wife said that she had been told of a lesser rate on the phone and the girl obligingly reduced the rate to one hundred eighty dollars. "No," said his wife. "The guy on the phone said that it was one hundred fifty and might even be less when we walked in."

"Whom did you talk to?"

"I don't know his name, but it was last night and it was a guy."

"Then I suggest you phone and make a reservation."

"That's idiotic. Why don't you call the staff that works the reservation phone and ask one of them?."

"That's not the way it works. You can go and phone from the house phone right there."

He followed this exchange and watched his wife getting more agitated. This was not a good sign and he knew her well enough to know that she was one step short of ballistic. Already people were turning around to look towards the desk. He hated this kind of scene. He was about to tug his wife away and suggest they could stay at the Best Western at the entrance to town when, thankfully, another woman stepped in to take charge. She called up and confirmed that 'Chris' had indeed quoted the lower rate. "Sometimes they don't tell us about specials," she murmured apologetically. There room would be ready at two o'clock.

They went to park the camper in the suggested lot next to the cathedral around the corner. A sign indicated the lot was full but just as they approached, the gatekeeper waved them in. A spot had just been vacated and they took this as a providential portent toward their weekend.

They loaded up with cameras and set off to do their tourist thing. The cathedral doors stood wide open and seemed the likely place to start. The church was old, beautifully maintained, and well used. There were quite a number of tourists wandering in hushed tones, but the pews also held a number of supplicants. The cathedral boasted a large organ and the organ master was warming up. The sounds filled every nook of the church and the Man settled into a pew to listen. He felt a sense of peace and contentment, and took great joy in listening to the organ—it was one of his favourite types of music.

They meandered through the streets, admiring the buildings and enjoying the sunshine in the squares and gardens. His wife darted into stores here and there, and occasionally he would step in for a brief look. She was particularly enchanted by the wreaths made of chilli peppers and took a photograph of a rack filled with the drying red spices.

They returned to the hotel a little early but their room wasn't ready yet. His wife had booked an appointment to get her hair cut and she hurried off. He would check in and would meet her later in the lobby bar at three-thirty.

He checked with the concierge about places to eat, and walked down the street to make a dinner reservation at Julian's. He meandered about and returned to the hotel. He picked up the key and retrieved the luggage from the car. It was only about a block away but in the mid-day sun it was hot work. He felt he'd earned a treat and headed off to the bar for a cold beer.

Though it was barely mid-afternoon, the bar in the lobby was doing a bristling business. He pulled up a stool at the bar and asked the bartender for the types of beer available. He settled on one that sounded micro brewed and was appreciative of the frosted glass. He watched the goings in the bar and in the lobby where a wedding party was gathering. Occasionally he glimpsed at the television showing American football, which didn't interest him in the least. Yet again he wondered why so many people were captivated by it when he felt the Canadian version was so much better.

Chiles in Santa Fe

He chatted with the bartender about Santa Fe, and soon the man sitting two stools down joined in the topic. He felt a tap on his shoulder and turned to see his wife sporting her new hairdo. It didn't look much different from when she left, just tidier. "I like it," he dutifully said. She plopped down on the bar stool next to him and asked the bartender for a Jack Daniels and ginger ale. The bartender returned shortly with another beer for him and a dark drink for his wife. "Ginger ale," she said, "not coke." The bartender apologized and poured her another drink. "I guess I'll drink that one myself," the bartender said, but left the drink in the tip well.

The man on the neighbouring barstool introduced himself as Henry. Henry seemed intent on joining in their conversation. His wife flicked an annoyed glance at him but said hello. They exchanged a few pleasantries and she subtly turned her back towards Henry.

Ignoring Henry, his wife pulled up a bag from the floor. "I bought you a present."

"Shopping, shopping, shopping," he teased. "Can't leave you alone for a minute. This one was born to shop." He aimed the last comment in the direction of Henry's male, understanding face.

His wife ignored the remark and handed him the bag. "Listen buster, I walked a long way for that so you better be nice."

He pulled a white denim shirt out of the bag. "It's nice, but I wanted blue." The words popped out. His wife grimaced. "Well we can exchange it later then. I thought you ripped your white one."

Henry broke into the conversation and asked where she had bought it. "I hope you didn't pay too much for it; the stores in town charge a fortune for everything."

"No," she replied frostily, still annoyed at the intrusion to their private conversation. "I walked to the mall and it was quite reasonable."

"The mall!" Henry exclaimed. "She did walk a long way—that's about two miles from here!"

"Sweetie, you walked all that way for me?"

"And back," she replied. "But I bought myself a present too" and showed him her new watch with a silver band inlaid with green stones. "A severance gift from my last employer," she laughed.

The bartender returned and asked after their drinks. The coke concoction was still there and his wife said she might as well drink it. "It doesn't taste too bad when it's free," the bartender winked. There seemed no dodging conversation with Henry and they chatted a bit longer before his wife again turned her back. His wife asked what their room looked like, and expressed her appreciation for bringing in all of the luggage. They said their goodbyes to Henry and the bartender, and walked into the lobby. A mariachi band was warming up and they waited to watch the band escort the bridal party up the stairs to the ballroom. It looked to be a very posh wedding. They had talked to the father of the groom earlier and now remarked that maybe he had looked so pale at the thought of the wedding cost.

On the way to the room, he teased his wife that the room was "OK." He opened the door and grinned at her reaction. The room was large and high-ceilinged. The king-size bed didn't diminish the proportions. She cooed with delight at the Spanish style furnishings and the silver accessories. Her delight grew at the size of the step up bathroom with enormous tub.

They enjoyed the room for a while and tested out the bed before heading off to find the hot tub and pool. The hot tubs were in a bright space lit by skylights, with doors leading off to the deck surrounding the pool in the courtyard. Even though the afternoon had cooled off appreciatively, the pool water felt warm enough after a good soak in the Jacuzzi. They had the place to themselves. He went into the locker room and weighed himself and came back pleased. She went into the male locker room to weigh herself and came back saying the scales were accurate.

Back in their room, he was ready for a nap but his wife insisted that they go to the roof bar to watch the sunset before dinner. They rode the elevator up and discovered the bar was outside, where a hearty wind was blowing. The small space was packed with a shivering crowd equally determined to enjoy the view. They talked with a couple at the adjoining table who divided their time between their homes here in Santa Fe and in Denver. The man owned his own plane so the travelling wasn't difficult. They in turn told of their plans to travel to Mexico, and that they had sold their home. "Homeless, jobless and cell phoneless!" he explained.

The bar closed as soon as the sun set and his wife said she knew of a western bar they could go to for a margarita before dinner. It was supposed to be in the Governors Palace on the square, but they walked right around the block without seeing anything resembling it. His wife stopped to listen to a man giving directions to other tourists and asked him if he knew the place. The man recognized the name of the bar and started to walk with them but he explained that it was a piano bar, upscale, and now doing show tunes. They expressed disappointment and their guide said, "I know just the kind of music you're looking for. It will be playing right here at the Ore House starting at nine tonight. The couple that play have opened for the likes of Ian Tyson and Lyle Lovett. I'm Pat, their road manager."

They went upstairs to the bar/restaurant and studied the menu that listed an extensive list of margaritas and martinis. The place had a good feel to it and they promised themselves that they would return after dinner to listen to the music. After one drink, his wife urged them to be off to the restaurant. He knew they were early but she didn't seem to be listening.

At Julian's they were told that it would be a half hour wait, which would put them right on schedule for their reservation. His wife was puzzled and he chided her for not paying attention to him. "Oh well," she shrugged "we'll just have to find another bar." They walked up half a block and found a promising spot. The bartender mixed her his specialty, a Lemonberry Coke. She looked sceptical but smiled after tasting it. The man tried it, and though a little to sweet for his taste, agreed it was not bad. "Lemon Bacardi, cranberry juice, and a splash of coke. I'll have to make that for our gang back home."

Santa Fe Sculpture

They returned to the restaurant and were seated promptly. The Italian restaurant had warm, apricot walls, and twinkling lights in the potted plants. The air was filled with good smells and soft chatter from the full tables. "Very nice," his wife murmured, "great choice.". She read on the menu that Julian's was originally set in Telluride, Colorado and she exclaimed that it was famous; that she had read about it in books. They ordered a bottle of wine and enjoyed it with their sumptuous dinner. To his amazement, his wife devoured the duck and polenta on her plate, leaving the platter as clean as his. The salad with mustard vinaigrette, the veal picatta with roasted potatoes had been excellent. "I have never tasted anything so good!" and he had to agree. They commemorated the moment by asking someone at the next table to take their picture.

They strolled back towards the promised music, pausing to admire pottery in the store windows and the incredible statuary scattered throughout Santa Fe. The town planners were very clever in their placement of these works of art, ensuring that the sculptures looked natural. In a school field, life size horses pranced, near a tree a bear reached up for a scratch, in other places children played.

At the Ore House they found Bonnie and Bill performing outside on the balcony. Heat lamps ensured comfort. They nodded hi to Pat who smiled back. The music was western and catchy. The couple playing were elderly, Bonnie on keyboards, Bill playing guitar. He had thick spectacles, and she was blind. Neither was bothered by the handicaps. Both had good voices, and if they faltered on a song, both laughed. Bonnie said she and Bill had been playing together for all of the thirty-two years they've been married and certainly knew the songs of by heart. They were still writing music, and the chemistry between them showed. The music prompted his wife to get the Man to dance and they two-stepped awkwardly between the closely placed tables. Amazingly, the couple played their last tune at only eleven o'clock and the soundman explained that was because of Sante Fe's bylaws. They bought two CDs, intending to send one to their friends in Calgary, and had the CDs autographed.

Not wanting the evening to end, they headed into their lobby bar for a nightcap. They were delighted to find a band playing good ol' fashioned rock and roll. He wanted to sit up close to the band, but his wife insisted on the quieter seats at the bar. There were a number of couples on the dance floor doing the two-step or jiving and they seemed almost professional. His wife wanted to dance, but he didn't want to look foolish against this competition and so declined. She shrugged and turned back to talk to the lady bartending. Out came the camera again and his wife and the bartender took turns taking pictures of each other. "I need one to send back to work to show them what an ex-clerk looks like!"

The band ended and the evening seemed too young to be over. The bartender suggested they might still find live music at the Catamount. This was the Lemonberry Coke bar and they tripped down the block. The downstairs of the bar was closed and upstairs they found a quiet room with a few customers shooting pool, but no music. Disappointed, they agreed to call it a night and returned to the hotel.

They woke late; too late for breakfast in bed. They went downstairs and he lugged their bags to the car while his wife checked out. He met her coming down the hall a little later saying that the restaurant wasn't serving breakfast or anything else as it was now after eleven. It was too late, as well, to take the city tour they'd planned on. Instead they drove to the mall where he bought a blue denim shirt and then, after brunch at a Sunday-crowded Denny's, headed off to the boarding kennel to pick up the dog.

The dog came out bouncing and jumping off the ground in her excitement to see them. The girl assured them that the dog had behaved herself and there were no problems. Pooch didn't look any worse for the wear, just exuberant from finding herself not abandoned. They got in the camper and the dog kept trying to worm herself into their laps, as if to say 'don't leave me again. See how loveable I am!' and they were both happy to have her back.

El Paso was still a good five hours drive from Santa Fe, and they decided to camp for the night at the State Park at Elephant Butte. A few miles from the turn-off they spotted a car on the shoulder with hood raised, and pulled over in response to the man waving. The stranger spoke broken English and said that he and his brother had run out of gas, and could they pick up his brother walking down the road. A little apprehensive, they picked up the other man and offered him a lift to the next turn off. The Indian/Mexican settled in the back with the dog constantly trying to jump into his lap. He seemed equally nervous, and kept pointing at the turnoff and where the gas stations were. They stopped to fill up and he jumped out with relief, offering thanks and unaccepted gas money for the ride.

The State Park had campsites placed along a ridge overlooking a large lake. The picnic tables were bolted down in solid, three-sided and roofed shelters filthy with bird droppings, dead bugs, and litter. They decided they would take their meals in the camper. The view was pretty but the vehicle area was cordoned off from the view by bollards. He left his wife and went back to register for the evening. When he returned, she suggested that he could drive between the bollards up onto the level ridge. They fit, just, and as there didn't seem to be any rangers around, he figured they would be all right for the night

He and the dog skidded down the sandy slope to the edge of the lake. The lake water was warm and people at the other end were swimming and water ski-ing. There were no people around this spot. The dog ran at her greyhound speed enjoying this unfettered freedom. He chased her and threw sticks trying to get her to swim. She wasn't a water dog, but was certainly appreciating the beach. She was a pleasure to watch. All of a sudden, the dog stopped and hackles up, started barking. She was trying to look fierce and he was amused to see that she was arguing with a log. He laughed at the dog and waved up the ridge to see if his wife was paying attention.

He returned to the campsite and joined his wife in their camp chairs set out for watching the sunset. For her entertainment and theirs, the dog flipped her stuffed animals around, shaking her head so vigorously she seemed in danger of whiplash. Inevitably, one of the stuffed animals landed on the roof of the shelter. Despite his wife's protests to leave it, he managed to scramble up onto the roof to retrieve it. Stuff like this made him feel like he was ten years old again, and he dropped back to the ground well satisfied with himself.

A relic of a big Chevy cruised by several times, stopping periodically just a few yards away. Something about it raised the hairs on the back of his neck. He pointed it out to his wife, and she agreed that there was something strange about it. They felt an uneasy twinge at the loneliness of the site and the lack of rangers. He told himself he would sleep with the fish bonker close at hand.

They had a dinner of barbecued chicken from the local IGA, and then walked down the hill to the washrooms. The old car had finally parked down the hill near a boat, and they were both relieved to see a woman. They decided that it was a group who just didn't want to pay the camping fees and so had kept driving around until the sun had gone down and there was no risk of rangers. Breathing easier, they returned to their site and built a campfire. They had been carting the wood with them since Moab and it would be good to free up the space. The night was clear and warm, and they sat a long time sipping liqueurs and gazing at the incredible star-studded sky. They talked about their travels, and how the stars at this latitude were in a different position from home.

The next morning, after giving the dog another run on the beach, he built the fire up and set the grill to cook breakfast. It was a beautiful cloudless morning and the sun had risen not too long ago. He settled in his camp chair, spatula in hand. Cooking breakfast like this was surely one of the best things in life.

They were just finishing their coffee when the rangers' truck passed them and then backed up. "Oh oh," his wife muttered "we're in trouble now ..." The ranger predictably told them they could not park on that side of the bollards. They reassured them that they were just leaving and that they had paid the camp fees. The ranger looked disappointed, but drove away. They broke camp with practiced efficiency, and he eased the camper back between the bollards.

They headed for Texas and their last stop before crossing the border into Mexico. They debated whether to stay in Las Cruces or in El Paso. He expressed the opinion that Las Cruces might be a bigger town with better prospects of a VW garage. His wife pointed out that each town had a corner in the map book outlining the city, and that usually indicated a large place. They agreed to go to El Paso.

They passed Las Cruces and moved into dairy country. This wasn't pretty, open fields of pasture, but rather thirty miles of milking barns and holding pens lined up side by side on both sides of the highway. The stench was horrible, and lasted until they came to El Paso city limits. Here the dairy operations were replaced by a large open mine with its own attendant ugliness. The freeway broadened into three lanes a side and then four. Traffic whizzed by at alarming speeds, with cars veering in and out of lanes. Exit ramps appeared on both sides and not knowing where they were going, he tried to stay in the middle lanes. He tensed up in concentration and hoped they didn't have to go far. His wife found the address of the Motel 6 in the hotel directory and guided him to the exit. The freeway had a connector road paralleling it and the traffic on this was every bit as frenzied. He hoped the motel would be acceptable because he just didn't want to drive in this any more.

They pulled into the parking lot and stared at the building. It was a large multi-storied complex, surrounded by parking lots—more hotel than motel. The camper would be out of sight of their room. There was a pool out back and some grassy areas, but it looked out of bounds to dogs. His wife checked in at the office and came back shaking her head. This was not a good location, none of their needed amenities near by. She mentioned another Motel 6 some ways further past town, and he reluctantly found himself facing the freeway nightmare again.

Thankfully the second Motel 6 was not too far down the road. He promised himself that he wouldn't do any serious driving for a couple of days. He needed to rest up for the concentration the Mexican highway system would surely tax out of him. In the meantime he would run down his list of preparations—oil change, spare tire, spare battery, fix the fan, check up for the dog.

His wife had left him in the company of the dog and the television, and with laundry bundled into two bulging pillowcases, had crossed the road to facilities at the opposing motel. She had come back briefly for additional quarters and a beer but that had been some time ago. He had been talking with a trucker whose vehicle had broken down. The trucker had approached him to see the dog and he had been amused that the trucker's eyes were a mismatched set just like the dog's. Now he wondered what was taking so long and decided to drive across the road to save his wife from having to cart the laundry back.

He found her sitting on the curb outside the motel's laundry room, book in hand. He said he had come to rescue her and she hugged him. They entered the small room and watched the clothes spin in the dryer. He cornered her with another hug but they broke apart like two guilty teenagers when another man came in.

Laundry stowed, they drove to a nearby mall to have dinner at a Japanese restaurant noticed earlier. The dog was well used to the routine by now, and yipped only a couple of times before settling down to sleep.

The restaurant had a sushi bar, and teppan tables where they cooked in front of you. The owners were actually Japanese! (Koreans and Chinese now ran a good portion of the Japanese restaurants in Vancouver and consequently the atmosphere wasn't quite the same.) It was wonderful to have a plate of raw fish in front of him again. It seemed a lifetime ago though it had been less than a month. He relished every mouthful, and helped his wife with the chicken and steak feast cooked for her. They washed it all down with several jars of sake, and crisp Sapporo beer. Towards the end of their meal, a group of patrons were seated at the teppan table opposite them. They seemed in a celebratory mood. One of the men was intent on having a martini and wondered about the sake martini listed on the menu. Ever helpful, his own wife had to jump into the conversation with an explanation. He kicked her under the table and whispered to her to mind her own business. She glared back it him; she never could understand his rules for when it was OK to strike up a conversation and when not.

They approached the camper, pleased with their meal and pleased with the quiet from within the vehicle. His wife peeked in the window and let out a gasp and a giggle. "Good Lord, the dog's had a party!" The camper interior was wall to wall with spilled corn chips, and spilled water, and dog grinned at them hugely. It did look as if she had just vacated the place of poker playing buddies and was sheepish at having been caught before cleaning up. Laughter was easier than anger, and they cleaned up.

He woke refreshed the next day and anxious to get on with the errands. The oil and lube job was completed without fuss only two blocks away. They drove down the hill and found the vet for the one o'clock appointment. The place smelled like antiseptic and had separate entrances for dogs and cats. The vet was brusque in his check-over of the dog and insisted that his assistant hold the dog for the temperature check. Both vet and assistant were a bit rough and the man felt his wife bristling next to him. The vet suggested the dog needed to be sedated, which they categorically refused. Then came a long discussion between vet and receptionist over what form needed to be completed for the border check. "I can't believe anyone would want to sedate a dog to look in its ears! I didn't like that guy and wouldn't trust him to clip the dog's nails." His wife was indignant.

They dropped film off at the drug store and returned to the motel. He busied himself bringing his journal up to date, and reviewing maps of their up coming route. He heard his wife talking outside and picked up bits of conversation about the war, the American economy, George W. Bush, the problems in Israel and the bible. He peeked out and was introduced to a huge hulk of a truck driver. He was the one with the Rottweiler that their dog was anxious to make friends with. Trouble was the Rottweiler had less manners than their pup and had bowled her over on their only encounter. The driver returned to his motel room, and his wife filled him in on their very redneck conversation. "That guy doesn't have a home." she said. "When he's not driving he holes up here for a couple of weeks. Tried marriage and didn't like it. Likes the Bible and trucking, period. Weird."

After two days in El Paso, spent running errands and resting, they were ready for the road again. He still didn't have the extra tire or the spare battery but decided that they would chance it. Mexico had one '*llantera*', tire shop, after another and at least those repairs could be readily had. He had tried to replace the switch for the fan, but even with the grill off, was flummoxed. In any case, the car had been running just fine and had probably benefited from the rest as much as he had. He hoped. If not, well they didn't have a timetable so could just deal with things as they came.

The drive to the border was short. "I suppose you want to go to the Duty Free?" he asked. She smiled sheepishly. In a manner of minutes, she was waving him into the store. "Look Tanqueray for ten bucks! I asked how much you're allowed to bring in and apparently it's a gallon … each." They stocked up on gin, Bailey's and a bottle of bourbon.

There was no traffic at the border. They had gotten away early to allow plenty of time for the Mexican bureaucracy. His wife directed him to the lane marked "Nothing to Declare" and the customs agent glanced at their passports and directed them to parking for *Migracion*. Inside they presented their passports and Mexican visas, which were duly stamped. He asked about customs, thinking particularly about the vehicle and was informed that vehicle permits were issued at a point on the highway thirty miles away. He started to ask about presenting the list of their household goods, but his wife interrupted him and said they had already gone through customs. The *Migracion* officer looked puzzled at the exchange but shrugged his shoulders. His wife asked about the dog's papers and they were directed around the corner to the agriculture control office. That officer didn't express the slightest interest in the fact that they had a dog. The vet visit had been a waste of time and money.

They got back in their vehicle and onto the highway. He kept looking in his rear view mirror expecting some official to come chasing after them. It had seemed just too easy. About forty-five minutes later they came to another customs post on the highway. They followed the signs regarding vehicle registration. This took a little longer, with line-ups at two separate wickets for photocopies and payments, but this too was simple. They found that they had to go through the customs checkpoint again, but his wife pointed him to the "Nothing to Declare" lane and they sailed through barely having to stop.

"Welcome to Mexico!" she exclaimed exultantly.

Hell Mexican Style

The highway stretched across flat plains, dry and dusty. Although the landscape was similar to what they'd recently driven through, here it also managed to look desolately poor. There weren't many houses along the way, but those that stood were often fabricated of cement blocks, with corrugated tin roofs.

His wife was even more quiet than usual. "I don't feel very well," she replied to his query. "Well you can't blame that on Mexico," he said. "You haven't eaten here yet."

"You remember a couple of nights ago when I suddenly felt weird and dizzy? It's like that but with major stomach cramps. Maybe I contracted anthrax in the post office when I mailed that parcel" she joked. Threats of Anthrax were the leading headlines in these post 9/11 days.

They stopped for a hamburger in a small town. His wife nibbled on some French fries, but even half of these were given to the dog. He felt absolutely no ill effects of any kind and so discounted his wife suffering from food poisoning from their Japanese dinner.

He had selected a motel from the guidebook and his wife looked for directions to it as they approached Chihuahua. It was a large sprawling city spread out across several hillsides. They were almost at the other end of town and hadn't been able to locate the motel. They asked for directions, but discounted them. The hesitation before he answered indicated that the man providing the directions didn't really have a clue of what they were looking for. They had noticed in the past that Mexicans were unfailingly polite and never wanted to disappoint so if an individual was asked for directions he provided them regardless of a total lack of accuracy.

They drove back through city, into rush hour traffic. The street was two lanes in each direction, but could have been four for the regard the other cars showed. Cars braking, turning, or parking didn't slow the drivers down one bit. They simply took this as encouragement to lean on their horns more. They passed some seedy looking motels and kept going. All of a sudden the camper's coolant light started flashing. He turned down a side street and the vehicle stalled. It wouldn't start, so his wife gave a push as he steered towards the curb. They would have to wait until the engine cooled.

His wife said she urgently needed to find a washroom and practically ran to the corner of the main street. He took the dog to stroll down the sidewalk, giving her the opportunity to relieve herself as well. It was hot, it was dusty, it was noisy and he was tired and worried.

His wife came back, looking pale but relieved. "Just got in in time, but no toilet paper," she relayed miserably.

They decided that they would not tax the camper's cooling system much further and would look for a place to stay in the vicinity, seedy or not. The camper started without hiccup and they drove around the block. Set back on a side street was a neon sign indicating Motel California. It looked fairly clean and tidy and was at least far enough from the main street to cut down on the noise. They pulled into the driveway and noticed that the carports all had blue tarps hanging in front like curtains.

A man came out of the office and his wife asked, in Spanish, if they had rooms available and how much they cost. She turned to her husband, puzzled. "He said it's three hundred pesos for eight hours." She turned back to the motel employee and was just asking what it cost for the whole night when realization dawned on her. The motel's purpose was to accommodate trysts. "I guess the carports have tarps across so that you don't recognize someone's car!" They turned away from the employee's lurid looks and headed back to the main street.

They finally turned in to El Capitan, right on the main drag. The administrator said dogs were not allowed but gave in in response to his wife's pleading. "*Ella es muy tranquille y muy limpia. Ella dorme en suelo.*" She is very quiet and very clean and sleeps on the ground.

Their room had seen better days, though in Mexico it was difficult to determine if that meant two years ago or twenty. It was dark with the only light offered being from a bare overhead bulb. The double bed had cushioned many bodies and presented a definite trough down the middle. The curtains hung half-torn on the window, and the bathroom door had warped to a slant. But the tile floors were clean, and effort had been made to cheer the place up with pictures of flowers on the wall. The requisite crucifix hung over the bed.

By this time his wife was curled up on one side of the bed. She clutched her stomach when the cramps attacked, and advised him she had a killer headache. She didn't want any food and urged him to go out to eat on his own. He left with the dog and walked down the street looking for green space for the dog to relieve herself. No luck there, and he returned to the motel, stopping only to buy a bottle of water. He wasn't hungry and was ready for bed. He gave the dog food, which she ignored, and water. He suggested his wife take a Tylenol 3; she said she had but asked for another one. He lay down and closed his eyes, trying to sleep.

The night was long and awful. They could hear every sound from the room next door, where a couple was partying. Anytime he or his wife moved on the bed, the other felt as if they were being bounced on a trampoline. His wife got up several times during the night to use the washroom or to look for more pain relievers. Just as he had drifted off to sleep, the dog woke him with her own urgency. Around three in the morning, their neighbour on the other side started up his truck parked just outside their window. He left it idling noisily and filling their room with exhaust fumes while he chatted with the night watchman across the courtyard. After a half hour of this, his wife threw open their door, and with disregard to her skimpy nightshirt, yelled across at the men. "*Por favor, senors …* *un poco de tranquille. Su motor!*" This had no success whatever and only elicited leering appreciation at her backlit silhouette. The truck kept roaring and spewing for another twenty minutes before the driver finally drove off.

They were up early and anxious to get out of this hellhole. His wife gave up trying to follow the map and just kept suggesting turns following the rising sun. Amazingly, they found themselves on the correct highway without much trouble.

They drove a couple of hours to Hidalgo El Parral. The guidebook promised a quaint Mexican town with curving, hillside streets, and interesting architecture. They passed a couple of motels at the entrance to the town but drove on. These looked like fancy resorts with sculpted gardens and swimming pools, and would probably be beyond their budget. He had selected a promising sounding hotel in town.

They found the hotel but his wife reported back that they didn't allow dogs. The receptionist had said the dog would have to sleep in the camper to be parked in the lot out back. They knew there was no way the dog would sleep all night left alone, and set off to find another hotel. The town was on a hillside, and had the curving streets, but these were jammed full and parking was scarce. There wasn't a scrap of green to be found anywhere; even the central square was all cement.

He found a place to park and they set off on foot to find a place to stay. 'No dogs' was the answer everywhere. He grew steadily more annoyed. It was hot and crowded and he didn't like the way the Mexicans jumped off the sidewalk in fear of his pup. How could people be so stupid about a beautiful pet on a short leash? His agitation showed through and he snapped at his wife "Now what? We're going to have the same problem with the dog everywhere we go. We may as well stay in that hotel and I'll sleep in the camper with the dog. At least you can get some sleep."

His wife tried to reassure him that they would find some place but she was at a loss to say where. She still felt really ill and had wanted to just curl up for a sleep, dog at her side, and let her husband explore this town. Personally she found it ugly and unappealing. But there was no way she would consider having him sleep in the camper. She suggested that he use the bank machine and that they then try the expensive looking motels. She trailed after him down the street and couldn't stem the tears. She pulled herself together while he was in the bank. She didn't want to add her misery to his aggravation.

They had no more luck at the expensive complexes. They consulted the guidebook again and decided to take a detour to a place called El Palmito. Though another two hours away, it was reportedly on a lake and promised bungalows, or failing that, a nice campground. There was supposed to be good fishing, and wildlife including pumas.

They passed through a small town and he realized that he needed gas. They had passed by the Pemex in Parral without a thought. A hand lettered sign on the highway said *Gasolina*. They asked directions and were steered into the village to a house where the man obviously did machine repairs. He had gas available from a barrel. No indication of the grade or purity and they took seventy pesos worth on faith.

The turn off to El Palmito wasn't marked, and he drove right past it. His wife gave instructions to back up to the dirt road that looked like a driveway to a farm. It soon turned to pavement and they barrelled along across the plain. The road started to curve and they wound down at least one thousand feet. The town of El Palmito was small and basically L shaped. They stopped and asked about camping and were assured camping was available at the lake edge, only a kilometer away. The road ended at the village limits turning into a forked choice of goat tracks. They chose left and came to what looked like an enormous dam complex. It was peculiar in its size and in that both sides dropped to dry land.

They turned back and followed the goat tracks to the right. After bouncing along for five minutes, the muddy edge of the lake came into view. Boats were pulled up onto the grassy shore indicating that fishing was a pastime here. They got out of the camper and stared around. No cabins in sight, only quite a number of cows that stopped chewing their cuds to stare at them with indifferent curiosity. The dog was anxious to get a closer look at the beasts, but the cows loped off at her approach. He gazed around at the cow-clapped field and said, "Surely this can't be the campground...."

They drove back to the dam like structure and across it. Two men were on the other side constructing a shrine to the virgin of nowhere. His wife asked them about the lake and they nodded enthusiastically. "*Si, si,* just follow this road around the bend for about three kilometers." They started to ascend the hill, when the camper's coolant light came on, and the vehicle stalled, unwilling to travel further. "Perfect," he thought. He let the dog out of the car for a run. His wife grabbed her Spanish-English dictionary and walked back to the shrine constructors.

She returned and informed him that according to those locals, the river had once flooded with catastrophic results. The owner of the house above the shrine had petitioned the government to spend ten million dollars on the spillway control. The river had never again even breached its banks and the spillway had never been used.

The VW was sufficiently cooled off to start again. They followed the gravel road for the prescribed three kilometers and came to the top of another spillway/dam. The lake below appeared man-made, and there certainly wasn't any camping area to be seen. There was no more road to follow.

They returned to the town. They stopped at the lone hotel and discovered that it was full. Would there be no end to the day's misery? Around the corner, the VW protested again. His wife fairly leapt from the vehicle and said that she was going to check out the room for rent she had seen advertised back around the corner. He said nothing, beyond words with the exasperations of the day.

He watched her walking back. She was smiling but shaking her head. "That room was such a hell-hole, it made the El Capitan look like a four star resort."

"We'll just have to camp by the side of the road somewhere," he said. "The car won't drive much further, and I've no desire to tackle that curvy hill in the dark."

Just outside of town, where the highway curved to start the ascent, there was a cleared triangle of land. They pulled over. At least here they would be out of traffic's way. His wife dragged some brambles out of the path of the door and suffered a deep scratch on the back of her calf. "Perfect," she muttered, reaching for antiseptic. Her stomach let out its ominous rumble and she scrambled for some privacy behind the camper. "Please don't let any cars come down the hill now," she wished. Diarrhoea without a toilet—surely there couldn't be any more torture left to this day.

She covered her deposit with several rocks and returned to the camper. She declined her husband's offer of canned beans for dinner; one of the few staples in their pantry but guaranteed to not help her situation. "Well this surely has been the day from hell, hasn't it?" He answered with an exceedingly appropriate expletive. She looked at him and gave him a wry smile. "Tomorrow has got to be a better day!"

The sun sets early and promptly in Mexico. By 8:00 pm it had been pitch dark for almost an hour. They crawled into bed and settled down for sleep. But eight is early for sleep, even if you have been awake for half the previous night, and especially when you lie in wait for *banditos*. They didn't talk, but each felt the other stiffen with tension every time a car passed by. Individually they reassured themselves: the doors are locked, the dog will alert us, this isn't a violent country … and eventually they slept.

Into the Sierra Madres

His wife awoke to the pleasant realization that she had slept and that she had to pee, but her stomach was calm. This in itself was enough to mark the day with a positive note. She furthered her consciousness with the sound of the kettle beginning to whistle and silently appreciated that her husband had obviously been up, let the dog out, and gotten the kettle going without disturbing her sleep. She took a further minute to be grateful for the lack of *bandito* attacks the night before. Everything was going to be all right. Still, there was the lack of the toilet.... well the traffic seemed calm at the moment and she knew where the rocks were kept.

The climb back up over the ridge and onto the main highway didn't take nearly as long as their descent the afternoon before. They were flying on the wings of restored optimism.

Their route bore them through a substantial roadside town—one that she couldn't find on the map. They decided coffee was in order, and backtracked to the beginning of this highway fronting town to an inviting *"restaurant familiar"* that boasted clean swept dirt floors and an abundance of bougainvillea. It was late enough for the place to be deserted, though to be truthful these roadside stops appeared deserted at almost any time of day. They looped the dog's leash handle around the bottom of the plastic Corona emblazoned chair and waited. Eventually, a middle-aged woman came to serve them. *"Solo dos café, per favor senora"* his wife politely declined the menus. Minutes later the small Nescafe instant coffee jar was presented, along with two cups of hot, not boiling, water and an economy size jar of some powdered dairy substitute. They thanked her and proceeded to unsuccessfully mix the blend to a lump free consistency.

They sipped the familiar concoction and looked at the numerous birds—parakeets, parrots, and canaries—in the cages hanging around them. An old woman approached from the house next door, hobbling carefully behind her walker. *"Muerde? Muerde?"* she called querulously spotting the dog. *"No es brava ... ella es uno cachorro"* his wife tried to reassure her. She didn't know what '*muerde*' meant, it wasn't in her dictionary, but wanted to reassure the old lady. Eventually and with much trepidation, she hobbled past them and into the kitchen of the restaurant. They sat a while longer and decided to risk another cup of evil Mexican coffee. His wife went and poked her head into the kitchen to order, apologizing for interrupting the woman's breakfast.

When the owner brought the new warm water out, she had decided to stay for a chat. She machine-gunned her Spanish at them and his wife answered: More rapid fire, more response. When there was a pause, his wife turned and explained. "She wanted to know where we're from, where we're going. She has over eighty birds. She wanted know if the dog was a wolf. We're in a town called Rodeo."

The man's attention was diverted by the sound of small cats. A four-year-old child appeared, with buddy in tow, and scooped up a kitten. He manhandled the kitten as only a child can, with total disregard of distress calls from kitten or mother. He seemed very interested in the non-Mexicans sitting at his table, but was too shy to come close. He showed off by holding the kitten on his head. The Man's wife took a picture with her digital camera, though it took some coaxing for him to place the cat in that position again, and charmed both boys and mother by demonstrating the likeness on the camera's small screen.

They were halfway through their second cup, when a second person joined them at the table. It took them quite a number of sentences to determine the sex of the mid-thirties person speaking to them; they learned she was the owner's daughter. She plunked down a pair of cowboy boots in front of them, and offered them for sale. They were made in Leon, but the leather came from her. It was soft, and had a beautiful texture. Ostrich. In response to their disbelieving queries, she led them around to view the backyard—full of birds, and two ostrich in sight. There were reportedly eight on the property. She informed them that ostrich lived long lives. "Longer than most of us," the owner cackled at her own quip. They thanked the owner for her hospitality, paid the twenty pesos for the awful coffee, and declined the purchase of the boots. As they climbed back in the camper, his wife wondered what the real life span of ostriches was in this country when there were boots to be made.

They drove on. They came to a major intersection of roads, each fork demarcated with trucks and people thrusting apples at them through the window. This was the town of Las Delicias—original home of the Delicious Apple. The realization came too late, however, and the traffic too pushy at the *topes* (speed bumps) to allow for discovery or purchase.

The landscape mellowed into rich farmland, with the highway bordered by wild flowering plants in brilliant hues of orange, pink and purple. The scent through the windows was heady. It would have been wonderful to stop, but there was no place, with the fields wired off. The mountains beckoned in the distance, the temperature was perfect.

They came to a lake, surrounded by trees, with a convenient pull off. It looked the perfect spot to let the dog run, but they opened the car doors, and discovered broken glass littering the ground. He took the dog on the leash, and picked their way carefully towards the lake edge. The dog wanted to run, but even in the open field, the results of many a drunken party spoiled the opportunity. They returned, carefully, to the vehicle and bemoaned this sad part of Mexican life—the tendency to spoil the most pristine parts with illogical tosses of garbage.

A mile or so down the road, the camper flicked on its temperamental gauge. They were on the other corner of the lake, and turned into a private holiday camp. There was a house off to one side, with chickens in the yard and loud disco tunes blasting from its stereo, but otherwise the place was deserted, and they were unchallenged. They parked to let the vehicle cool, and the dog run. It would have been a nice spot to stay longer, but the last night's experience lingered and they were anxious to find a place to stay for the night.

The highway wound around and came to Durango. The guidebook-promised movie set came first on their left, but a quick glance suggested that it was more a Mexican conception of what a movie set should be. It was probably true that a movie had been filmed at that location, but the Mexicans had embellished it with a movie town that even Hollywood would find too cheesy.

As they came into town, they spotted the tourist information centre and pulled over. Despite the hours of operation proclaimed on the door, it was closed. Not wanting a repeat of Hidalgo del Parral and its anti-dog attitudes, they followed the guidebook directions to the trailer park. No one could object to a dog camping. The trailer park also advertised hotel rooms, and his wife, desperate for a functioning toilet and a warm shower, asked for one of these. The receptionist quoted a rate that he supposed his wife found reasonable in her desperation, and held a finger to her lips in response to the enquiry about the dog. His wife came out bearing a key and the curt instruction to "Drive."

The hotel was in reality a motel, with a long semi-circular curve of rooms fronting a large field (the campground) and a swimming pool. Their room was large, with two beds, and room enough to swing several cats. The curtain sheers were torn in places, and the room generally looked a little forlorn. His wife peeked in the bathroom, at the television, at the rocking chair on the brick veranda outside and expressed a sigh of relief so loud that one would think they had just checked into a posh resort.

She picked up her handbag and announced she was going to the bank. When she had gone, he organized the room: bathroom kit neatly hung up, towel on the counter and glasses inverted on top, liquor bottles to one side, cooler handy below on the floor. He fidgeted a bit, took the dog for a walk in the field, and waited for her return. He had noted the bank machine on the corner and wondered what was taking so long.

She came back, hot and sweaty. "I found the bank ok, but wandered for blocks looking to get us something to eat. *Nada, nada, nada.* I guess we'll have to go into town later."

She looked around and noticed all the arrangements. "Didn't I marry well!" she delighted.

They watched a little bit of television and laughed at the novelty of the Mexican programs. For a while they watched a corny made-for-television drama in English with Spanish subtitles. His wife said it was a good way to learn Spanish, but he quickly got bored and enticed her into other activities.

At the Durango Pool

Eventually they pulled on swimsuits and set off to the pool, dog in tow. They attached her long lead to a cement bench and slipped gingerly into the cold water, pushing drowned wasps and beetles out of the way. The air temperature hovered around eighty degrees Fahrenheit but not even the sun had heated the pool. The dog barked and pranced, wanting to join in the fun. He led her over to the wading pool, only knee deep, and as the dog leaned over he gave her a gentle nudge in for a swim. She barely got wet and was out of the pool, racing in every direction as far as her lead would allow. To the dog, this was obviously some wild game of tag, and they laughed heartily at her antics. She raced with speed, but wet paws gave no purchase on the cement and there were numerous wipe-outs.

After a hot shower and cocktails on their veranda, they set off for downtown in search of dinner. They left the dog in the camper—it was cool in the evening—and she settled down quickly, now used to the routine. They packed a plethora of cameras, just in case, and crossed the square to the big cathedral. Standing at the entrance, they watched a ceremony taking place. At first glance it appeared to be a wedding, but the bride was seated alone on a chair directly in front of the altar. The rest of the party was ranged at a respectful distance to either side, and there didn't appear to be a groom. A young girl came down the aisle, handing out cards to everyone in the congregation, including them at the door. It turned out to be a confirmation of sorts; something called a "*quinze*" where girls fifteen years of age were welcomed into the Church as adults, and now marriageable.

They left the church before the ceremony was over, and strolled the streets. They came upon an internet shop and his wife pulled him in to send a couple of quick messages. She was disappointed again to see that there weren't any messages in return. "It costs ten pesos for a half hour here to use the computer. In Moab it cost ten dollars!"

They walked back around to the square, and peeked in on the dog. She was sound asleep on the back bench of the camper. They walked around the corner and up into a bar overlooking the square. The place was decorated for Halloween, with skeletons propped up at the window tables like patrons much too long at the bar. One skeleton held a cigarette in its bony hand.... an irony that tickled him deeply. It was happy hour still, though only with minutes to go and they managed to snag the waiter's attention. They added a club sandwich and an onion soup to their drink order. He was sobered by the high prices on the menu and mentioned it to his wife. "Look at the prices ... and we're inland, not in some tourist spot!" They ate the mediocre food and left. If there had been a band playing they might have lingered, but the entertainment was promised only for eleven o'clock and that seemed too long and too expensive to wait.

The next day they returned to the downtown core to have a closer look at historic Durango. They managed to find a shady spot to park the camper but it was too hot to leave the dog so all three set off. They took pictures here and there, and watched a march go by the government offices. It was a protest of some sort. His wife asked a security man what the protest was in aid of and learned that it was a general protest. Quite a number of different groups and organizations were participating, all with individual causes which they took turns shouting to the people watching. The march circled around and gathered at the square, where speeches were made to varying degrees of crowd approval. The Health Department had taken advantage of the gathering of people and had a series of trailers parked along one side of the square. Persons in white uniforms milled on the sidewalk trying to entice customers into the trailers for a variety of free dental work. There wasn't a throng lining up for the opportunity.

They drove back to their motel/campground, mutually agreeing that Durango had been a bit of a disappointment. It seemed they had both conceived ideas of a charming colonial town, oozing charm and photo opportunities rather than the businesslike city they had found.

They changed and headed back to the pool. One of the delights of this place was its few occupants and they found they had the pool area all to themselves. This time they tethered the dog to the swim ladder of the pool and tried to coax her in. She barked, and tried to catch their splashes and did her mad dash from one side to the other. They howled with laughter and enjoyed her antics. They lifted her gently into the wading pool to cool her off, and again she spurted out and galloped crazily from side to side. She obviously was not a water dog, but greatly enjoyed the poolside ambience.

Later they went out for dinner. He had spotted a nice looking restaurant not too far from the hotel, and thought it was Italian. It turned out to be Mexican-Continental but the maitre'd appeared so crestfallen at the thought they might go elsewhere, they decided to give it a try. His wife ordered a banana daiquiri that put a puzzled look on the waiter's face. No bananas this side of the mountains apparently, and she settled for a lime daiquiri instead. The waiter happily scurried away and came back with a thimble size drink in a champagne glass that put a puzzled look on his wife's face in return. No concept of daiquiris on this side of the mountains either. They had dinner and pronounced it passable—classic cuisine it could never pretend to be. But then, this was Durango and on the opposite side of the mountains from fine cuisine.

They set off in the morning to conquer the Sierras. He was very pleased with how the camper had held up thus far, and said a silent prayer to the gods of travel that this good fortune carry them through the most challenging portion of their trip. As they climbed out of Durango, the scenery changed to pine forests. The altimeter crept up though there weren't any steep hills. They passed through towns with crude sawmills and passed an old steam engine that bespoke of the area's early mining days.

Just passed Salto, the road began to dip and curve. It spiralled up and down, and he found himself constantly changing between second and third gears. Their attention was held by the sway of the road itself and it seemed that after rounding every corner, there was another hill and another corner to transit. Then, abruptly, as they rounded onto a bridge, the world opened up before them, and their breath was taken away. The Sierras spread out before them at their 9000-foot vantage point.

Sierra Madre Ouest at 9000 feet

Gripping the wheel tightly, he drove on. There were at least ten thousand curves to this road with no indication of what lay around the corner. There was no margin for error as the two-lane highway had no shoulder, and the flimsiest of guard rails only in occasional places. He geared up, and geared down, sparing his brakes as much as possible. His wife sat in the passenger seat with her feet only mildly braced. He felt grateful that she seemed so at ease with his driving. A nervous passenger would have made the trip that much more tense.

Four hours later they started their final winding descent. The pines were interspersed with jungle until finally, at three thousand feet the jungle won out. The air, pristine and fresh in the high mountains, grew thick and humid as the altimeter spun down. By the time they reached the straight highway approaching Mazatlan they were sweating despite the air rushing in through all the open windows. The humid air took on a salty smell—they were approaching beach country. It had taken five and half hours to cross the mountains. He was ready for an ice-cold beer and a swim.

La Zona Dorado

They drove directly to the Mar y Rosa Trailer Park, which proved empty save for a few large trailers, mostly at the beach edge. The camp hosts, escapees from Arizona who had come last year for two weeks and ended up staying four months, advised that the park wasn't officially open, and that when it would open it was fully booked. He told them they planned to stay only a few days and they allowed him a choice of spots. The further from the beach, the less the rental cost. He settled on a spot three rows back, and popped the top of the camper.

He and his wife set about setting up their temporary home. It was unmercifully hot and humid, and the slightest exertion produced buckets of sweat. They changed into swimsuits and headed to the beach to cool off.

Dog's first coconut

The dog rediscovered her joy of beaches but was distinctly leery of the surf and would only approach the very edge. If any wave approached, she scampered well back, but then came back to the water's edge to drink despite the salt. They waded in over occasional rocks and found the water to be bath warm. Certainly at this temperature the ocean didn't have any cooling properties. While they were in the water, the dog took advantage of their distraction and raced down the beach towards a group of people. The beachgoers, all Mexican, jumped back in fear even though the dog was obviously trying to show her friendliest side. When his wife had coaxed the dog back to them, they clipped on her long wire lead. Here at least, they would have to take turns swimming while the other stayed with the dog.

They returned to the campsite and showered. The campground was littered with fallen coconuts and palm fronds. The dog, who loved to rip things apart, discovered these new toys and kept herself busy for hours.

They sat in their camp chairs, sipping cold drinks and doing their best not to move. Eventually they decided that dinner of some type was in order. Their camp hosts had named a restaurant on the beach where the food was good and the dog would be welcome. They didn't want to drive because that would mean disassembling camp and wandered out to the street to see how far they would have to walk.

Mazatlan's Pullomonio Cabs

His wife suggested taking a cab—one of Mazatlan's open-air cabs. He expressed his doubts that the cab would take the dog as a passenger but was quickly proved wrong.

The open air Volkswagens were a godsend especially for the welcoming breeze as you traveled along. It took them into the heart of the golden zone, the *Zona Dorada*, where hotels, shops and restaurants abounded. It was a typical tourist zone with large, multi-storeyed hotels blocking access to the beach. The only Mexicans here were those in the service industry. It was the type of Mexico they usually avoided. Their restaurant of choice did have tables out on the beach and the dog was certainly welcome. His wife ordered drinks for them, insisting that he have a very large margarita in celebration of his successful drive through the mountains. They ordered a light supper, a club sandwich and onion soup, and a second drink.

There were four little girls from the neighbouring table, who to show their bravado, raced around their table, shrieking and taunting the dog. They were very cute in their dress-up clothes, but very annoying in their noise and games. His wife chided them for throwing sand at the dog, and eventually decided that there would only be peace if they were introduced to the dog. She spoke to them in quiet tones, and holding the dog still, encouraged them to pet her. The eldest one came first and expressed a love of animals. She found petting the dog to be quite amazing and was even more delighted when his wife helped her to feed the dog some of his sandwich.

The margaritas had gone completely to his head and he would confess in the morning that he didn't remember paying the bill or leaving the restaurant. They took another cab ride back to the campground with a very accommodating driver. He stopped to let them purchase eggs for breakfast, and then drove them directly to their campsite rather than leaving them at the gate.

They had another shower and climbed into bed. Even with the side door open and all the vents unzipped, it was hot and airless. Sleep was difficult, and the heat barely dissipated even in the early hours of the morning. The next night they would sleep with the hatch lifted part way. This allowed more air to penetrate and still ensured a modicum of privacy. He didn't tolerate heat or humidity well, and would have had the hatch open completely but his wife was a little more prudish.

Getting to know Dog

Yet other people seemed to find the heat quite bearable. He pointed out to his wife that the woman in the trailer in the next row was wearing white opaque pantyhose under her shorts. The woman with the pantyhose was travelling with her husband, retired. She came over one morning and explained their trailer had developed a leak from the air conditioner and she and her husband had had a surprise shower in bed that morning. The story had kinky overtones from these, the most unkinky looking people. When they pulled out of the campsite later on, their trailer was still streaming water from the roof.

The man who moved into the side to their left was travelling solo. He was late middle-aged, and amused himself watching television or roaring around the campsite on his dirt bike.

One afternoon, an old panel van arrived and took up the space behind them. It had been camperized after a fashion, and would have been popular in the sixties. In fact it looked like it had been popular in the sixties, and the occupant could well have been the original owner. They watched in fascination as he set about unpacking. First large metal bars were taken out and fashioned into tripod.

This took quite a while, as they were unwieldy and heavy. Eventually a satellite dish, large enough to serve as weather station for China, was set on top. Next a dirt bike was unloaded and propped up. Then some mysterious metal boxes were set on the pad. He was totally uncommunicative and a bit furtive in his movements. They wondered if he could be some sort of spy. These preparations made, he pulled out a beaten up lawn chair, and turned on a television inside the van. He would make a great partner for their other neighbour and sure enough, by next morning the two were discussing the merits of their respective bikes.

Old Mazatlan

It continued to be unseasonably hot and humid. Showers were de rigueur every couple of hours just to stay comfortable. They took a *pulmonio* (the open air taxis) ride to Old Mazatlan and were impressed with the architecture. The old part of the city was miles past the Golden Zone, passed central Mazatlan, which was shabby and unremarkable. Here in the old part they discovered the history and character of the Mexican city, and were surprised at the lack of tourists.

They visited some of the beaches and let the dog chase after seagulls while they enjoyed a cold beer. They walked through the Golden Zone and brought back pizza for dinner. They showered, and napped, and read books. And after three days, they were ready to move on.

Magic

Their guidebook spoke of a camping place near Tepic and this was their destination. They reached Tepic in early afternoon and drove into the heart of the city. It was at a higher altitude and considerably cooler here, a welcome relief. The city itself had large tree-lined squares and the typical cathedral fronting the main *zocolo*. Larger than the cathedral, a soccer stadium looked the dominant feature of the city.

They stopped in at the large Soriana grocery store to pick up some food for camping, and a bag of charcoal so that they could barbecue steaks. Nourishment ensured, they pushed on to Santa Maria del Oro some fifty kilometers distant.

The town of Santa Maria del Oro was eight kilometers off the toll free highway. It was a typical small Mexican town but was remarkably clean. There was no debris littering any of the roadsides, and a sidewalk was being installed at the approach to the town. The town appeared wealthy, its funding no doubt stemming from the lush farms surrounding it.

They drove through the town and came to the volcano crater that housed the lake where they would camp. The lake was set in the crater pocket, some two thousand feet below them, and sparkled like a flawless sapphire in the afternoon sun.

They found the campsite compound, Koala, run by an ex-patriot Australian who had made Mexico his home for the last twenty years. The grounds swept back from the lake with a large expanse of lawn. There were a number of bungalows and full size houses set on the property. In the back of one set of bungalows, hibiscus and sword plants delineated trailer sites. The road up through the property followed a line of palm trees, with ornamental light poles set at intervals. To one side sat a building housing bathrooms and showers. Several long-term residents were set up in some of the trailer sites, their permanence indicated by the add-ons to their trailers.

They chose a site and popped the top of the camper. They walked down to the lake and found access via a cement boat ramp. The water was pleasantly cool and very clean and clear. Small fish could be seen feeding near the lake's edge. They walked back and were challenged by a dog rushing out from one of the sites. This site belonged to one of the long time residents as evidenced by the large collections of driftwood decorating the site, one of which proclaimed "Old Salt". His wife asked the resident if the dog was friendly, thinking their own dog would enjoy some playtime. "Depends on how she feels," the crusty looking owner replied. Old salt indeed … they kept their dog on the leash and returned to their own site.

The sun was setting and the odd mosquito made its presence known. He piled pieces of charcoal into the hibachi and asked his wife how she proposed he light it—there was no starter. The charcoal itself was true charcoal—aged bits of blackened sticks. She presented him with a can of lighter fluid but this quickly burned itself out, and he rebuilt the fire with newspaper at its base. The charcoal burned quickly, and even supplemented with dry bits of wood found around the campsite, they just barely managed to cook the thin steaks. The steaks were tough and unappealing. His wife fed most of hers to the dog. Despite this, the ambiance was enjoyable, the meal eaten at a table out under the stars.

They sat, after the dishes were done, and watched the stars. He noticed little flashes of light here and there, flickering through the dark sky. "Have you never seen fireflies?" his wife asked. "We used to catch them and keep them in jars when I was little." He admitted he had never seen such a thing before.

A little while later, his wife scooped a bug that had landed on a rock near her. She placed it on his finger. In a few seconds, it started flashing but didn't fly away. He could feel its soft feet brushing his hand as it walked this way and that, but not in any hurry to depart. It flashed its bright white light at regular intervals, and it looked like a mobile diamond on his hand. "It's magic!" he murmured.

"We used to pretend they were fairies," his wife said.

He sat for a long time with this flashing pulse travelling over one finger and then another. He hadn't felt this kind of enchantment since he was a small boy.

To Puerto Vallarta: Home

In the morning, they swam in the lake, relishing the silkiness of the fresh water. They managed to drag the dog a short ways into the water, but she obviously didn't like being wet. As soon as she found herself on dry land, she raced from one end of her tether to the other. This was a familiar trick of hers, and extremely funny to watch; she so patently enjoyed herself, pretending it was all a big game of tag. The dog managed to yank her tether free, and then it was a real game of tag until they could corral her again. The dog loved this game and was hard to catch. She was a very smart dog, but also very obstinate and the game ended only when she was good and ready.

They paddled in the lake for a while longer, the dog secure again. The water was a perfect temperature and it felt good to be wet but not salty. They talked about staying another day, but his wife said she was feeling anxious to get to their ultimate destination and set up a more permanent home. It was nearing the end of October and the tourists would be descending in force. They didn't have any reservations booked, and it was imperative to get settled before the tourists arrived. They decided to leave that day and push on to Puerto Vallarta, their pen-ultimate destination.

His wife studied the map. Where possible, they tried to avoid retracing their steps and looked for new vistas. Part of this trip was to experience as much of unseen Mexico as possible. She was also anxious to continue the journey and advised that the *Cuota* (toll) highway should cut a considerable number of miles off their journey: a shortcut on a previously unseen road. So instead of taking the free road, they turned away from the coast onto the super highway. The shortcut proved longer than the free road by thirty miles and included the insult of two expensive tolls. At one toll booth the attendant seemed bent on adding to a private fund until a state police car providentially pulled up behind them, and the fee was quickly reduced. President Fox, newly elected, had promised to rid Mexico of corruption but obviously the word was slow getting out.

They saw and recognized the town at the other side of the toll from their trip to Guadalajara on a previous journey. From here to Puerto Vallarta the road was familiar, and the journey passed quickly. Soon they passed by San Francisco,

Sayulita, La Penita and Rincon de Guayabitos. As they grew closer and closer to Puerto Vallarta, they leaned forward in their seats as if to hurry these last few miles. They reminisced about past experiences, and looked forward to "coming home".

He passed the airport and joined the hectic flow of cars, trucks, taxis and buses flowing in an intertwining stream into Puerto Vallarta. He congratulated himself on the ease of driving in this traffic. It was so very familiar.

They looked for changes in the town, and found few. Soon they pulled into the cul de sac outside their home away from home, the Posada Lily. His wife jumped out and suggested he wait with the dog while she negotiated a room. They were unsure of the dog's reception. She came back in short order, disappointed that there was no one in the office. They decided to just sit and wait, and their patience was rewarded in short order. She recognized the owner, Pepe, though he showed no recognition of them.

It was not yet full tourist season and so they had their pick of rooms, and the owner reluctantly agreed to the dog. They chose the second floor corner room as opposed to their normal choice of the third and top floor. The room was large and had the same corner balcony with the terrific views of the main street, the hills, and the beach. Being one floor down had its advantage in that it was one less long flight of stairs to climb; this was particularly important given the dog's inclination to want a stroll in the wee hours.

They hauled the bags up. His wife typically loaded herself like a camel on a nine-day trip on the first go. At his insistence, she then waited with the dog while he brought up the rest of the luggage, and a bag of ice. That accomplished, they poured a celebratory drink and moved to the balcony to survey their kingdom. The stresses and strains of the previous seven months fell away. The tiredness of the travel and adventure of the past three weeks mellowed. This felt like home; they had arrived, unscathed. They had done it.

After a reviving shower, filled with the tingling excitement of revisiting a beloved place, they set off to rediscover old haunts. First stop was Andeles Bar, home of old friend, bartender Carlos. He waved at Carlos from the street, and was reluctant to bring the dog in. His wife took thirty seconds to say "For gods' sake, they bring a donkey in here every night; they're not going to object to a dog in the corner!" and tugged the dog in.

Carlos showed his pleasure at seeing them again. They delightedly explained that they were in Mexico to stay for six months or more this time. They told of where they had been, how they got to the trip, and what their plans were. His wife teased Carlos about his new wife and asked whether he was a papa yet. Carlos' face plunged and he curtly told them he was divorced. A year or so earlier, Carlos news of marriage to a girl ten years his junior had been a huge surprise: he'd been the perpetual, handsome, young bachelor. They expressed distress and understanding at this turn of events. Carlos provided some further small details and then shrugged the whole matter off. "I'm over it," he proclaimed, though his eyes still showed heartbreak.

They walked around the old town trying to decide where to eat. They went over to Torritos Sports Bar to check the hockey television schedule. As luck would have it, there was a game in progress between the Canucks and the Avalanche. He lingered longingly at the door. His wife noticed and asked the burly doorman if they could go in with the dog. The doorman apologized but declined. "You can watch through the window," he said. She looked at him tartly and replied "Yes, but you can't drink out here." He weighed the thought of revenue lost and escorted them to a table just inside the door. The dog was to stay quiet and out of sight. The dog, obligingly, settled on the cool tile floor and snoozed. "See?" his wife asked. "No problems about dogs." She advised her husband she didn't need any dinner after filling up on Carlos' hefty banana daiquiris. He settled back to watch the game—beer in an ice bucket, a quiet uncomplaining wife, dog asleep at his feet, and his home hockey team to watch on television in a tropical country. Life was good.

They ended their evening with a stroll on the beach. Music played by a duo enticed them to a table set on the beach. His wife ordered a salad for him, and chatted to another couple of the origins of the dog. The salad was new-age and delicious. They let the dog loose for a final run, and then returned to their balcony for a final nightcap.

The next morning, he answered the dog's cue and took her for a dawn visit to the beach. The tide was out, and there weren't any people about so he let her off leash for a run. She did her business, which he cleaned up, and then she took off for one of her mad dashes. He watched with amusement. He had bonded with this dog, even though he was still frustrated by her obstinacy in not coming when called. She was fun to watch when she ran, and she was smart and funny with her toys. He noticed through the dim dawn light that her attention had focused on some mounds on the beach near one of the palapa bars. She was snuffling and nosing at a pile of sand as he drew closer for a look. All of a sudden all three piles of sand erupted into Mexican youths. They had obviously been sleeping off the previous night's tequila in the cheapest of places, only to be awoken by this "*lobo*" in the early light. Normally he was embarrassed and stricken by his dog's lack of manners, but this situation was too funny to warrant being apologetic. He called the dog back and she came. He chortled all the way back to the hotel, patting his personal "*lobo*".

They spent a few days in Puerto Vallarta, never even venturing across the bridge into Centro. They breakfasted on the beach at Fidencio's and continued the day their people watching, swimming, and napping in the sun. They would return in late afternoon to their room for a shower and more people watching from the balcony. They ate at favourite restaurants, although disappointed that their number one favourite was not yet open for the season. They looked forward to returning for those great steak dinners, and to show expected visitors from Canada their second home.

The Homecoming

With the weekend approaching, they thought it best to head for Melaque, their ultimate destination. The end of the month was approaching and it was time to find a permanent home for the winter. It would be best to reach Melaque before the weekend rush of Mexican tourists.

The three and a half hour drive to Melaque had been made many times before and each bend in the road was familiar. They talked on the way about where they would stay and how they would find a permanent home. Prices in Mexico had soared even from a year ago and they worried about maintaining their budget.

They pulled up in front of the Vista Hermosa Hotel—their home in Melaque on all previous trips in the last eight years. They hoped that Paty would be on duty as she tended to be much more welcoming and amenable than her husband Pablo. Pablo was very tight-fisted. He had once approached them in the street and asked that their rent, always paid promptly, be given to him by a certain hour the following day; he wanted to pay the electric bill. This was a most un-Mexican and rude attitude and so very typical of Pablo.

They walked into the office and found, to their dismay, that Pablo was manning the desk. He barely acknowledged them. When asked about vacancies and rates, Pablo responded that the hotel's rates had increased. Skyrocketed would have been a better term—where in the past the most they had paid was three hundred pesos a night, Pablo was now asking five hundred fify and telling them that was a discount. The rates remained unchanged whether for a day's stay or a month's. They said "no thanks" and left.

"I don't get it," he turned to his wife. "The place is obviously next to empty but he still won't reduce his rates. You would think that he would rather have some cash in hand."

"Pablo is and always will be stubborn," his wife replied. "We'll check with Paty later in the week." (As it turned out when they eventually did check back, Paty reluctantly informed them she would have to consult Pablo. It was obvious Pablo was now dominating the hotel management.)

They walked a couple of doors down the street to the Hotel Monterrey. His wife inquired about rates on the basis of a week's stay and they were shown upstairs to view the room. It was on the top floor, with screened windows open to the foyer. Inside was one large room with beds and kitchen sharing the floor space. The appliances looked old, the beds and wooden shutters even older, with the two burner stove taking the prize for antiquity. She shook her head and backed out. Across the foyer, she spotted another bungalow, this with a separate bedroom. The key was asked for, and they looked in.

The kitchen was large with a floor one step up, and oddly for Mexico, done in wood. The wooden floorboards were broken in some places. The appliances were a bit newer, but what sold them on the place was the extremely large separate bedroom with tile floor, and the fact that both rooms opened to a spacious rooftop patio. They could enjoy the breeze out there and there was ample room for the dog to play. They ascertained the rent was the same three hundred pesos per night and moved in. They would use this as a base while they looked for a more permanent house or apartment.

Settled, they donned swimsuits and headed downstairs to the beach, and to say hello to their old friend Meli at Cesar y Charlys. Meli was delighted to welcome them back and shook his hand vigorously, then gave his wife a big hug. His wife and Meli exchanged news. Meli was fine though his wife and nine children were currently living far away in Michoacan looking after her aging parents, and he missed his family.

The ocean was inviting and they took turns having a dip and playing with the dog. He suggested they return to their room for a shower, cocktails on their rooftop, and then dinner back at Cesar y Charlys. They strolled through the town first, to buy ice and stopped in at the bus station across the street to greet other friends. Lupita and Vincente. Lupita recognized him, not his wife, and complimented him as usual on his movie star looks. Lupita told him he looked different, very relaxed. He preened slightly at the outrageous compliment and explained that he was retired, hence relaxed

They had their drinks on the rooftop. "Don't you think the town is looking a little seedy somehow?" he asked his wife.

She glanced at him apprehensively. "It's the way it's always looked." She wondered if he might be changing his mind about staying here and it worried her.

They returned to Meli's care and dined. His wife had fried chicken with fries, and he had a shrimp salad, which was more like coleslaw with shrimp mixed in. One had to be cautious ordering shrimp dishes and the results were always something different that what one expected. Shrimp cocktails, for instance, bore no resemblance to the shrimp and avocado concoctions had at home; in Mexico they were served hot and like a soup in a sundae glass.

They enjoyed the pleasant evening air and then decided to walk into town—roughly two blocks—to buy dessert from the street vendor cake ladies. His wife chose an extra piece of flan, saying she was going to visit with Lupita a while. He returned to the room with the dog, enjoyed his pastries with his habitual night time tea and turned in. He never heard his wife come in well past midnight.

They spent the next day relaxing on the beach. His wife made occasional forays into town. She came back and told him of a bungalow she had located and they went out in late afternoon to have a look. It was large and accommodating with two bedrooms, but was dark and unprivate. The owners were in Guadalajara and so a price couldn't be quoted, but he told his wife he didn't like it at all so there was no point in pursuing this further. She expressed disappointment, but acceded to his wishes.

She cooked pasta for dinner that night, though it was a trying effort. The stove was unreliable, and they had left their dishes, pots and pans in the camper. Still, he was always amazed at what she could come up with in the most difficult circumstances. They moved the table out of the rickety kitchen onto the patio and ate by candlelight.

The morning brought a couple of nasty surprises. The kitchen floor was overrun with ants, and the fridge was obviously not working. Water from the bag of ice had flooded the floor, and the milk, butter and bacon were spoiled. They cleaned up as best they could and decided that looking for a permanent place had just taken on a new urgency. He didn't say anything to his wife about the cockroaches he had spotted.

They set off walking in the direction of Barra, mostly along the streets fronting the beach, occasionally on the beach itself. They stopped in at all hotels and bungalows on the way to make enquiries. At many there were simply no vacancies for a long-term stay, but in any case, the costs were well beyond their budget. They were quoted five hundred pesos per night and up—sometimes as high as two thousand US dollars per month. They moved further and further away from town, and grew more despondent and frustrated with each block. It was frustrating to think that after all their struggles the past nine months, and all of their travels, that their plans would be thwarted at the very end by a lack of accommodation.

They reached the very end of the town, now actually in Villa Obregon, and the last hope of a place to live. They enquired at Bungalows de Laguna del Tule. A woman showed them a lovely new one-bedroom apartment overlooking the beach and a swimming pool. It was so new that the building had not yet been painted, and the third floor balustrade consisted of a green wire fence. Unfortunately the woman, a maid, could not tell them the cost and called for help. A young girl, arrived and said that her mother, the owner, would only be back at four o'clock and asked that they return then.

They walked the dusty streets back the several kilometers to their hotel. Even not knowing the rates, they felt a cautious optimism. The apartment was very nice; some of the expensive places they had looked at earlier were dingy beyond hope. "It will work out," he said. "Yes," his wife agreed, "everything else has fallen into place so this will too."

They played on the beach, keeping a close track of the time. At four o'clock promptly they drove back to the hotel between the lagoon and the beach. They met the owner, and talked to her about their plans. She explained, very apologetically, that she could only accommodate them until Christmas. Over Christmas the place was fully booked, but she added, she could possibly find room again in January. She showed them to a different room, away from the pool, but with a balcony still facing the sea. Her normal rate was six hundred US dollars per month, but she was willing to drop that one hundred dollars in recognition of their proposed long-term stay. This room, on the third floor, was away from the pool and the lagoon but would be quieter. They did quick calculations (it would cost one hundred fifty pesos per night) and happily agreed. They would move in the morning.

By ten thirty the following morning, they were unloading the camper and settling into room 19 at *calle Zafiro* 43, Villa Obregon. They had left the Hotel Monterrey citing the broken fridge and the ants as the reason for their early departure. The girl at reception had merely shrugged.

They made countless trips up and down the stairs carrying bags, dishes, stereo, blender, and computer. They made a trip back into town for groceries. They set up their camp chairs on the balcony outside their apartment. They tied the dog's lead to the balcony railing so that she could move about with some freedom. Finally, they were settled.

His wife poured drinks and brought them out to where he was sitting on the balcony. Their stereo issued the Spanish sounds of the Jesse Cook CD. It was restful watching the waves lap onto the shore. Occasionally the big rollers would come in and echo in a row down the long beach as if some order had been given for artillery fire. The palm fronds rustled gently against their balcony. They would have a magnificent view of sunsets here. There were no neighbouring hotels on the far side of the complex; only miles of beach where he could take the dog to play.

Looking towards Barra

He knew that they would likely have to move again before Christmas, but that was seven weeks away and as it always had, everything would work out. He sat back with contentment. They had fulfilled their plans and could now start the Mexican portion of their life together. It had seemed such a long way to come, both in distance and in thought but this was worth it. The reality was every bit as good as the dream.

He looked at his watch. It was November first, and he had lived through October of his sixty-first year.

Tales from the Gringa

Posadas

Mid December found the Gringa, husband and dog still living in San Patricio de Melaque. This was familiar stomping ground as they had holidayed in this town of five thousand frequently over the last ten years. Melaque is situated at one end of the Bahia de Navidad, with the slightly more trendy Barra de Navidad located at the opposite end of the three mile beach. Melaque is a town devoted largely to Guadalajaran and other Mexican tourists, while Barra holds appeal for funky *Norte Americanos*. Both have an almost cult following among Canadians and Americans and although the "secret" was closely guarded, it seemed that the number of non-Mexican license plates was threatening to outnumber locals.

Around the pool at their complex the population consisted mainly of the Canadian and American snowbirds taking refuge for two weeks to three months, although the longer stays were the more common. All were quite accustomed to the weekender buses from Guadalajara which disgorged circus levels of Mexicans anxious to party, without sleep, for their short vacations. As the buses arrived, so the local *gringos* retreated to their rooms—the beaches would be noisy and polluted for the weekend's duration and the pool waters took on a murkiness that discouraged cooling off.

It was the consensus of Melaquans and snowbirds alike that of all the creatures under the sun, none was more slovenly than the Mexican tourist. Their love of holidaying and partying with family totally obliterated their normally cleanly habits—litter was dropped where convenient to the user (often within two feet of a rubbish container), broken glass was left to sparkle on the beach sand, the pool waters were murky because … And the locals, while realizing that extra unpaid work hours would follow the departures, nonetheless actively encouraged this branch of tourism. Room rates were charged on a per person basis and increased each weekend or holiday period a base rate of eight hundred pesos plus one hundred fifty pesos per person per night. The demand for rooms was high and the prices undisputed so these Mexican tourists were paying for the otherwise slow economy. The Gringa and her husband occupied a one-bedroom apartment with rent set at four thousand five hundred pesos per month (roughly four hundred fifty dollars US). Next door was a two-bedroom apartment. One morning while breakfasting on the balcony, they counted twenty-two Mexicans of various ages disappearing into that room for a weekend's stay. Their luggage consisted of the omnipresent vinyl shopping bags, blown up beach toys, bags of farina and assorted grocery bags clinking with promise of good times. The innkeeper was collecting almost four thousand pesos for the suite per night. Apparently they meant to sleep in shifts, if at all.

Now at mid December, the holiday season was about to swing into high gear with this holiday second in importance only to Easter in Mexican festivities. The loaded down tourist buses would start arriving in earnest in a few days time, and the inn keeper was forcing Gringa, husband and dog out of their apartment until further notice. Monthly rent could not compare with the holiday rents paid by Mexicans over the next three weeks. She wouldn't confirm the availability of apartments in the New Year but promised to constantly "checky checky" and keep in mind that they would be returning mid-January.

The Gringa and her husband had decided that they would travel to the mountains—sure to be deserted as all the mountain people flocked to the beaches. They had neither reservations, nor specific destinations other than heading to the State of Michoacan—touted highly by their German American neighbour as one of the more beautiful places in Mexico.

Before their travels began again in earnest, there was time to sample the festivities. Melaque loved a good fiesta and practically any occasion was sufficient to loudly rejoice. So far in their six week stay there had been several parades for the Revolution Day. There had been at least two crownings of very junior queens as the numerous nursery schools and kindergartens took to the streets in parade. The pint size youngsters were arrayed in their very shiniest tiaras, fancy dresses and garlands, with the to-be queens arrayed decorously on the hoods of new model cars.

The Christmas season was celebrated in almost every town and village with *Posadas*—a triumphal procession re-enacting the Blessed Virgin and Joseph seeking room at the inn. Having recently spent many hours seeking her own room at the inn, (though happily not in a blessed state), the Gringa was eager to witness the Mexican version. Fed by street rumour of a *posada* that night, she set off just as the sun was setting to find the parade in their suburb of Obregon, home to the working poor.

Unusually the evening promised rain, and the streets were strangely deserted in advent of a Mexican parade. Asking passers by of the location of the *posada*, she was given typically vague and conflicting directions. Certainly there were no crowds lining the streets to cheer on the participants in their quest. Finally she found herself outside the open doors of the local church. Catechism class was in full swing with the congregation of mostly children answering in one voice. Having assured herself that this must be the starting point for the *posada*, the Gringa popped open a can of pop and lit up a cigarillo to wait. She was perched on a nearby wall and had a good view of the proceedings through the wide open doors. The supervising adults motioned for her to join in the congregation but being non-Catholic and mid cigar, she smiled and declined. It was a very progressive church with its doors open to all—several of the neighbourhood dogs wandered freely through the chanting children.

After a lengthy time, there was much stir and excitement within the church. The children were mustered into formation and all handed lit candles. The wealthier of the children were easily identified—they had on good clothes, with the boys wearing ties and the girls fancy confirmation dresses (though those fortunate enough for lace concoctions were often paraded at the Sunday night ritual walks around the town square). Glow sticks in addition to the traditional candles evidenced further proof of wealth. Some of their poorer compatriots were in clean pants long outgrown and barefoot.

The Gringa moved down the block and set in place with her digital camera to record the ritual. She was quite stunned and amused to see that reality had a place in Mexican life—the lead Mary was quite expectant with pillow, though the round belly was at odds with her nine year old face and figure. One had to wonder how prophetic that belly was in this youngster's life and how few years would pass before she would be parading the real thing in the village square.

The children sang hymns as they walked along, candles carefully shielded against the raindrops. Oddly, no one came out of his or her house to salute their march and so the children were quite delighted with presence of the Gringa, and more particularly her camera. Mary and Joseph remained serious while the rest of the villagers jumped about and aped for the camera.

After about a six-block walk, the group came to parade in the courtyard of a house. There they sang to the owners that a room was desperately needed, with promises of sacred enticements for pity shown the poor, holy couple. The owner responded with applause but rather than a welcome into the home/inn, the childrens' attention was directed to a swinging piñata. And thus ended all sacred ritual, evolving instead into a barely controlled free for all for the goodies held within the piñata.

The children formed a circle, just, and children were chosen at random to be blindfolded and handed a bat. After being turned about several times, the blindfolded child would start swinging wildly at the elusive target. The piñata was made that much more difficult a target by sadistic adults who constantly raised and lowered the target by ropes, making the child's rate of success almost futile. Finally one child succeeded with a lucky swing and the piñata cracked satisfyingly open, spraying its candy contents into a general melee. The Gringa decided that the posada had been strangely passive by Mexican standards of celebration but amusing nonetheless. She returned to their apartment through the still quiet streets—the Mexicans at home and disinterested in Mary and Joseph's travails.

On the Road Again

The morning brought a flurry of packing as their inn keeper had apparently checky-checkied her reservation "book" (a pile of loose scraps of paper) and discovered that their apartment was required by a tour bus group a day sooner than expected. She could squeeze them into bachelor's quarters for a night or two though, and the innkeeper seemed to expect great thanks for this inconvenience.

They shifted lodgings and managed to divide their goods into pack along and stay behind. They had made arrangements with one of their snowbird neighbours to store items like beach floats and coffee machines for them until they returned from the mountains. Not being sure of accommodations anywhere during the Christmas season, they felt it was prudent to keep as much living space free as possible in the Westfalia camper. Efficient as they were at stowage after so many months of travel, their efforts were a little hampered by mutual needs to be furtive in hiding away Christmas presents. Of particular concern to the Gringa was the need to hide a gift-wrapped hammock. There's not much room to hide anything in a VW, and finally she secreted the present in the closet and then had to tell her husband that the closet, for undisclosed reasons, was off limits to him until further notice. He, sheepishly in turn, told her that a certain other portion of the camper was off limits to her. They agreed to terms and the last item packed was the eighteen inch high, fully decorated, artificial Christmas tree.

On this, their last evening in Melaque for this year, they set off for a dinner out at Barney's—home of real homemade whole wheat bread, and fabulous *enchiladas suiza*. At the neighbouring table, their snowbird neighbour was entertaining her newly adult sons and girlfriends. Barney's margaritas had apparently been more potent than usual as the whole table stayed in paroxysms of laughter over farting sounds produced with the aid of straws and crooked elbows.

Having had fewer of the potent potables but well satisfied with food and drink they joined the group for a nightcap while the dog finished up her bounty of spare ribs. They offered the group a ride home, gratefully accepted as walking the several miles would have been just too sobering for thought. Seven people and the dog piled into the VW, and the Man decided that it was time to play tour host again. He determined that a trip to the town square was in order to best view the illuminations, and more particularly to see if the Jesus had arrived at the crèche.

They bounced over the back street potholes and parked at the town square. Several of the enterprising youngsters headed for the nearest store to stock up with beer for the long five-minute drive back. The rest of the group gathered at the newly fenced off square to admire the many adorned Christmas trees with oversize wrapped parcels beneath, and the all important nativity scene. The Son was not present, it being nearly a week before Christmas Day, but they all wondered at the symbolism of the very bright red devil standing in the manger.

The ride back was bumpy and raucous, with a good deal of very loud off-key sing-a-longs to the Mexican radio station. Back at the compound, the Gringa and her husband said a polite good night to the crew—and everyone headed off for further partying. The Gringa, the Man and the dog followed the lure of a campfire on the beach and found a group of young tour busers ensconced. Their backs were to the fire, lit for atmosphere and light, while they were engrossed in a game of spin the bottle.

In age anywhere from fifteen to early twenties, the group of twelve or more, invited the Gringa and the Man to join them. The beer bottle was spun in the air and landed facing the Man. The males promptly handed the Man a full bottle of beer that they explained to the Gringa he had to chug in one go or suffer the consequences. Apparently if one didn't down the beer in one long swallow, to accompanying cries of what sounded like Blue! Blue! Blue!, the loser would have to kiss one of the females. Strange rules, but of no worry to the Man who was feeling thirsty in any case. On the next spin, the bottle faced the Gringa and a group crowed that a kiss was required. The Gringa smiled mischievously and pointed to a male and female on the other side of the fire and said, "Ok, they should kiss!" She wasn't sure if it was in the rules or not, but the couple obliged much to the fury of yet another female in the group. Apparently the Gringa had stirred up some trouble.

Jealousy and hard feelings were short lived with those young people. They were soon distracted by music; in particular polka tapes being played on a ghetto blaster near the pool. The group quickly gave up their beach game in favour of some poolside dancing. It was quite amazing to see such a young, hip crowd so thoroughly caught up in old-fashioned music and dance.

But the young will be young, and the edge of the pool too inviting to some and so some of the dancers found themselves helped into the pool. The Man was not far behind in this kind of horseplay, and soon not only was he in the pool but he had dragged the poor dog in to join him.

They left the kids partying at the pool and returned to their room about three am, wet and only mildly sober. They planned an early start to their travels that morning, as much to get some miles traveled as to escape the wrath of the inn-keeper who would be able to easily identify the fur clogging the murkier pool's filter.

Mazalmita

In the morning they piled the remainder of their clothing bags into the camper. Half the compound appeared to wish them a safe and happy trip, and by ten in the morning they were on their way.

The road out of town was familiar and they headed south past Manzanillo's busy port, up past the salt flats and onto the freeway south. She practiced her Spanish on the various road signs, although the one about dimming your lights was proving a bit confusing. Most signs were familiar—*topes* for the speed bumps, *cuervo peligroso* for the dangerous curves. The toll highways are very efficient in Mexico, but can be extremely expensive. Tollbooths are set at random intervals, and toll costs fluctuate without rhyme or reason as well. A six-kilometer stretch of road could cost thirty pesos, and then a thirty kilometer bit exacted a one hundred peso toll. They generally avoided the toll highways not only because of the cost, but the highways tended to be flat and boring. In this case, it was the most expedient route to the Michoacan turn off and they were anxious to cut some time off an anticipated eight-hour drive.

They took the turn off for Highway 14 and started the climb away from the sea. The countryside was typical semi-desert scrub with the occasional *rancho* and small village thrown in. Their destination was Mazalmita—reported to be the Switzerland of Mexico. Just as they were starting to doubt aloud the guide talents of their pushy neighbour, the landscape changed to pine forests. Climbing further, they were astonished to spot Bavarian style lodges set back amongst the forest and it did seem as if they had boarded a magic bus to be transported to middle Europe.

Not half an hour further, they arrived in Mazalmita—a small town set on a hillside with its main street lined with gingerbread houses and alpine lodges. It kept its Mexican tones with the ubiquitous central square leading to a dominating church. The alpine atmosphere was made further enchanting with large, lit stars, comets, and bells criss-crossing the avenues and threading into stately trees. Quaint and charming were the first words to leap out of their mouths.

Mazalmita

The first priority was to find a room. They chose a hotel just up from the square. The hotel had an appealing veranda on the second floor, complete with gingerbread mouldings. They debated leaving the dog in the camper while they secured a room but decided that up front honesty was the best policy. Two teen-age girls were manning the reception desk and provided acceptable room rates (three hundred twenty-five pesos per night) and offered to show the room. The Gringa agreed that they would like to view the room and added they were travelling with a well behaved and clean dog. The gum snapping girl simply shrugged her shoulders at this news, and retrieved a key. The room was on the floor above reception and fronted the veranda that had attracted them in the first place. It was a pleasant spot with marble tile floors and numerous large plants interspersed amongst rustic benches. The room itself was quite typical of a modest Mexican hotel with heavy furniture and a hard bed, and an ensuite bathroom with questionable plumbing.

The room paid for, they set off to explore the town. Mazalmita was several thousand feet above sea level and they needed jackets for warmth even though it was still late afternoon. The Man took charge of the dog and set off in search of green space for pooch hygiene. The Gringa took herself off to explore the shops along the main road. Christmas was of course the sacred shopping season as well, she rationalized. It was interesting to note that handicrafts here in the mountains were more wood than glass or papier-mache and she treated herself (and her far away sister) to a pair of gilt painted crosses adorned with angels.

The square, lighting up with Christmas lights in the setting sun invited the religious with stalls selling saints' cards and votive candles. The jewel of the shopping expedition, however, was a food store set up in an old fashioned mode. Wooden floors warped with age, shelves filled with home made preserves, peppers and oils, a deli counter filled with *dulce de leche*, and some crunchy looking nut bars which turned out to be a toffee and almond brittle. The *dulce de leche* was as smooth as any vanilla fudge. This kind of shopping she knew needed no justification for the husband with the sweet tooth.

By now the sun had set and a chill permeated the air. She caught up with husband and dog admiring the saints in the square, and they headed back to their room for a pre-dinner cocktail. As they passed the reception desk of the hotel, the man now presiding behind the desk hailed them. "You cannot take a dog into your room," he announced. "It is not permitted." The Gringa whirled on him and replied equally in Spanish "We told the girl that we had a dog and she did not say it was not permitted." The man blustered that she did not know the rules and he was in charge.

"Very well," replied the Gringa. "Give us our money back and we will find some other hotel." There had not been very many tourists in evidence in the streets and she banked that he would be loathe to part with money already in hand. "Besides," she added, "the dog is clean and quiet and will not be left alone."

"Alright!" the man threw up his hands. "But you can stay only one night!"

After their drink, they strolled around the town looking for a place for dinner. A funky café with very modernistic lines drew them to look at the menu. "La Luna" promised a variety of food, and a bearded giant of a man called for them to come in—dog and all. The interior was sparsely furnished with rough furniture set off against whitewashed walls and a roaring fire in the fireplace. The fireplace had a massive wooden cross above it, and there were odd adornments hanging from the ceiling—a brass bed, a suitcase, a bicycle and a birdcage.

The Gringa ordered soup and enchiladas for dinner, while her husband opted for the specialty of the house—a mixed grill of meats and vegetables. While they sipped drinks and waited for dinner, they were amused by a tiny kitten that fearlessly climbed legs—table or human—and leapt from tabletop to tabletop. The kitten couldn't have been much older than eight weeks and newly separated from its mother but it already knew the hardship of Mexican petdom and took no time to swat the dog into submission. The dog, enormous by comparison, looked quite the coward straining at its leash to get a safe distance for this spitting demon.

The meals were delicious. As they ate, the owner came to sit with them. He told the story, in Spanish mixed with English, of the spinster owner of this house in revolutionary times. She fell in love with the dashing army captain who rode his horse into her sitting room. Such love they had, he explained, particularly in the afternoons when the bedsprings could be heard to creak throughout the house. He pointed at the brass bed frame. But the revolution called and the army captain was sent away and the maiden fell into great sadness. She did not hear from her lover, and she confessed her love to the priest. The priest claimed that she had sinned and it was due to her sins that the captain was not heard from. For her penance, she was to carry the heavy cross (that very one above the fireplace) around the square. She did this every year for five years on the anniversary of meeting the captain. And then miraculously she received a telegram from her lover saying he was alive and well and posted in deep Oaxaca, and longed for her to come to him. He sent her a train ticket and told her that he would meet her precisely at two pm on the thirty-first of December of that year. She hurriedly packed her luggage (yes that very one hanging from the ceiling), and set of on the journey. The train arrived, precisely on time at two pm on the thirty-first of December at the very station where her lover waited as promised. But it seemed the maiden had disappeared and she was never heard from again.

"But what about the birdcage and the bicycle?" the Gringa asked.

"That is the second part of the story," the owner replied, "and I will tell it to you when you next come to visit our town and my restaurant." And no amount of pleading would coax the story out of him.

Christmas and New Years at 7000 Feet

The following morning, they nipped across the street to a well-patronized Mexican café. The breakfast choices were decidedly Mexican and without any mention of bacon. They both decided on *huevos divorcados*—fried eggs in red and green salsa respectively—and of course, Nescafe from the jar on the table.

The water wasn't boiling hot and the caffeine mixture bore little resemblance to coffee. The eggs arrived, runny and swimming in their Christmas colour sauces, accompanied by a basket of warm tortillas. Her husband sopped up most of his eggs, while the Gringa managed only a few mouthfuls. "I can't believe fried eggs can be so badly ruined! These are called divorcados because that's what would happen if you served them to your spouse!"

They quickly left the restaurant, leaving barely enough pesos to cover the alleged meal, and hunger revolted enough to last until lunchtime.

Next stop on their hand drawn tourist map was Uruapan, location of a fabulous botanical garden and top quality market. It was not too far up the road and they arrived near noon. Uruapan did not have anything quaint to recommend it. The highway was intercepted by a long string of traffic lights diverting traffic into the city centre. The botanical garden was fenced and posted a hefty entrance fee. Perhaps it would have been worthwhile, but the streets surrounding it were log jammed with traffic and there wasn't a parking spot to be found.

The streets leading through the residential district towards town centre were narrow, with high sidewalks, and two-way traffic on one-lane streets. The overall impression of the city was a gray one. The centre was highlighted by six story cement blocks without character, an incomprehensible one-way system and nary a sign of a market. The Gringa could tell that her husband was feeling stressed by the traffic and suggested the best route would be the quickest one out of town, and to hell with the market.

The highway continued to climb towards their next destination, Patzcuaro at elevation seven thousand feet. It was a two-lane highway and the traffic was moderate allowing both driver and passenger to appreciate the surrounding beauty.

The countryside was lush with vegetation; the hillsides dotted with coffee plants and mango trees, peas and tomatoes, and assorted other produce. The earth, where turned over to receive new crops was almost black in its richness. The surrounding mountains were volcanic in shape and mystical with shreds of cloud clinging to them.

Traffic gradually increased as they approached Patzcuaro—a cultural and artisan centre since its establishment in 1540. The road veered off to the right and they circled a congested round-about before climbing a road lined with large, leafy overhanging trees. Traffic was brisk, and they missed the entryway to the hotel/campground they had picked out of the guidebook. It would have been difficult to execute a left turn across the opposing traffic in any case, particularly as the target driveway was largely obscured by construction trenches. They continued up the hill to have a look at the town itself, and hoped fervently that it would have more character than disappointing Uruapan.

The road led past houses built into the hills, crested, and let down into a square. Bedlam reigned! The square was occupied by a vast number of kiosks with tarps protecting their wares, open space was largely littered, and the surrounding one-way streets impassable with clogged traffic and blaring horns. To one side of the square, a sea of tarps branched off innumerable alleyways, but it was impossible to get a good look—too many cars, too many people, too many tarps! Her husband cursed and did his best to creep along, braking frequently for the cars and trucks pulling in and out of traffic on either side; the two lane street appeared to mean five lanes as far as the Mexican drivers were concerned and there was much laying on horns just on sheer principle.

It took a good half hour to circumnavigate the square and that was enough to speed them out of town. They headed back down the hill in search of the dug up driveway that would hopefully lead to a home for few days, if not the holiday season.

The Villa Patzcuaro was located at the end of the dug up lane way. The main house and a row of attached cabin/rooms blocked the rest of the compound from view. Behind the main house was a swimming pool, still filled with water but obviously closed for the season. The cabin/rooms veered to the right, with a further expanse of six units. The units were all fronted by a continuous covered porch, with various types of tropical plants set in pots, or planted to trail up supporting posts giving the whole structure a very cosy and appealing look. The veranda faced onto a several acre field, with two tennis courts, some landscaping, lovely trees and lots of lawn. To the left side of this field was the camping portion though this was only definable by the communal kitchen and bathroom/shower building

The lady of the house spoke no English and was tolerant of Gringa's Spanish attempts to explain their need of a room over the course of the Christmas season and lack of a reservation. She willingly showed them the rooms and in the end they settled on the furthermost cabana. The bags were brought in. Gringa photographed her husband standing on the lanai, looking like a homesteader of yesteryear.

Patzcuaro Home

By mid afternoon they were settled; the clothes were hung in the walk-in closet, and the shelf on one side of said closet had been turned into a bar/pantry. The stereo had been assembled and the Christmas tree put in place of pride at one end of the room. The room was functional and cosy. That accomplished, they repaired to the veranda for teensy hour. The dog was given a long lead line and secured to one of the veranda posts. They were just commenting on the tranquillity of the spot when an elderly man came from around the main building.

"Buenos tardes, senor" they greeted him but he was having none of it. He shook his finger at Gringa's husband and launched into a tirade in English.

"You may love your dog, senor, but I love my plants more! And if your dog harms one leaf you will have to go!"

Both Gringa and her husband were stupefied. The dog was placidly lying on the lawn. Husband recovered first.

"My dog has not harmed anything and if that's your attitude, we'll leave right now!"

Gringa was alarmed. She understood her husband's defence of the dog but where on earth would they go?

"Well just see that it doesn't" the elderly man blustered and stomped off.

Gringa and her husband looked at each other. The attack had been so vehement and so unprovoked. She tried to reassure her husband that there was no reason to leave and offered to have a further conversation with the lady of the house. Still she suggested that it might be prudent to relocate the dog's lead to a pole not surrounded by landscaping. Her husband had just finished retying the lead to the fence of the tennis courts when the elderly man came back. His face was very red.

"I am sorry I was so angry. I am sorry that I yelled at you. It is just that I have spent a lot of time to grow these plants and they very much matter to me. Here is the history of the region that I have written, which you may find of passing interest. I hope you enjoy your stay." And he left.

Gringa and her husband looked at each other mystified. "Drinking?" she asked. "Bipolar?" he replied.

The air cooled rapidly as the sun went down. T-shirts were covered up with sweatshirts, and then further sweatshirts. By six o'clock the sun had set and they moved indoors. In the corner of their room was a curiously built fireplace. The back part of the fireplace featured an inverted pyramid with the purpose of deflecting heat down and back into the room. A skinny fire had been laid with no paper in place to help start the fire. However a lighted match set to one of the kindling sticks quickly started a healthy flame and released a lovely scent into the room. It was strange to think of needing a fireplace in Mexico but here in the high altitude the generated heat was much appreciated. They glanced at the few sticks left for their use and quickly assessed that this would certainly not keep the fire going long.

Under cover of darkness and pretext of walking the dog, they snuck off to scavenge the woodpile at the top of the property. There was a healthy pile of chopped wood there, but they didn't want to get caught by the elderly man and suffer only God knew what kind of tirade.

The next morning her husband woke at his usual early hour and took the dog out to do her business. He returned to bed and reported, with wonder in his voice, that there was a hard frost on the grass. Later he rose before his wife and set flame to the fire to take the chill out of the room. While his wife showered, he went out to the camper and boiled eggs, brewed coffee, and flamed toast for breakfast. His wife reported that the shower barely trickled and suggested he hurry his shower as the duration of the hot water was suspect.

After breakfast they set off to give Patzcuaro another look. Today, in the quiet of the morning, they could be forgiven for thinking there were in a completely different town. The square was clean and the little traffic orderly. They parked and walked to explore.

Patzcuaro featured three large squares and numerous churches. The architecture is spectacular Spanish colonial and many of the predominantly stone buildings date back to 1500 something. Some of the hotels had large gates to let cars and passengers into central, flowered and fountained courtyards. All of the buildings were three or more stories and each had lovely surrounding balconies. Enquiries proved that the room rates were very reasonable, but typical to most interior Mexican towns, dogs were not permitted. The husband sighed wistfully that if they didn't have the dog with them they could have stayed in town. Gringa tried to pacify him with "we'll come back some other time" though his wistful comments irritated her.

The squares boasted a mix of fountains, statues, trees, and grass spaces. The paved pathways cut across in major compass directions offering short cuts to the other side. The commercial establishments ringing the squares consisted of sidewalk cafes and ice cream vendors along with a variety of intriguing stores to shop in. There was much to explore, and lots of opportunities for Christmas purchases, the Gringa thought happily, but it would require some plausible excuse to send her husband off on his own.

Streets radiated up from the squares and at the top of one was a cathedral of considerable proportion, as well as a beautiful and very old church attached to a monastery—though whether there were monks still in attendance was uncertain.

During their walk, they perused menus posted on restaurant walls and found quite a number of restaurants offering interesting cuisine. The photo opportunities promised the need for several rolls of film. The coffee shops dispersed real coffee aromas and they were delighted to learn that the region was famous for coffee production. (They had often wondered at the specialty shops at home boasting about Mexican coffee when in all their travels the only drinkable coffee was instant.)

They discovered that market day was twice weekly and that they had happened onto one of them at their arrival the previous day. The market was a large one serving communities all around the region, with focus on food products as opposed to the flea market affairs on the coast. The Gringa looked forward to the next market day—she found them especially intriguing and enjoyable without being able to put reasons into words.

They read all the plaques on the statues in the square with Gringa translating for her husband. They learned about Papa Quiroga, a Spanish bishop first sent to the area when the Spaniards settled in the sixteenth century. Unlike the other tales of the conquering and proselytizing Spanish, this bishop practiced a more tolerant and benevolent form of conversion that earned him many faithful. It also endeared him to the people so that they called him 'father' in the familial sense. Bishop Quiroga recognized that each of the surrounding towns had a history for a particular form of craftsmanship and he encouraged the villages to retain that heritage and practice. The guidebooks spoke of towns and villages that specialized in such diverse artisanry as woodworking, straw weaving, guitar making, coppersmithing, and all within an hour's drive of Patzcuaro. Gringa felt she had arrived in shopping heaven. Her husband groaned teasingly at the gleam in his wife's eye, but look equally forward to the touring possibilities.

They participated in the local pastime of people watching from one of the many sidewalk cafes and bars, and ate passable *hamburguesas* for lunch. They walked the back streets and noted the location of the grocery store, while the Gringa counted shoe stores—there had to be at least three on one block alone! They purchased a half-pound of real ground coffee for the next day's breakfast. Well satisfied with their choice of Christmas vacation locale, they returned to Villa Patzcuaro

A day or two later, they were sitting on the veranda enjoying the warmth of the afternoon sun. A motor home with California plates pulled in and commenced the rv dance of to-ing and fro-ing to get the right position and level over near the communal kitchen. A young couple emerged, both looking blonde and California fit, followed by a very squat bulldog.

Later that evening, they observed the young couple cooking at the outdoor barbecue at the top of the property. They were having a good time and had availed themselves heartily of the woodpile. But what attracted attention even at the distance, especially of Gringa's Irish husband, was the very pronounced Northern Irish accent of the female.

Shortly after the barbecuing couple had returned to their motor home, the elderly hotel owner tromped onto the scene brandishing his fist at the couple.

"Listen," he blustered, "You used too much wood. Who said you could take it? And by the way, I love my plants more than you love your dog. Your dog had better behave and if you don't like it, you can leave right now!" The young couple stood there with their jaws hanging.

The Gringa and her husband looked at each other and laughed. "So I guess that's the welcoming speech!"

The Irish girl visited later that evening, bringing along beverages to be sociable. Her husband had declared an early night thanks to the twelve hour drive they had had from Acapulco. The Gringa's husband and the Irish lass compared and confirmed mutual roots, and discussed how long they had both been away from the "Old Country." (Amusing to the Gringa is the fact that virtually every Irish person refers to the "Old Country" as if theirs was the only old country and that everyone else in the world universally understood that.) The Irish lass relayed that she used to sing in a full jazz orchestra at the Ritz in London, but that her roots were in the small Northern Ireland town of Bushmiill's near where Gringa's husband had frequently summered as a lad. The Irish lass had met her Californian husband in England and they were on a six month honeymoon in Mexico before returning to settle in California. Their work background was in computers, and they hoped to fund their trip by selling Mexican artisan work on Ebay.

Further details were tipsily exchanged—the bulldog was a puppy weighing a current forty pounds (and wasted no time throwing her weight at the Gringa's dog, albeit in a friendly manner), and Californian husband was an avid surfer (of course!). They were planning to spend quite some time in the Patzcuaro region but intended to take surfing side trips to the coast. The Gringa and her husband in turn shared their song and dance about chucking jobs, packing up and selling the house and being homeless for an expected eight month period. They exchanged stories about the welcome to the property and had a good laugh. As the Irish put it, the craic was great.

The days leading up to Christmas passed quickly. The routine for breakfast was by now well established, and portions of the day were devoted into trips up the hill to the town centre for sight seeing and shopping. Market day became a quick favourite, and one full afternoon was devoted to simply strolling the aisles of the massive building and tarp city full of vendors of every imaginable product.

In the main building were kiosks and counters set up for butchers and fish-mongers. The initial aromas greeting patrons were mouth-watering ones of roasted pork, available for sale by the pound, complete with well-salted crackling. Roasted pork or *carnitas* is a specialty of the region and is offered up to snack on, in sandwiches, or in bulk pieces for the family dinner. However, once past the *carnitas* vendors, the uncooked meats were on offer and the smells and sights in here were not for the faint of heart. It was quite common to see whole animals hanging waiting for the customer's selection. Pig heads dangling from hooks adorned the stalls of the vendors specializing in pork. The meat cases offered every part of every animal for sale from chicken head to chicken feet, pig snout to pig tail, cuts of beef from heart and liver to hooves.

Outside the building, the vendors set up produce tables sheltered by tarps. The variety was simply amazing—from tropical pineapple and mango to cooler weather coffee and peas. Enormous heads of snow-white cauliflower sat next to fist sized strawberries. Herbs, spices and assortments of barks for cooking and for medicinal purposes offered mysterious allure. Vendors handed out samples of tangerines and pistachios to munch on while shopping. Chickens sat balefully in wire cages next to eggs that were likely their last productive efforts on earth. Past the foodstuffs, were stall upon stall of household gadgets and goods, bootlegged CDs and tapes, belts and shoes and underwear by the gross. And all the alleyways were jammed with people, sounds of vendors hawking their wares as *el primo*, and greetings being exchanged. The atmosphere of the market offered a feast for all of the senses and one felt a real part of the Mexican community just being there.

On some afternoons, they took to the road and visited the surrounding villages. The Gringa loved the musical sounding Tzinzunzan (meaning place of hummingbirds—can't you just hear them?) where the local talent was focused on straw goods. She bought garlands of straw Christmas bells, and straw wreaths to decorate their home away from home.

Tzinzunzan had been the capital city for the Purapecha Indians and still featured the remains of two large pyramids. The presence of these posed a challenge to the conquering Spaniards who built a competing cathedral. The Gringa and her husband visited the old church and its grounds. Here, despite the magnificent, gold adornments of the interior, the Indians had been afraid to step inside the church and so an outdoor stage had been built to perform plays about Christianity in an effort to convert the locals. Next to the large stone constructed stage was a baptismal well, also of stone, in a six by four foot wide dimension with steps leading seven feet down into the ground for full immersion. The surrounding gardens displayed the stations of the cross and the hushed atmosphere even managed to mute the happy cries of playing children.

They visited Paracho, a very small town with world renown for the guitars hand built there. It was amazing that virtually every single shop made and sold guitars.

Paracho Guitars

They drove around Lago Patzcuaro, famous for its Day of the Dead festivities when lit candles were set adrift on the lake from historic Janitzio, and for the boats with butterfly nets used in fishing the now almost extinct whitefish. They had lunch at a German hotel and restaurant set in the countryside away from everything, and where the schnitzel was accompanied with the entertainment of a waiter trying to chase down a fast moving chicken.

But of all the towns, it was Santa Clara del Cobre that sang to the Gringa's cooking and shopping loving soul. Here the entire town was devoted to fashioning goods from the copper mined nearby. Religious artefacts, decorative vessels, statuary was available in any size or form, all copper. The Gringa almost wept with pleasure at the extraordinarily inexpensive price of two hand beaten copper frying pans lined with silver, and a matching paella pan. Her shopping there would have taken on magnificent proportions had not space been at such a premium in their camper.

Santa Clara del Cobre

Some evenings they dined out in Patzcuaro. They learned the hard way that in Patzcuaro, unlike the rest of Mexico, dining was at a relatively early hour. By nine o'clock in the evening, most restaurants had closed their doors for the night. The majority of the buildings didn't have any sort of heating system and by the time the sun had set for a couple of hours, diners had to resort to wearing coats even indoors, and so early closures were the rule.

An exception occurred one evening dining at La Campagna. They had enjoyed their dinner and enjoyed even more the talents of the guitarist/singer on stage. A local accordionist joined him and together they delighted the crowd with an impromptu jam session. Just as the restaurant doors were being closed for the evening, a family came in with a young girl in their midst. She was practising to be a vocalist and asked if she could join the jam session for a song. The players and the audience were delighted with the resulting sound and the jam session was carried on enthusiastically well past midnight.

Christmas

On Christmas Eve day Gringa and her husband set off for the market to purchase their Christmas feast. It had been their tradition to barbecue on Christmas Eve, but with the early dark and cold here in Patzcuaro, they decided to break with tradition. At the market they picked up a large chunk of roast pork, a few varieties of cheeses, grapes, strawberries and fresh bread. They stopped in at the *supermercado* to purchase an affordable yet drinkable Mexican wine.

The Gringa asked to stop at one of the nativity scenes before heading back to their compound. "I'm curious to find out when they put Baby Jesus in the crèche. My Dad was the biggest kid when it came to Christmas and he always told me that Baby Jesus was born at four o'clock in the afternoon on the twenty-fourth so that's when Christmas officially starts. I realize it was just his way of speeding up the festivities, but it's always worked for me!"

The crèche was empty still and the Gringa wondered if the priests had to come out at midnight to perform the sacred birth.

Back at the complex, they stowed the foods in their walk-in closet kitchen, and collected a sufficient quantity of wood from the woodpile while keeping an eye out for the old man. The fireplace was extremely efficient, and a helper came in daily to clean it out and lay a new fire for the evening. The daily allotment only ran to a few sticks and they knew that on Christmas Eve the fire would need to be kept going to the wee hours.

They made separate trips to the camper and laid gift-wrapped parcels all around the tree. Most of the packages dwarfed the tree in size. Each was amused to see two three-foot high gift-wrapped rolls side-by-side—reciprocal hammocks! And each wondered how they had not stumbled across the other's gift in the tight space of the camper!

At four o'clock her husband declared "It's Christmas!" and let her finally play the Christmas CDs she had packed from Canada. They poured themselves a holiday libation and sat on the veranda. The old man and his son were busy making tens of paper-wrapped lanterns and hanging them in the trees around the property. "Feliz Navidad!" they called out. As the sun set, the old man went around and lit every lantern in every tree. In the darkened evening, the entire property was transformed into a magical fairyland.

That evening they lit the fire early and sat down to their market feast. They gave the dog an enormous gift wrapped bone and she settled in quiet contentment. They talked about their travels, and reminisced about Christmas' past.

The Gringa handed her husband a package with a tag that read "I'll love you till death do us part and beyond." He laughed delightedly at the contents—a pair of well-dressed dancing skeletons. The famous "*Katrina*" dolls could be found all over the region, and in many shapes and sizes. Most of the ceramic statues were of female skeletons in elaborate Victorian or flamenco dress and were in tribute to the region's Day of the Dead celebrations. The dancing couple was in honour to the Gringa and husband's love of dancing. The Gringa told him about some of the other humorous statuettes she had seen, including one of a very pregnant skeleton sitting on a park bench.

They exchanged hammocks and laughingly compared shopping excursions, price, and hiding place.

She thanked him, the dog and the absent cat for the box of chocolates they traditionally gave her. Her eyes gleamed with pleasure at the silver bracelet with each link depicting a different piece of Mexican culture.

The Gringa handed her husband a flat box and waited with held breath for his reaction. Inside was a leather wrapped binder containing the story "In October of his Sixty First Year." "I'll be interested to see what you think—I kind of took the liberty of writing it from your point of view."

"When did you do this?" he exclaimed.

"I wrote whenever you took the dog for runs on the beach, and I wrote a lot at night after you had gone to bed."

And yes, she agreed, that was why she had insisted on buying a new printer in Manzanillo. And yes she confessed, the trip to the town to buy leather to make toys for the dog was really to look for binding material. "But I miscalculated. Remember the piece of leather we tied into a knot and wet for the dog to use as a toy? I ran short on the cover and had a cut an extra piece from that—if you look on the back you can see teeth marks!"

They settled into companionable silence. He read his new book, she read Harry Potter. They sipped liqueurs and were comfortable in front of the fire. Occasionally he would look up and comment "This is fantastic!" or to her amusement, "I can hardly wait to see how this ends!"

Some time past midnight, they took the dog out for an off leash run and wandered among the lanterns in the garden. They returned to the cosy fire lit room and snuggled into bed for a long winter night's sleep, well content with their gifts, and each other.

They agreed to stay on in Patzcuaro until after New Year's. The days were warm enough to wear shorts, the evenings and nights cold enough to require the fire. The hammocks were strung between the trees by the tennis court. The Gringa settled in, wrapped in sleeping bag for extra warmth and immersed herself in all five volumes of the Harry Potter story.

They played tennis one day but the seven thousand foot altitude had them both puffing and breathless after one set.

They socialized with the California/Irish couple and watched their dogs play together. The Bulldog was amazingly agile with a soccer ball, while their dog made a pretty good goalie. The dogs were now allowed off leash as the old man had relented on his threats and had quite taken to both sets of tenants.

One evening they all sat in front of the fire in the Gringa and husband's room, sharing a bottle of wine and talking well into the night. The conversation drifted into the effects of alcohol and other enhancements. The Irish lass produced a tablet and said "We have just one tablet of Ecstasy left and we want to share it with you. It makes you shag like rabbits! Brilliant!" The Gringa started in horror, visions of a four-way sex popping into her brain. Neither she nor her husband was into illicit drugs of any kind, including pot. To her surprise, her husband said "Great! Thanks!" To her relief, the tablet was cut in half and the California couple left, with lots of winks and "Have a good night!"

"You're kidding me, aren't you?" she asked her husband.

"Sure, why not?" he replied. And so they split the half into half again and each swallowed their portion. They got ready for bed and lay down under the covers, holding hands and waiting for the magic to take hold. In the morning the Irish lass exclaimed "Well we had a great night. How about you two?" The Gringa and her husband blushed … and admitted they had fallen asleep. So much for Ecstasy.

There was only one other family that rented a cabin for a few days over New Year's. The Gringa watched in amazement as her husband conducted a several hours long conversation with this family from Mexico City—his Spanish was very limited. He nonetheless came away and reported to the Gringa that they had a standing invitation to stay with the university professor and his family in Mexico City.

The California man's parents flew in for a visit. The dad was quite a blustery hale-and-hearty type, while the redheaded mother quickly had the old man of the complex completely smitten and offering any number of favours. Their son and daughter-in-law took them sightseeing and having left the bulldog unattended in the rental car, returned to fine the gearshift knob completely chewed away. There was great hilarity at the possible explanations to be given to the rental agency.

The Gringa and her husband drove the hour and half distance to visit Morelia. They were awestruck by the beauty of the architecture, the cleanliness of the streets, and the number of parks. They strolled the streets in the sunshine, savouring ice cream made with fresh fruit. They visited the cathedral, which had two pipe organs. They watched a wedding in progress, the Gringa's husband waiting for the pipe organ to sound the recessional. Sadly this extravagance had been beyond the purse of the wedding party, and the music was only of taped variety.

Morelia Cathedral

Exploration of Morelia's outskirts revealed a Costco Warehouse and Walmart! They browsed through both just to compare products and prices to those at home. Costco proved a little more irresistible and they came away with cheeses, wines, rice crackers and other assorted goodies not normally associated with Mexico.

During the week they exchanged dinner 'parties' with the California/Irish couple. One night the Gringa cooked and served spaghetti Bolognese in the communal kitchen. Another night the Irish lass made UK style boiled ham and potatoes. Both dinners were very convivial with lots of good conversation and drink. Almost too much so as one evening the Irish lass twisted her ankle stepping out of the communal kitchen. The fault actually lay in a wobbly rock serving as a step stone. The next day Gringa's husband and the Californian took the girl to the hospital where she was diagnosed with a bad sprain. The old man of the complex felt very bad about the incident and promptly poured a new flush, concrete step. The Irish lass took her moment for posterity and carved her initials into the step before the concrete dried.

The sprain didn't prove to be much of an impediment. Her able young husband was quite willing to fetch and carry for her or herself if need be. One night the four of them returned to La Campagna Restaurant to listen to music. With the Irish lass' experience in singing with the big band in London, she would be a natural for the audience. When she was announced, her husband carried her up the steps to the stage. A terrific rendition of "Summertime" brought the crowd to their feet before our chanteuse was carried off the stage again.

New Year's Eve, the Gringa and her husband decided to eat out. They had scoped out a few of their favourite restaurants, including La Campagna, but found their celebratory meals unreasonably priced. Most restaurants weren't offering any type of special and they decided that they would just take their chances. It was around nine o'clock when they started their walk about Patzcuaro and they were stunned to find that even those restaurants with the special New Year's menus were already closing for the evening. One waiter informed them that for Mexicans New Year's Eve is a home and neighbourhood celebration. The restaurants were closing even earlier than normal (or not opening at all) so that their staff could be at home for the festivities.

They got back in the camper to head back to Villa Patzcuaro but detoured through one of the residential neighbourhoods. Celebrations indeed! They counted numerous bonfires in the street, children playing with the exuberance of those allowed up past their bedtimes, and adults visiting. Overall though, the celebrations seemed to be very low key but they assumed the frolic factor would increase with the advent of midnight.

On their return trip, they noticed that the newly opened French restaurant on the boulevard approach to Patzcuaro was brightly lit. Inside the owner assured them that full service was available, even at this late (by Patzcuaran standards) hour. They were offered a complimentary drink and provided menus. The

French lady owner explained that they were newly opened, and she and her husband were quite puzzled at the poor turn out on what is traditionally a big night to restauranteurs the world over. The Gringa and her husband shared their new-found knowledge on local customs.

"Never mind then" said the owner. "We are expecting some good friends from Morelia tonight, and there is one other group here. We will simply join all the tables and celebrate *en famille* ourselves!"

And so all the tables were joined and introductions made. The French husband and co-owner cooked all of their meals and joined them at the table. The food was delicious. The group was an eclectic mix of French, Canadian, Mexican, and German, adults and children—all well educated and well traveled. Conversation flowed in a curious melange of French, English and Spanish, and by the time the New Year's countdown came they were fast friends. They toasted the New Year and threw streamers. The volume was turned up on the music and a dance or two had in the empty part of the restaurant. By one am, goodnights were exchanged with lots of accompanying hugs and kisses.

The first day of the new year dawned with a cloudless sky. The shepherd from the adjoining property guided his flock onto the vacant field adjoining the complex for some grazing. The Gringa walked over to take some photographs. The shepherd pointed proudly to a tiny lamb in the midst, chasing after its mother. "It was born just after midnight and is a New Year's baby—very lucky!" He wore a half toothless and very indulgent smile as he gave permission to the Gringa to hold the newborn for a photograph. And the Gringa felt very lucky indeed to have held the small miracle on the first day of the year.

No Butterflies

They left Patzcuaro on the fourth day of the new year, feeling like they were leaving home again. The old man seemed sorry to see them leave and offered a fifteen percent discount on their bill. How different the departure from the reception!

They traveled the winding back roads of the mountain country heading for the butterfly sanctuary at Angangueo, a purported two hour drive from Morelia. The guidebooks promised pathways and hillsides of orange and black with monarch butterflies so thick that visitors had to be careful not to step on them.

The turn off to Angangueo stated a distance of thirty-four kilometers from the highway. Her husband asked whether they should gas up and find a bank before they traveled further but the Gringa, anxious to get there, said "No, we can gas up in Angangueo and get money there." As the road wound ever higher, and deteriorated to frequent potholes, the country became more and more remote. They passed through a village that was little more that a church and two speed humps. Their speedometer indicated forty kilometers traveled and still no town in sight. The gas gauge needle moved steadily towards empty and the Gringa nervously joked about having to hitchhike back to the highway. Her husband didn't see the humour.

Finally the road culminated in a town set on a steep hillside. At the top of the hill was the omnipresent church and typical businesses ran down either side of the street. There was no going further as the road seemed to simply vanish. They noted, thankfully, the presence of a gas station, parked the camper and set out to find a bank machine. There were quite a number of 4x4 vehicles parked along the road, virtually all sporting signs "See the butterflies—400 pesos per person" and "Butterflies—3 hours". Certainly there weren't any butterflies in sight, even though they were already at eight thousand feet altitude.

A couple of enquiries later, they faced disappointment: One—no bank or ATM in town, nowhere to cash cheques or exchange money and they only had about three hundred pesos between them. Two—the butterfly sanctuary was a further two to three hour four-wheel drive up the mountain and the cost was at cheapest three hundred fifty pesos each. (The guidebook had indicated an entry fee of $3.50 per person but made no mention of the exorbitant fee to get to the entry). Three—no available rooms that would take dogs but this was a moot point as they didn't have the ready funds to pay for the room. Four—even if all else was well, the dog would be forced to wait alone in the camper for a good six hours should they undertake the butterfly excursion.

By this point, husband was a bit on the grumpy side. The Gringa was totally unhappy herself but didn't feel allowed to grumble as she felt responsible for rushing them off the highway and into this fund-less state. They had a cheap and mediocre meal at a café. Her husband wanted to look around the town and explore its mining history a little but the Gringa saw no point and hustled him along. No doubt her disappointment was colouring her vision, but she saw nothing attractive about the place and was anxious to move on.

Two hours later the miseries of the day were compounded as they circled through the streets of Ziticuaro in search of parking, a bank machine and accommodation for the night. They managed to find an ATM but the rest was an exercise in frustration. Even the girl at the information centre seemed particularly obtuse and unhelpful, and the Gringa's and husband's tempers frayed to snapping point. They finally managed to settle in the Bungabillo Motel well out of town—and well away from any kind of amenities. They cooked a can of soup in the camper as this was about the only food choice available. Still they took good news where they could and were heartened by the dog (usually reluctant in strange places) having a poop, albeit in the middle of the driveway.

The next morning they decided to forego butterflies and continue on their journey. They traveled the back roads through beautiful mountainous countryside. Their travels led them to Vallee de Bravo, touted as a weekend playground for wealthy Mexico City residents. Nestled above a pristine looking lake, the town exuded charm. It had serpentine streets lined with shops and attractive houses. The feel of the town was a mixture of European alp villages and old Mexican. They looked longingly at a lovely home, complete with three chimneys, overlooking the lake. Vallee de Bravo seemed like a good place to live, particularly if one was experiencing the rootless pangs of the recently homeless.

They had a hearty breakfast in the central courtyard of a restaurant. The day had already made up for the foibles of yesterday's travels. Outside, in the square fronting a lovely church, the weekly market was in full swing. They bought some luscious,fist sized strawberries to munch on as they walked. The local Indians were there in very colourful dress although to the Gringa's shock, one lady demanded 50 pesos for having her photo taken. Long tables were laden with *Rosco des Reyes* cakes—a traditional sweet bread with saffron and dried fruits made in commemoration of the kings' arrival at Baby Jesus' side—and the bakers were quite aggressive in their desire to prove their goods' superiority, thrusting samples at everyone. The Gringa was delighted with the treat—it tasted very similar to her native Latvian krengels and was a taste of home.

They retraced their miles back through the pastoral countryside and rejoined the main highway once again. The road climbed ever higher and they watched with awe as their altimeter registered ten thousand feet. Amazingly, even at this altitude farms continued to line the roads although their crops looked increasingly more meagre. The Gringa asked her husband to stop at the top as she wanted to get a photograph of a herd of ponies with the ring of volcano tops in the background. She hopped out and trotted back a hundred feet for the right angle. Even that short exertion left her absolutely gasping for breath. "How do these people get any work done around here?" she marvelled.

The road descended to the basin of the ring of volcanoes that flanked Mexico City. They approached Toluca, a suburb a full hour's drive from the capital and commented on the urban sprawl. The Gringa and her husband debated driving to Mexico City, but with suburb already demonstrating massive volumes of congested traffic, decided to pass on the opportunity.

They veered west instead and headed for the silver capital, Taxco.

As soon as they crossed the state line into Guerrero, the difference in state affluence was evidenced in the poor condition of the road. In Michoacan, the roads were in good condition. In Guerrero the highway was narrow and so potholed that driving became an exercise in obstacle avoidance. The countryside faded into a uniform brown, relieved only by straggly vegetation. The road developed a roller coaster form with ups and downs and hairpin corners. Their conversation dwindled as her husband's concentration on the road intensified. A *topes* (speed bump) placed incongruously in a shaded patch in the middle of nowhere took them unawares and her husband swore as the camper thumped over it at speed. There was a cracking sound but the camper didn't falter so they drove on, her husband berating himself for not having anticipated the bump. The camper seemed to sway more around the corners and her husband offered the opinion that they might have broken a rocker arm. The Gringa was alarmed—she had no idea what a rocker arm was or its function, but it sounded important and these decrepit roads were no place to have a faulty vehicle. Not to mention that if they got stuck somewhere, the lack of traffic on the highway promised that they could be marooned for days. One look at her husband's grim concentration, however, and she kept her dooming thoughts to herself.

Finally, as the afternoon waned, they turned a corner and Taxco suddenly presented itself. The town spread before them across a u shaped gorge. The buildings and streets seemed to tumble down a mountainside, and with the late afternoon sun hitting it full on, the effect was mystical. Here was a silver capital that sprang forth directly from the mountain that gave it its riches.

The highway bisected the town across the middle and as they drove through they craned their necks up and down to get a better look. It was difficult to do as the traffic was dense with honking taxis and trucks. The side streets seemed impossibly steep and narrow and so they stayed on the highway. No way to meander to the town square in this layout! The highway stretch through town was only a few kilometers in length, and they soon had to turn around and back-track. They spotted a multi-storey hotel perched on the down slope and turned in to try their luck at a room. Even the entry ramp to the parking lot was impossibly steep and the husband had to take several runs at it before they were able to park on level ground. He took the dog for a toilet expedition while the Gringa went to inquire about rooms. They rendezvoused in the parking lot—she successful, the dog obstinately not. "A lot of sniffing but no action," her husband reported.

They moved their luggage into their room on one of the upper floors. The building was relatively modern in that it had an elevator, but the atmosphere and décor was more communist block unchic than Mexican. They did have a balcony overlooking the poor parts of Taxco at the bottom of the mountain. The rate was reasonable, and the dog was welcome so they were satisfied.

By now the dog had gone the whole day without relieving itself, so Gringa took the pooch on another expedition while her husband relaxed with a cocktail. Outside the hotel, there was a sea of concrete, very little sidewalk and nothing green. Gringa decided to try their luck at the construction site across the road—it held several appealing looking mounds of earth. The dog sniffed and sniffed and they moved from one section to the other. The dog growled at the caterpillar tractor and then sniffed hopefully at the tires. Each mound was carefully checked out, but no deposits were made. After twenty minutes of frustration, Gringa gave up and they returned to the hotel room.

They decided visit the town centre by taxi instead of trying to negotiate the winding narrow streets in the camper. The dog would also be happier if left in the camper in the quiet of their current parking spot. Gringa checked at the desk for the cost of a taxi to *Centro* so that they would not be conned by the taxi driver, and they managed to flag one down on the street.

The taxi was a VW bug, common in Mexico and in good shape except that the front passenger seat was missing. Later they would notice this was common to all taxis in Taxco though the reason was unexplained. They negotiated the price and the destination with the cab driver and climbed into the back. They wanted to go to the main square up the mountain.

The cab driver shifted into gear and floored the accelerator. He turned right and headed down the mountain at breakneck speed. Gringa and her husband gasped at the manoeuvre and held on tightly, too astonished to question the direction. The streets were all very narrow, barely wide enough for a car to navigate. Despite this, the traffic was two-way and compounded with pedestrians. The ride turned into an exhilarating game of 'chicken' with their driver charging at full speed towards anything in his path, honking the horn all the way. Opposing traffic was suitably cowed to back up and give way, while pedestrians jumped into doorways to save their lives. Eventually the driver turned and headed up the mountain, increasing speed to perhaps get a run at the steep hills. Maybe he wasn't comfortable starting from a dead stop on a hill driving a manual transmission, or maybe his brakes wouldn't hold; either way Gringa and her husband agreed it was a better ride than any amusement park could offer and they moaned at their lack of foresight to bring the video camera.

A large and ornate cathedral dominated the main square. Thirteen workers had plunged to their death during its construction, and this added to its mystery and aura. Streets meandered in every direction from the main square like a spider web, and lured the visitor with curves and corners, restaurants and silver filled shops.

They had pizza for dinner in a restaurant flanking the square and their terrace table gave them a great view of the town. The Gringa questioned the waiter about mail delivery in Taxco, but he didn't understand. She wondered at how long mail delivery would take for the poor postman who had to climb the steep hills. Given the size of the mountain and the town, every errand would seem daunting, By night, with some Christmas lights still decorating the houses, Taxco looked like a fairyland.

Their drive back to the hotel was considerably more sedate although they still instinctively braced themselves against imminent impact. At the hotel, her husband liberated the dog from the camper and set off again for the dog to do her necessaries. He returned a half hour later with the report that there were some incredibly nasty dogs running loose, and that despite a variety of locations, their dog was still holding all in. They decided to leave their balcony door ajar that night in the hopes that if the dog had to relieve herself, she would at least do so on the balcony.

Gringa slept poorly. She had drifted off to sleep only to be awoken by the sounds of a dogfight below, which in turn had their dog whimpering. She calmed their dog but sleep was now impeded by the sounds of a very loud argument and breaking glass. The cacophony went on for hours, and she eventually shut the balcony door in an effort to block out some of the noise. She managed to drift off to sleep again, but woke to each sound her own dog made, ready to leap into some kind of action if the dog decided to relieve itself. By morning she was exhausted.

Taxco

They decided to go back into the central part of town to have breakfast and take some photographs before setting out of town. They put the dog in the camper—she had again refused to do any business on her morning walk—and hailed another cab. This time, husband had the video camera to his eye to record the ride. While the journey would have turned the average person's hair grey, it was nowhere near as perilous as the previous evening's and they were oddly disappointed. They were equally let down by the return ride—strange to be disappointed because your life wasn't put at risk.

They collected their belongings and turned back onto the highway, destination Acapulco. Gringa looked back on Taxco and thought about her sleepless night. With the difficulties with the dog she was glad they weren't staying on longer. But she was astounded that she, Gringa Shopping Queen, was leaving behind the silver capital without so much as a pair of earrings to attest to her presence.

About an hour's drive further, they came across a flat and accessible pull out area near a dry riverbed. They pulled well off the highway and let the dog out without her leash. Gringa kept her eye on her, watching for the elusive pee movements. Her husband crawled under the VW to have a look at the rocker arm. He called to the Gringa and she leaned underneath to get an idea of what this critical/non-critical part was. A few minutes later they both emerged and looked around for the dog—nowhere in sight. They both whistled, to no avail. Gringa spotted movement out of the corner of her eye and looked far down the riverbed. There, about a half kilometer away, she saw her dog streaking at full run towards a herd of goats. She also spotted the shepherd on horseback angling towards the dog. "*Es mi pera! Es mi pera!*" she screamed at the top of her lungs, trying to alert the Mexican to the fact that it was a dog and not a wolf about to attack his goats. The dog succeeded in scattering the herd before she finally gave in to her masters' frantic calls and whistles and came happily trotting back. "You're lucky you weren't shot!" the Gringa chastised. The dog panted with a big grin on her face, and to put a finally punctuation on the moment, walked out a big long pee. (She always walked on her two front paws while she peed, so as not get her rear paws accidentally wet—it was a talent she had cultivated since early puppy hood.) All parties now greatly relieved, they jumped back into the VW for the rest of the drive to Acapulco.

Highlights and Lowlifes of
Acapulco

They entered the city through the tunnel, with Gringa's husband grousing at her because she hadn't spotted the "*libre*" road signs fast enough and they were now faced with another eighty peso toll. The highways had cost them over two hundred pesos that day already. As they emerged from the tunnel the road forked with an option to go left or right along the bay, though the bay wasn't visible, hidden behind the buildings lining the avenue. This highway, divided by a large grassy boulevard, was the "*Costera*" and paralleled the breadth of Acapulco Bay.

Gringa directed them right and started the lookout for a reasonable motel. She spotted one that her guidebook stated as affordable and they pulled into the parking lot. She trotted in to the reception area and was quickly back out—no reservations/no room, no dogs and very expensive daily rates in any case. The worrisome part was that the guidebook didn't offer many other options. They continued further on until they reached the residential section at the furthest northern part of the bay and had to backtrack. The *Costera* was two or three lanes in each direction. It was hard to determine if there were two or three lanes as for the most part cars, buses and bicycles were four, five and even six abreast. The traffic sped at an alarming rate, punctuated by brake squealing at the *topes* and horns blaring just for sheer exuberance. It was very unnerving to have horns sound immediately behind and beside you without apparent reason. Gringa could tell her husband was anxious to have the driving done with.

On their third pass of this section of Acapulco, they managed to find a parking spot and set out on foot to scout out the hotels/motels in the area. As luck would have it, the one closest to their vehicle, the Playa Suave proved to have a vacancy and accepted dogs. It was a two star motel, even by Mexican standards, but it did have a nice pool, the rooms were clean and it was directly across from the beach. It also had the bonus, in their eyes, of being located on the fringe of the old town. A room was only two hundred pesos per night.

They dumped their luggage in their room, quickly changed into bathing suits and headed across the road to the beach. The water was quite a distance from the edge of the road, and yet the normal beachfront restaurants hugged the street edge. They wandered down the beach until they found some vacant beach chairs and settled in. The bar for these chairs was a good hundred feet away and she felt sorry for the waiters having to make the constant long trek. In the end, her sympathy was misplaced as the only waiter who approached them was one who demanded a fifty peso payment for use of each of the chairs and advised that the bar was self serve only. Gringa was quite miffed at both statements—in other places if you were charged chair rental you were compensated with drinks. Still, thirst was thirst and hubby deserved a cold beer or two to decompress from the drive. She hiked towards the bar and then spotted a convenience store across the road—beer would be cheaper there. She loaded up with *cervezas*, some pop for her and some chips. She was shocked at the checkout counter to be charged a further ten pesos per bottle for a deposit. (She would be even further shocked when she tried to return the empties without a purchase slip and they wouldn't take back their own bottles!)

They made themselves comfortable on the beach, admiring the view of the big bay. It looked just like the fifties' postcards of Acapulco at its heyday. The bay made almost a full circle having a quite narrow entrance. Unfortunately, the narrow entrance and the long flat beach also served to keep out a cleansing tide, and when they ventured into the water, she was disgusted to find empty plastic bags and other trash swirling around her legs. The swim, therefore, was quite short and they repaired to the beach chairs for sun and people watching.

A fishing boat, one of the common fibreglass *pangas*, roared in as close to shore as it could get, and two of the occupants came ashore. They started reefing in a fishing net, straining almost horizontal with the effort. Another couple of passersby took up the lines to assist. Soon there were two lines of five each pulling mightily to haul the net and catch ashore. It took a full half hour to drag in the bounty that was more net than fish. What fish there were in the net were parcelled out to the helpers, leaving the original fisherman with scarcely a bucket full of an assortment of small fish. Not a very profitable day it seemed.

Back at their hotel, they discovered that the majority of fellow tenants were French Canadians. They seemed a little distant and the Gringa wasn't sure if they were annoyed by the presence of the dog or by the presence of English. Either way, they would have to put up with each other.

After showering, Gringa put on a sundress and some makeup, and snapped her new bracelet on to her wrist. They were going to check out one of the beach side restaurants. The one they picked seemed to have a varied menu and a fair amount of clientele—mostly Mexican. They ordered a carafe of very terrible

Mexican red wine, and pasta for dinner. Dinner turned out to be as awful as the wine, and they didn't linger. They returned to their hotel and sat outside to have a nightcap. She took the dog to the grassy verge across the boulevard for one last pee and they turned in for the night.

Acapulco Catch

Gringa and her husband both awoke with a start around two am when there were a couple of thumps against their door. It didn't repeat and they lay awake listening for further sounds of intrusion. "What is that smell?" Gringa asked her husband. They lay still a while longer and the smell grew stronger. Gringa got out of bed and opened the door. There, partially smeared on the door and still steaming on the floor was a pile of faeces. She thought maybe this was someone's retaliation about the presence of the dog and she was not amused. Her husband got up to clean up the mess, but the Gringa angrily told him to leave it; she would have the hotel staff deal with it. She quickly got dressed and stormed down to the sleepy desk clerk. He didn't seem to understand her Spanish but followed her back to the landing outside their room. His face expressed his horror and distaste and now the Gringa's reason for agitation was clear. He reassured her that they would investigate and would clean up immediately, and that he would report this to the owner tomorrow morning. Gringa thanked him and went back to bed—the sickly fumes soon replaced with those of ammonia and bleach.

In the morning, Gringa bought coffee from the hotel's bar and they sat outside, eyeing all the other tenants to see who looked guilty, or who wore a smirk. All seemed normal and if anything, the other residents were friendlier. The hotel owner introduced himself and explained that a couple of guests had returned from a night of heavy drinking and had confused their own room with the Gringa's. Apparently one of the men had a bit of an emergency and failed to make it to the bathroom in time. In any case, these patrons had been asked to leave that morning, and the hotel manager extended his fervent apologies.

Gringa sipped her coffee pondering how best to tell her husband that her new bracelet was missing. She remembered wearing it to the restaurant, but she didn't remember taking it off or where she might have put it. She hoped it hadn't been stolen ...

They spent several days in Acapulco. One day they drove out the thirty kilometers to Pie de la Cuesta where campsites were located, but found that the sites were far from town, and the campgrounds more expensive per night than the hotel they were staying in.

On another day, they drove to the south end of the bay and had a look at the lifestyles of the wealthy. Here the five star hotels stood shoulder to shoulder, along with bars and restaurants where a pina colada cost fifty pesos. Gringa daydreamed about her upcoming birthday and thought how nice it would be to be treated to a night at the fivestar Princess hotel—though admittedly the presence of the dog would be a cramp in style.

They noticed a Japanese restaurant one evening and went inside to check out the menu. The décor was classy and impressive. The menu prices had them hustling quickly out again—who could pay three hundred pesos for a single plate of sushi? Instead they found themselves at the lower scale McSushi type restaurant where they had their fill of Japanese delicacies and sake for a cost just slightly less than the cost of their hotel room.

Another evening they headed out to La Quebrada to watch the famed cliff divers. They set off in good time, which was a fortunate thing. The Gringa was navigating using maps in the guidebook and they found themselves travelling in circles, to the great annoyance of her husband. It was not to be helped. The maps were not as detailed as required, and were typical of Mexican maps—places that existed weren't on the map, places that had vanished were clearly marked. Asking for directions only proved the five-person rule, as explained to them by a Mexican friend: If you want directions in Mexico, find five people standing on a corner and get a consensus, otherwise you'll get five different and opposing sets of directions. But at last they found the spot.

Ticket booths were set up, although the tickets only enabled one to stand in a general public park to watch, no preferred seating—actually no seating at all. They spied a restaurant with a terrace overlooking the bay and for the additional price of drinks ensconced themselves at the terrace edge with a terrific view.

At show time, five divers ran down the steps of the promenade and climbed down to the waters edge. They swam across the small bay and then scaled the cliffs to the top. It was amazing to see their agility as the cliff was high, steep and rocky and yet they scampered up barefoot and clad only in bathing suits. At the top, a searchlight shone on the five divers as they each prayed at the shrine atop the cliffs. Individually, and then in a pair, they timed their dives with the swelling surf below. It was indeed a leap of faith to fly off the cliff face in an elegant swan dive to the perils of the black waters and rocks below. The crowd cheered and shouted their appreciation with each dive. And after all these exertions, the divers swam back across and ran back up the promenade where they solicited donations as payment, and had their photographs taken by admiring tourists. Gringa and her husband decided to come back for the day show the following day to be able to photograph the *Clevados*.

Following the show, Gringa and her husband headed back into town following a number of buses. The buses in Acapulco were fabulous, particularly at night. The drivers took a very proprietary interest in their vehicles and decorated them to reflect their personalities. The results were buses with garish designs of semi-clad and overdeveloped women, or fantastical beasts, occasional religious scenes, and all outlined in neon. The ever-sounding horns played "Tequila" and other popular favourites and stereo speakers were set on the outside of the vehicles for the sure entertainment of every neighbourhood they passed through.

Next morning the Gringa and her husband parted company—he set off on a ramble with the dog, she set off on a shopping expedition. They agreed to rendez-vous at the hotel by noon so that they could attend the one o'clock cliff diver show. Gringa took the bus to the upscale part of Acapulco to pick up sundries at Walmart and to browse the tourist shops on the way back. She wanted to buy herself a cute sundress as a birthday present. She sauntered along happily, though without success where the dress was concerned, and about eleven thirty boarded a bus heading in the right direction to return her to the hotel

The bus traveled to the main intersection of the approach to town and turned right. Gringa didn't panic—she knew city buses often had routes which meandered through residential areas before returning to the main road. She enjoyed watching her fellow passengers and was amused by a man performing an infomercial at the front of the bus in the hopes of selling miracle cream to the passengers—talk about a captive audience! Within a dozen blocks, the bus was in a commercial area unknown to the Gringa, and traffic totally gridlocked. She glanced repeatedly at her watch and realized that a) they were pointed in a direction opposite to where she needed to go, b) she was pretty much lost and c) the likelihood of making it back to the hotel in time was slim to marginal. In a sweat, she had the bus driver let her out in the middle of the street, and she ran weaving between cars to the opposite side to flag a taxi. "How much to the Hotel Playa Suave?" she asked. The driver replied "How much to you want to pay?"

"*Mire* (look), I'm in a hurry. *Rapido! Rapido!*" she snarled at the cab driver and he obliged by gunning the engine for every ten feet the jammed traffic allowed. Once she recognized the neighbourhood again, Gringa decided she would be faster on foot. She ordered the startled cab driver to the curb about three blocks short of her destination and paid the fare (money she had earmarked for the dress). She ran the last distance to the hotel and arrived hot, sweating and out of breath to find her husband nowhere in sight. None of the pool loungers reported seeing him, so the Gringa looking at her watch indicating one fifteen, sat down to fume. By the time her husband wandered in at one thirty she had reconciled to missing the divers show and was almost back on Mexican time—no *problema*. No point in venting her misadventures on her husband and ruining his day. Instead she agreed to lounge by the pool for the afternoon in the company of the dog, so husband could explore the old fort to his historical senses' delight.

He returned late afternoon with many tales of the grandeur of the Spanish shipping enterprise, but physically not feeling all that well. After considering their horrible Italian meal, and their expensive sushi meal, they opted for good old-fashioned Kentucky Fried Chicken—take out to eat by the pool.

They had a last swim and a nightcap back at their hotel. The next day they would travel on and the Gringa looked forward to spending her birthday, two days hence, in Zihuatenejo. The Acapulco Princess stay had not materialized so maybe her husband would treat her to a steak dinner at one of Ixtapa's fancy restaurants.

At Last the Birthday Celebration

On the ninth of January, they set off for the one hundred fifty mile journey up Highway 200 from Acapulco to Zihuatenejo. It wasn't a long distance but they were familiar with the State of Guerrero's lack of highway funding and knew it would take them twice as long as expected. Guerrero is one of the poorer states in Mexico and its roads, including the main state thoroughfares, have fallen into great disrepair. At one point, they circled the edge of a "pot hole" by driving on the verge. The VW Bug coming from the opposite direction took the direct route through the hole and actually disappeared from sight. This was off-roading territory conveniently placed on the main drag!

By one o'clock and tired from the intense driving concentration, they pull into Zihuatenejo. Their first stop was to check out room availability at the hotel they had stayed in on a previous trip. Gringa made enquiries and returned to the vehicle with a shocked expression. "They're now charging eight hundred pesos a night for the room we paid three hundred for a couple of years ago!" Her husband replied "No way I'm paying that! That's crazy!"

Gringa set off on foot to scout out all of the neighbouring hotels—it was easier to do this on foot rather than experience parking and reparking on the narrow and steep streets. It didn't take her long to come back with the grim news that all of the hotels had similar price structures and few vacancies. She was hot, sweating and discouraged to the point of tears.

They opted to try their luck a little further from town at Playa Ropa but met zero vacancies. Amazingly, the room prices here were even higher. Neither Gringa nor her husband wanted to drive any further that day and so in desperation decide to look for a room right downtown despite the difficulties this would create with the dog. There too they experienced a low availability. There was one very old hotel that had rooms available at a rate affordable to them, but Gringa took one look and said "We're not that desperate."

Their only remaining option was to travel a further two hours to Playa Azul. They had visited this "resort" town in years past and had discovered a decent, cheap and mostly deserted hotel with nice rooms, and a great swimming pool in the central landscaped courtyard.

Another long drive followed. The roads improved radically once they entered the State of Michoacan and they were happy to see the loading cranes in the port of Lazaro Cardena, last stop before Playa Azul. They drove into the outskirts in search of an ATM as the chances of this service being available in their destination were slim.

Finally, they turned off the highway onto the dirt road approach to Playa. All of a sudden, the VW listed to one side. Gringa's husband pulled over and took a look. Their lack of luck that day was continuing unabated and he reported they had a flat tire. Gringa jumped out and secured the dog's leash to the door handle. She helped move bags and goods out of the way so that her husband could access the jack. The tires on the VW always seemed small to her, but the spare looked positively miniature and it was obvious it wouldn't take them far or at any great speed.

A man came running out of the house they were parked in front of. He seemed a little gruff and hostile until he noticed the problem tire. He offered his assistance, which husband graciously declined but also gave the hopeful news about a tire shop around the corner. Amazingly, despite it being the dinner hour, the garage was still in full operation. The offending tire was examined and pronounced patchable—in Mexico if a tire was completely bald but still round it would be deemed still serviceable—and the repair was effected in minutes. Even more incredibly, the price of the repair was only thirty pesos, to which the Gringa felt compelled to add a substantial tip.

At long last they pulled into the parking lot of the hotel. To their intense relief, rooms were available, dogs were allowed and the rate was three hundred one pesos per night. Gringa poured her husband stiff and well deserved drinks, which they sat outside to enjoy. In their memory the hotel's restaurant was quite good and Gringa pronounced that she was satisfied to spend her birthday here in Playa Azul.

At the restaurant they were quickly seated. There was only one other couple patronizing the establishment. Gringa scanned the menu—it offered a wide variety of traditional Mexican and more *norte americano* foods. She settled on a club sandwich, while her husband ordered a hamburger. A short time later, their waiter reappeared. "I'm sorry, *senora*," he apologized, "but we are out of club sandwiches." This seemed a bit strange, and the Gringa asked "What part of the sandwich are you out of? The chicken? The bacon?" thinking that she would just have a modified version.

"We are out of bread, *senora*."

Gringa was stunned by the response and ordered a pasta dish she didn't particularly want. "I don't get it" she fumed to her husband, "why wouldn't they just go to the store across the street?"

The next morning was the Gringa's celebrated birthday. Her husband brought her a cup of coffee in bed, and presented her with a beautiful black and purple *rebezo* (all purpose shawl) made in the Patzcuaro region. They breakfasted in the same hotel restaurant on a miniscule portion of hotcakes. The Gringa quizzed the waiter:

"Do you have thick t-bone steaks"

"*Si*, of course *Senora*."

"Are you sure they are thick and not skinny like used in fajitas? Today is my birthday and I will want a thick steak for dinner tonight."

"Of course *Senora*."

After breakfast, Gringa and her husband went their separate ways. She was going to lounge by the pool in the courtyard; he was going to Lazaro Cardenas to see if there was a VW dealership that could deal with the broken strut. Gringa spent the day moving from one lawn chair to another as the sun dictated. She had the pool, and in fact the entire courtyard, to herself. Occasionally she would go to the restaurant for a Coke or a plate of french fries but she was their only customer.

Part way through the day, she slipped on shorts and set off to explore the town and buy herself a birthday treat. There really wasn't much to explore. The town was basically two parallel streets with just the one hotel. She didn't see any other restaurants though there were the occasional street vendors. Behind the hotel the amusement arcade with the waterslides stood empty. A side street offered a market for tourist goods, but they were cheap and poorly made. She returned to the poolside empty handed. Still, it was a pleasant, peaceful day and she was enjoying her book. She looked forward to dinner that night and shrugged wistfully at the thought of the Acapulco Princess or the Ixtapa steakhouses.

At dinnertime, Gringa put on a dress for her birthday celebration, and her husband dressed in nice slacks and a silk shirt. They strolled over to the restaurant where again they were one of very few patrons. A young and very nervous waiter approached them with menus. The Gringa noted that the rather extensive bar list included white vermouth and so ordered a martini. The young man looked very uncertain but promised to deliver two vodka martinis. Not trusting the message to get translated properly, the Gringa went over to the bar to speak to the manager. She gave him very precise instructions—mostly vodka with just a capful of vermouth.

Back at their table, the drinks arrived in sherry glasses. They were also the colour of sherry and the Gringa saw maraschino cherries floating in her amber drink. She asked the trembling waiter to summon the manager. In the meantime, they ordered two rib eye steaks for dinner.

After a long wait, the manager turned up at their tableside. "What is this?" the Gringa asked, "It's certainly not a martini."

"*Si senora*. I made it as you said. Vodka and vermouth,"

At her insistence, the manager brought over the bottle—amber sweet vermouth. The manager informed her this was all they had. Then he said "Also, *senora*, I regret to say we do not have any rib steak."

This was too much for Gringa and an outrage on her birthday. She went into ballistic mode. She ranted about preordering the steak that morning, about last night's lack of bread, about putting items on the menu when they clearly had no intention of supplying them. She asked "If you knew this morning that I had ordered steak for tonight, why didn't you go and buy one?"

"We had steak this morning, *senora*. Unfortunately we are now sold out."

Gringa exploded. "You have not had any customers today. I sat over there all day and had a good view of your restaurant and I was your only customer. And I certainly did not have steak for lunch. Today is my birthday and you have not made it very happy!"

The manager simply shrugged and said "Sorry."

"Forget it. Let's go honey. I don't want to eat here." Gringa urged her husband out of his chair. Gringa's husband summoned the waiter for their bill. To Gringa's astonishment, the bill for two martinis came to a whopping sixty pesos. "I can't believe they're even charging us when they got everything so wrong. Talk about no customer service!"

As they were leaving the restaurant, the Gringa asked her husband to wait a minute. She went towards the kitchen area in search of the manager. "Look" she said, "it is my birthday and if you don't have the dinner I want, do you at least have flan for my dessert?" Flan is available everywhere in Mexico, including on street corners on weekend nights. "You have flan on the menu; do you actually have any flan?"

The Manager checked with the kitchen help, and replied "Maybe tomorrow."

Gringa and her husband walked from one end of town to the other and back. The only option available for dinner was a sidewalk vendor selling *taquitos*—deep-fried rolled up tacos. Business was brisk, hopefully a positive sign, and they squeezed onto two remaining stools. They ordered beer and *taquitos* and the Gringa laughed at how low her expectations for her birthday dinner had sunk.

Dinner was served and no amount of hot sauce or salsa could disguise the oil soaked taste. They requested permission to take away the beer (vendors are ever mindful of deposits paid) and took their Styrofoam containers to a more private venue on the beach.

They found a seat at a deserted and darkened beachside open-air restaurant. They had brought the dog along, and released her from the leash to explore the beach at will. The dog tore off to the water's edge and relieved herself—she was always selective about doing her business below the tide line—and then streaked off to investigate something in the shadows. She came back accompanied by a very emaciated and badly limping stray. Gringa divided her birthday dinner between the two dogs, offering the larger portion including the rice to the starving beach wanderer. Her own dog seemed to sense her companion's greater need and did not attempt to wrestle any titbits away.

Gringa and her husband finished their beers and sat companionably watching the moonlight reflect fluorescently on the breakers. They wandered back along the beach and turned up the road to their hotel. The little stray limped determinedly behind them. The man noticed the little dog and tried in vain to send it on its way. Gringa said "Wait here—I'll run to our room and get some kibble."

She returned with a plastic bag filled with kibble and set it open before the stray. "Now, while she's eating…. let's make a run for it and hopefully she won't sniff us out at home!" And they set off, giggling and laughing like school kids with their own dog dancing beside them. It had certainly been a memorable birthday.

Last Stop Before Home to Melaque

From Playa Azul it was a relatively short five hundred kilometer scenic drive back to Melaque—the beautiful *Costa Allegre*. Their funds were running low but it was too soon to return to Melaque; they would only find themselves homeless again. A decision was made to visit *Faro de Buceria* (Divers' Lighthouse) beach and perhaps camp there a few days.

Faro proved a disappointment. On their last visit the small bay had been virtually deserted but for one palapa restaurant and the swimable cove. Now palapas lined the entire beach making it inaccessible for the camper. The only spot to camp was a designated area behind one of the restaurants where one would have a less than charming view of outhouses and laundry.

They traveled further up the highway and turned off at a sign marking Las Brisas Hotel. A short and bumpy road led to a small hotel complex that looked empty of customers. The road continued to the right, flanking the beach. There were housing sites bordering the road but whether these were homes razed to the ground or the foundations for a new development was unclear. They pulled off at the very last lot and found a perfect clearing on a short bluff with a path to access the beach. There wasn't anyone around and they decided it would be a perfect camping spot. There was some garbage to clean up but thankfully the site was devoid of broken glass.

They set up camp and then walked back to the hotel to ask for permission to camp. The hotel was vacant but the people at the neighbouring restaurant seemed completely indifferent to their request. There was no charge and the owners even agreed to let them use the stand-alone shower and toilet on the edge of the parking lot. Gringa thanked them and promised to come back for a meal (though Gringa was doubtful as this menu was seafood only and she was allergic).

They settled into a routine of reading books and taking walks on the dark sand beach. The dog was in her glory on the flat, soft sand and didn't even mind following her owners part way out to the surf as the waves were gentle and unthreatening.

Road to Manzanillo

At night they would sit outside and gaze at the stars so close above them. They identified constellations and made up names for those they didn't know. The nights were restful with only the sounds of crickets and gentle surf to lull them into sweet dreams.

They ate from the camper's stores and had uncomplicated, simple meals. It was good to give their stomachs a rest from Mexican fare. Gringa was especially grateful because a case of *tourista* would have been very unwelcome. They had a portable toilet in the camper but her husband designated this "pee only" and it would have been an urgent and dangerous run the three hundred yards or so to the restaurant's facilities during a dark night.

Las Brisas

One morning they looked out and noticed a bundle in the middle of the low-tide beach. They moved closer and identified it as a pelican. It was oddly nestled into the sand and didn't seem in any hurry to leave. When they approached, it madly flapped one wing and stretched out it huge bill in anger, but did not take off. It was crippled but whether at the wing or leg or both was unclear and they couldn't get close enough to check further.

Over the course of the day, they watched the stranded bird from their bluff viewpoint. A flock of pelicans flew in to the shallow waters and the injured bird struggled madly to join them. But it could only drag itself a couple of feet before it subsided in exhaustion, and the flock abandoned it.

Gringa and the Man felt really bad for the bird. She asked her husband if he couldn't shift it to the water's edge but he pointed out that it likely couldn't swim—nor could he get close to it. She wondered if she should go to the restaurant to buy some fish to feed it ... but what would be the point. "It's like being in the middle of a National Geographic episode where you have to let nature take its course, but it's horrible. I don't know how those photographers and filmmakers stand it."

The next morning the pelican was still there and lying still. A group of people came along the beach from the direction of the hotel. The children ran up to investigate the bird. The pelican roused itself and flapped one good wing angrily. The children were called away and the bird was left in peace. As night fell, the bird moved only occasionally and sadly the end seemed near.

They woke the following day and looked out for the bird. The beach was completely empty and the tide had receded. Nature had cleaned up and the sands were again pristine. Gringa and her husband felt sad for the death of the bird and yet somehow relieved.

They enjoyed one last day at their private little spot of Mexico. Their food stores and water were running low. It was time to move on, to get back to Melaque where hopefully their innkeeper had checky-checkied into finding them an apartment for the next two months. Their travels had taken them in a big circle and they were ready to settle down again for a while. Friends and family were due to visit and they were looking forward to sharing Mexico with the folks from back home.

The Dog Days of Mexico

Introducing Dog

She rested her head on her dad's slippers and sniffing the comforting scent, closed her eyes for a snooze. It had been another busy day in this noisy place full of strange and exotic scents. It was all a lot for a young pup to take in.

As she drifted off into dreams, her inner projector flashed through her short six-month life. There was the scary plane ride when she traveled from Montreal to Vancouver to meet her new family. There was the wonder of discovering that cats did not play by the same rules as polite dog society. Some of them were fun, but that one black thing with the yellow eyes was positively evil with her hissing and scratching and yowling.

There was that trauma of being left alone while Mum and Dad went to some-place called work, and the hard job of aiming her bodily functions to the mats laid down. And then later the terror of going through the dog flap; it did get you outdoors but you had to move fast not to get swatted on the backside on your way.

Worst was the terror that she had been abandoned. She had known something was up when things started disappearing into boxes. She was loaded into a box (with windows) too and carted off to that place with the horrible medicine smells. The people at the vet's kennel were very nice, but she had been so worried that Mum and Dad weren't coming back that she made herself sick. She was so relieved to see them again that she peed everywhere and Dad had yelled.

She had stayed sick with a nervous stomach for that first week on the road—she could hear the arguments between Mum and Dad about her being too young and undisciplined for this journey—and she worried herself sick thinking that every time the car stopped it might be the end of the line for her. They finally got her some medicine to stop her throwing up, but it made her woozy and sleepy, and she couldn't understand those commands to pee every time she was let out of the camper.

After a while she learned the routine. Wake Dad up in the morning to let him know she wanted to go out. Then, when she got distracted by all the new smells, listen to Dad (or occasionally Mum) say in exasperation "Come on! Pee now or you'll have to hold it ...") Then into the camper to be left alone while Mum and

Dad had breakfast somewhere. They always came back with a napkin filled with goodies, but she was too excited and too worried about where they were going to eat. Then the food would sit in her bowl and she could smell it while trying to contain the whoopsies her stomach was doing any time they were on a hilly or curvy road (or, God forbid, a hilly and curvy road—to this day she couldn't hold down her cookies on those). Sometimes she ate the food just to get rid of the smell; Mum and Dad just didn't get that she liked quiet peaceful mealtimes with her dog food and her stomach stationary.

Hurry Up!

Despite the occasional bouts of motion sickness, she had become quite the seasoned traveller. The camper was quite comfortable particularly since she was allowed to sleep on the backseat bench, and even had a cushy pillow for her head. The very back was the best place, though, because it had all kinds of pillows and blankets. It wasn't worth the hassle though, because the parents would get quite bent out of shape about a few shed hairs. Dad didn't understand either that the front seat was the best place to keep a lookout. She could watch in all directions for the parents to come back, and sometime stick her head out the window to hurry them along. But he sure was touchy about the driver's seat—it was definitely Dad's throne. There was a good scolding every time he caught her at it, and he was good at catching her even when she was lying innocently on the proper bench pretending to be asleep. Must be those pesky hairs giving her away.

Mom came into the kitchen and dog lifted her head. Dinner time? Yes!! Out of the fridge came the yellow container that dog knew contained her supper. It was a yummy mixture of rice and cooked chicken livers. She had gone to the market with Mom to do the shopping—lots of good smells there and what sights! There were piles of vegetables, and although she liked carrots, these didn't interest her half as much as the cases displaying chickens and meats. She was also fascinated by the heads hanging from hooks above the cases; she supposed that they were set up that high to keep them out of her reach because what a great treat it would be to get a hold of one of those pig skulls. Mom bought chickens and asked for the head and feet to be removed—the lady serving her argued these made the best soup but Mom was quite adamant in her refusal. She didn't scrimp on the chicken livers, though, and there would be delicious aroma of sautéing livers and Mom would add garlic. The livers were all blended in with rice and made a much tastier alternative to the awful dry kibble that was in her bowl all the time.

She watched Mom spoon some of the dinner into her bowl. Dog dutifully got up and stretched and meandered over for a sniff. Even though she really liked the stuff, it wasn't smart to show too much enthusiasm. If you faked indifference, most of the time some other titbits from Mom and Dad's dinner would be added—it was a great way to ensure variety. She poked through the food with nose and went back to her nap. She flopped down with a heartfelt sign. Mom looked at her and said "eat it up, dog—there's nothing else for you". "Ha! We'll see who can outlast who," thought dog, and went back to her nap.

Dad came in and mixed cocktails for him and Mom. They took them out to the balcony overlooking the street, and dog followed. The apartment they were in right now was over the corner store and there was lots of interesting activity below. The balcony wall was solid concrete and Dog had to get up on her hind legs to get a view, but this was quite comfortable. It was a great location to survey the world and she felt like royalty watching her subjects.

There was always something going on—her favourite parade had been when the circus came to town and the pickup trucks careened around the corners with live monkeys hanging off the sides. It was noisy from the loudspeakers and the band, with the bandmembers trying to keep their balance in the back while they

blasted out tunes. It was funny to see the camel chewing its cud and ignoring the
fracas. They didn't go to the circus because Mom had seen the animals in their
cages at the circus grounds and had been quite upset at the condition of the
scrawny bears. Of course the bears were no worse off than most Mexican farm
animals, but they looked pathetic and out of place sweltering in the sun

Surveying her kingdom

There were lots of trucks coming and going in this area and they all advertised
their presence with loudspeakers. "Ayyyy Gazzzzzz" was the long, drawn call of
the propane man, and the water truck had lots of bells. The man selling tamales
and corn pushed a pedal bike with a bike bell as a he called out his wares "*Hay
tamale, hay elote*". The street vendor with the steam powered oven had an especially loud and ear piercing steam whistle. The fruit trucks used loud speakers to
advertise tomatoes and watermelons. The politicians honked their horns and
droned on through the loudspeakers to the disinterest of all. Interspersed through
it all was the boom, boom, boom of car stereos played at a level to ensure everyone could share the enjoyment. Mexico was never quiet.

Dog watched the activity below and then started wagging her tail frantically. There was her pal Cassan—he is so handsome! She hoped that he would still be around later when she got taken for her after dinner walk. Maybe it would be one of the times when she was let off the leash....

Mom noticed the tail wagging, and the handsome Cassan below. "Shall we take in the sunset from the beach?" she asked Dad. Dog hustled them along. She ran to the back door and back again. She ran to her leash and back again. "Come on! Hurry!" She let out a yip—she didn't bark much—so her excitement was in her body language and that one staccato bark. Mom snapped the leash to dog's collar and then yanked back. "Oops!" thought dog. "Got to remember they've only got two slow legs and don't like being pulled down stairs."

Cassan

Dog pulled her Mom around the corner, but Cassan was gone. She gave a whimper of disappointment then squatted to relieve herself. Her Mom watched with amusement as Dog's back legs came up and she walked on her front paws while the urine trickled out. Her record distance was twenty feet. Personally Dog didn't see the humour—this was simply a practical way to ensure that her feet stayed dry and she'd perfected the technique from early puppy hood.

Dad caught up with them, and they walked down the sandy alley to the beach. Dog trotted dutifully at their side, tail high and proud. They reached the tide mark and stopped. Mom and Dad scoped out the beach and determined that there weren't many people about—Dog could be a right pest about saying hello to everyone whether they wished to be greeted or not. And the sight of their husky-cross bearing down on visitors at great speed often as not instilled real terror in Mexican hearts who thought a wolf/lobo had appeared out of the gates of hell. This evening the beach was relatively deserted and so Dog got her freedom from the confines of the leash.

Dog accelerated from zero to sixty in the space of ten yards. Her face creased into an exuberant smile—she loved to run almost better than anything—and her long distance, high-speed husky genes kicked in. She streaked off, a group of boys playing soccer on the beach her target. Then as she neared them, out of the corner of her eye she caught sight of Cassan. Could life get any better!! She dashed up to Cassan and politely bowed, urging him to take up the chase game. Cassan was a worldly year older and tried to show his sophistication by ignoring her. Dog gave an encouraging bark, and feinted in one direction and then the other. Cassan couldn't resist and the game was on.

They tore up and down the beach, taking turns being the leader. Cassan veered off and went through the gate to the pool complex. Dog was almost faked out but caught sight of the manoeuvre at the last second and vaulted the four foot wall instead of using the gate. She had to put the brakes on and skidded across wet tiles but avoided the swimming pool. She caught up and passed Cassan as they rounded the corner back out into the street. Cassan regained the lead when he again changed direction and Dog found herself following pell-mell down unfamiliar backyards. She could hear Mom and Dad calling but was too caught up in the game to pay any attention. Eventually, Cassan led her back out to the beach and abruptly ended the game by lying down. Dog tried her best to get him back in the chase. She jumped over his prostate body from side to side to side, but he wouldn't get up. Game over. She trotted back to her parents, grinning wildly, and tongue lolling out the side. She was so thirsty she even took sips of the salty waves puddling around her feet. Now that built up an appetite—bring on the chicken livers!

Beach Patrol

After breakfast, Dog watched her dad stuff the backpack with the things they would need on their daily walk. He put in his eyeglasses and sunglasses, a book, a beach towel, a bottle of water, her water dish, and her favourite ball—the one that was all textured and used to squeak before she'd managed to chew the squeaker out of it. Her leash was snapped on and she wagged a goodbye to her Mom.

Once Dog and Dad arrived on the beach, they turned left and headed for the long strip that separated Melaque from Barra de Navidad. The beach dune fell away to ocean and rolling waves on one side, and to a marshy fresh water lagoon on the other. Their daily hike took them to a spot mid way, where they would set themselves up facing the lagoon. Dog liked to wade through reeds here and Dad would toss pebbles that she would try to catch mid-air. There were supposed to be caimans in this lagoon but they had never seen one. The cows grazing nearby seemed unbothered as well. Dog liked it here because although the water was a bit brackish, it wasn't salty like the other stuff. After a while, Dad would pull out his book and settle in for a good read leaving Dog to freely wander along exploring frogs and bugs in and about the marsh.

Sometimes they beached themselves on the ocean side. It was fun there too because Dad would throw the ball into the water and Dog was supposed to chase after it. She and Dad had a game where Dad would try to trick her into getting rolled by the waves, and sometimes she let him think he was winning. She'd wander out chest deep and bark at her ball, but would always scamper back before a roller hit. In all their time by the sea she had only been bowled over by waves three or four times, and at least twice it was because she had been dragged by the collar into deeper water. It hadn't taken her long to figure out both her ball, and the coconuts she liked to play with, floated. No matter how far out Dad tossed them, if you were a patient dog, the surf would gradually push them back to you.

Well, ok, there was that one day when she had totally lost her focus and her ball had been swept away. Dad had chastised her for losing her favourite toy—but let's face it he was the one who had thrown it in the first place. Anyway, the beach police had brought it back. "That was a funny one," snorted Dog.

"Dad was so worried when those police showed up on their all terrain vehicles. I was really cool and went bounding up to say hi. Dad had a fit and thought the police were going to give him a ticket because I didn't have my leash on. As if … duh … this is Mexico where they don't even have dog licences."

Playing coconuts

The beach police were a lot of fun once you got to know them. They would pull up on the top of the dune above where Dog and Dad were playing. If Dog didn't notice them, they would rev their ATVs to catch her attention. Once she looked up, they would take off at top speed. Of course Dog knew this was a challenge and would run after them. They usually only managed to get about a third of a mile along before she passed them. Dog wouldn't slow up, and neither would they. They would continue to ride, full throttle towards Melaque with Dog weaving porpoise-style back and forth in front of them. It quite startled her Dad the first time it happened and he was pretty mad when she came panting back. But since then it was almost a weekly ritual and Dad barely glanced up when he heard the revving engines.

Once Dad and Dog had spent a couple of hours on the beach, they continued on with their walk to Barra. Sometimes they would go visit Polly. Dog had never seen a bird that could whistle as well as Dad. It could talk too, but it obviously didn't speak dog.

By that point Dad was pretty thirsty and would stop in a store for a beer. They would find a nice shady spot in the square. Dog would lie next to the bench and Dad would sip his beer. Barra was a pretty interesting place too. There weren't too many free dogs in the area they stuck to, so Dog was unbothered by the sometimes less than friendly locals. The 'free' dogs had a pretty tough life without parents to look after them and had to scrounge for scraps to sustain them. Sex was pretty available if you were that kind of dog, and Dog wasn't, and you had to feel sorry for a lot of the females who had suffered through raising numerous litters in the street. The 'free' dogs tended to be tough and very unwelcoming to strangers—they could be very aggressive and this was always a surprise to Dog who just wanted to be pals. Still, it could be very overwhelming when they traveled in groups, and Dog was grateful for Dad's protection.

Dog meets Polly

In Barra there was a wolf dog who looked particularly interesting. He had some physical characteristics similar to Dog, but despite the wolf cross' pedigree, Dog felt she looked more like a wolf and had better manners as well. Maybe it was the owner's fault because he always played up the wolf side and warned how unpredictable the wolf-cross was. Dog knew that real wolves are generally very playful and polite. But warned was warned, and so she kept her distance.

After Dad had finished his beer and cooled off, it was time to walk back to their apartment. They played the surf game off and on along the mile walk back and so were both usually pretty crusty with sand and saltwater by the time they got back to the complex. Then came the part that Dog hated the most—the daily shower by the pool! She didn't think it was fair to have to shower even when she hadn't rolled in any good smelling fish—that first shower had been a real shocker!

Sorry for dead fish roll

She really didn't like getting her back or head wet, but there was no struggling with Dad and the shower was pretty cooling in the end. More than anything, it was embarrassing to have so many people watch her lovely coat get matted down, and undignified to have your ears pressed flat back. Dog made sure to fluff up her coat as quickly as possible, regardless of who was nearby and got sprayed. Sometimes, when she was annoyed about the shower, she would shake before Dad let her out from the water so that he got a double shower. Of course the air was so warm that the shower didn't bother Dad either, though the laughing people sometimes did.

Mom was usually by the pool when they came back from their walk. She'd be lying comfortably on a lounge chair. If there weren't too many people around, Mom would let Dog lie on a lounge chair too. Dog liked that a lot—it made her feel like the special person she was, and it was way better than lying on concrete. Dad didn't like it at all and usually scolded both her and Mom.

The people from the complex who spent their time around the pool were used to her and were very friendly. They didn't think she was a scary wolf at all—what wolf plays with squeaky toys? Dog had an assortment of stuffed animals to play with. She liked the squeaky ones the best but somehow they always quickly lost their noise maker. Maybe it had something to do with her plucking skills—she could destuff a toy in minutes flat—and inevitably they lost their sound maker. She liked to see what was inside so the animals were a bit misshapen too, and some pieces just weren't made to last. Her favourite gorilla had quickly lost an eye, and his nose was half chewed off; he'd lost his squeak and his insides were kept intact with duct tape. Dad was the chief surgeon when it came to her stuffed friends. When he had patience, he would sit by the pool and carefully put in stitches with a darning needle and fishing line. His work was very fine and diffi-cult to undo—usually Dog just picked a new spot to tear into. The local ladies watched with admiration and called him King Neptune. Dog didn't think that nickname had anything to do with Dad's sewing ability and she noticed that Mom had a very weak smile whenever she heard it.

Today there was quite a crowd around the pool and all the chairs were occu-pied. Dad managed to find a seat but Dog had to settle for a towel on the ground next to Mom. Dad poured some water into her dish and Dog had a good long drink. There was a lot going on and she didn't want to miss any of the fun, but Mom firmly anchored her leash to the lounge chair. Dog watched a big German Shepherd named Ben escort his owner around the pool. Ben's Mom had been in a terrible car accident and she had trouble walking. It was Ben's job to hold her steady as she stepped down into the pool, and then to follow her around the perimeter to keep her safe. If his Mom slipped or had trouble, Ben would jump into the pool and pull her to safety. Dog was really impressed with this heroic canine, though she thought Ben was a bit standoffish. Ben never wanted to play; he was always focused on his Mom. Dog thought this was admirable but was too young to understand how someone could work all the time! Actually, Ben had plenty of chances to play but preferred this when he could be alone with his human siblings. When there were strangers around, he had to watch his Mom.

Dining Out

That evening Mom and Dad decided to go out to eat. Dog enjoyed this because she got to go along and in most places they treated her pretty nicely. Of all of them, the taco stand was her least favourite because she had to stay in the VW. Not that the taco stand was a snooty place. On the contrary, it was a very humble street-side establishment with an outdoor barbecue, tables covered with linoleum cloths set up under a tarp, and a television blaring Mexican soap operas from the corner. The *senora* would serve up a bowl of bean soup as an appetizer and Mom and Dad would order a selection of tacos. The meat was freshly barbecued and then placed on homemade tortillas. With beers to wash the good food down, the bill rarely came to more than thirty-five pesos including tip. Dog wasn't sure why she had to stay in the car but maybe it had to do with encroaching on someone else's turf. Or maybe Mom found it too much of a distraction to keep Dog from trying to say hi to all the other dinner guests.

Dog looked at Mom and Dad and decided that they weren't going to Maya's for dinner. They weren't dressed up enough. Maya's was a fabulous place with a candlelit courtyard and very romantic tables with some even perched over the beach. The food was incredible—the chef was a famous lady from Vancouver who used to be the chef at Delilahs. Mom found it amazing that the chef could put out all those gourmet meals by cooking on an apartment sized four-burner stove. Maya's was named after the owner's pet—a regal half Malamute, half wolf creature.

Maya the wolf didn't seem to mind people intruding on her turf though when Dog tried to engage her in conversation she snarled that she was busy. Dog's feelings were a bit hurt but were soothed by the tuna tartar appetizer she was served. She had actually received her appetizer before Mom and Dad got their cocktails—now this place had class and knew how to treat customers!

Tonight they were getting in the camper so that meant they weren't going to Pancho's, the fish and chip restaurant. That was just down the street and around the corner and they usually walked. The restaurant was the outside patio of the owner's house and was only open for certain months in the winter. The owner was from Quebec and knew to serve the chips with vinegar instead of ketchup.

He also made a really good homemade tartar sauce that Dad raved about. Dog had to sit very quietly in this place and didn't have much room to move. There weren't many treats coming her way either because she didn't really like French fries and Mom could be very stingy with her chicken. Mom was allergic to fish and so always had chicken Dad always had fish, but he was stingy too. There wasn't anything else on the menu. Dog never got any treats from the owners here, and always felt that she was being barely tolerated.

Regal Maya

Maybe they were going to Romeo's. Romeo's was an Italian restaurant about half way to town. It was upstairs on a balcony and could be quite crowded. It was named after a German Shepherd who had died a tragic death on the operating table. Apparently he went to get neutered (sounds unpleasant doesn't it—like losing your personality) but never woke up. Dog remembered going for a walk one day with Mom to find some new, tastier kibble. They were about to go into this veterinary store when Mom jerked Dog away in a hurry. Dog could smell the strong antiseptic coming from the back and had just barely got a glimpse of the boxer being operated on the table at the back in plain view of everyone. Anyway Romeo's, despite being named after a dog, wasn't all that great as far as Dog was concerned. She didn't get any treats there, though she could count on Mom asking for a doggy bag for all the pasta she never finished. Dog's favourite was the tortellini with the cream sauce because she found the meat sauce could be rather spicy.

But no, they had driven past the street with Romeo's and the upstairs was all dark. They drove all the way into town and parked in the courtyard of the Terrazzo. Dog butted her nose against Mom's shoulder to show her approval of the restaurant and to make sure she didn't get left behind. She really liked this place.

Their favourite table was on the roof top terrazzo at back where they were away from the street noise and could see the beach. Barney was the owner and cook, though he had help from his Mexican wife. They made really good enchiladas (another dish Mom could never finish and so shared with Dog), and homemade whole wheat bread that Dad tried hard not to fill up on (whole wheat bread was very unusual in Mexico). It didn't really matter to Dog what Mom and Dad ate because Barney and his wife, and often the other guests, kept Dog well plied with spareribs. Mom had been horrified the first time she noticed Dog scarfing these down because she was afraid the bones would splinter and Dog would choke. But she realized that Dog had already consumed quite a few without incident and now she relaxed and let Dog have as many as they cared to feed her. Of course great consumption of bones tended to repeat on Dog later on and there would be comments about her smelly air, but at least there were no windows in their apartment to impede air circulation.

Healing Dog

One day when Dog and Dad came home from their walk, they found their studio apartment crowded with plumbers, and the bathroom partially dismantled. Mom explained that the workers were in the process of putting the toilet back, and had run a piece of metal down the hole to see if they could find a blockage. So far they had not had any success and seemed to think that the toilet operated perfectly well. They had been there for several hours so Mom had her annoyed look on. Dad told her to take Dog to the pool and that he would supervise the cleanup.

They met the complex owner on the way, and Mom asked again about moving to a bigger apartment. She explained that they were expecting company from Canada and needed more room. The owner said she might have a three bedroom apartment later in the week. Mom said this was bigger than they needed (and more expensive) but if that was all that was available they would take it.

It was quite quiet at the pool. It seemed that most of the residents were either off on shopping trips or out sightseeing. Dog took advantage of the lack of people and the absence of Dad to park herself on the lounge chair next to Mom's. Mom just smiled and settled in with her book. Dog settled herself for a snooze but kept one ear cocked for the "down" command.

In a while, Dad wandered down and joined them. Dog didn't wait to be told and slunk off the chair, relinquishing it to Dad. There were plenty of other chairs available but she supposed Dad would specifically want the one she was on. She hoped he wasn't too mad, and set about making amends. She knew that Dad had a sore foot where the sand had rubbed a blister, and Dog set about cleaning the spot with her tongue. She knew she had a talent for getting the spot exactly—this amazed Dad, but Dog knew it was her great sense of smell that could tell healthy from unhealthy. Of course she was a very firm believer in the restorative powers of her saliva. To think some people thought that her licking was unsanitary!

Dog had further demonstrated her powers one evening when Mom had taken her to visit one of the women who lived near the pool. This woman's Dad was very ill and bedridden. The woman had asked if it would be okay for Dog to visit her father and so Dog had followed into the bedroom. A man lay on the bed, groaning unintelligibly and Dog licked the hand that was hanging to one side.

Dog's mom had asked the woman if it was all right to lift Dog onto the bed, and once there Dog zeroed in the poor man's head. She completely ignored the cat lying on the pillow beside him (now was not the time for chasing). Instead, Dog carefully snuggled up on the man's chest and gently licked at his face. Dog didn't know words like Alzheimer's or dementia, but it was obvious to her that his problem was in the head region. As she licked his face so very gently, the man's groaning stopped and he became peaceful. Mom called her a healing dog and said she was a very good girl.

Tenacatita

Mid morning the next day, Dog accompanied Mom and Dad and two Canadian women friends they'd met in Melaque to the camper. They were going to take the friends to see the caimans and then on to Tenacatita Beach. The caimans lived in the lagoon in a nearby town called La Manzanilla. Dog didn't think much of them—with her poor eyesight they just seemed like big logs in the water, but she noticed that Mum kept a really tight hold on her leash. They parked in front of a little bay of the lagoon, separated from the water and beach by a couple of thin strands of wire. All four people dutifully gathered around and stared out into the water. "Yikes!" Mom yelped as she noticed that instead of being in the water at a safe distance, one of the caimans had pulled itself up on the land not two feet away from them. It just lay there, unblinking, with its bottom teeth sticking up on the outer side of its mouth. Dog sniffed the air—there was a slightly delicious rancidness to the air, though seemingly undetected by the humans. "What is that?" Mum asked pointing out to an island in the middle of the lagoon. "Oh my God" one of the women exclaimed, "It's a dead cow."

Dad said "it's no wonder there are so many crocs around—that will keep them fed for a while. Look there's at least another four caimans in the water."

They got back in the camper, the women tittering excitedly about their close brush with wildlife. They drove around to the other side of the lagoon to show the visitors the adjacent campground and the sign that understatedly said "No swimming, Danger, Caimans". They all agreed that it was a very peculiar spot for a campground and doubted that the caimans knew that they were supposed to stay on the other side of the single strand of barbed wire.

They drove the 15 miles further to the village of Tenacatita. Mom told her favourite story of them being stopped by the army patrol on the road leading into the beach community. She had asked the soldier, in Spanish, what they were looking for. The soldier replied, in English, "Gons, drogs, knives … got any?"

Tenacatita village was a few kilometers from the water. It was a very poor and rustic place, although typical of all Mexican villages, it did boast a town square. The villagers were preparing for some festival or other because the community band was practicing in the band shell. The mooing cattle and barking dogs shared

Dog's opinion that these were far from talented musicians. Dog was very glad that Mom said not to stop—the cacophony hurt her ears.

They traveled on to the beach. Their passengers let out a gasp as they crossed the small rise and the bay came into view. It was a very large bay with a wide flat beach bordering brilliant blue water. At one end of the large bay was a series of palapa restaurants. Past the palapas was a very rudimentary camping area, without even the roughest facilities, and very few occupants. The beach at this end was rockier but the waters were still quite calm. Mom and Dad explained that this section of coastline had some of the best snorkelling on the Pacific side of Mexico, though it hardly compared to the Caribbean.

They drove past the palapas in the direction of the other end of the bay. In the centre, parked all along the rough road was another makeshift campground though some sites were considerably more elaborate. The occupants ranged from fancy bus rigs to tents and homemade palapas. Some had constructed little gardens, others a rough shower and the most ambitious had built a clay oven. It was obvious that these campers were here for the long haul. Their licence plates showed them to be from all over North America although there seemed to be more Quebec plates than others. They even had water delivery and a scheduled grocery delivery so that they did not have to go in to town. Dad always said he would like to camp here over a winter. Mom always said that having a shower and a bathroom were fairly critical to her happiness and therefore his.

They drove past the campers towards the headland and parked at the side of the road. Dog led the way as they slipped down the soft sand bank to the beach below. The sand was baby powder fine but very hot until you reached the wet line. Dog cranked up the speed and launched herself into a powerful, exuberant run. This was the best running spot—there were no people, the beach was flat and compact for good traction, and the rollers so gentle that even Dog felt comfortable wading knee deep. They were so far away from everyone that Mom and Dad sometimes swam naked, though with company today they were a little more decorous. After a very satisfying game of tag, Dog reluctantly followed them back to the camper. She could play "catch me if you can", but she was thirsty and Dad was pouring a bowl of fresh cool water.

They drove back to the palapa portion of the beach and chose a restaurant to hang out in by the comfort of its chairs and the availability of hammocks. Food in these restaurants was pretty standard fare and great if you liked fish and seafood. Mom spoke fondly of having had the best fried chicken ever on this beach, with thick crispy yellow skin and tender meat, but it seemed that particular owner had moved on. Dad liked shrimp but didn't like that they weren't peeled before serving so he was just planning on having beer. Their friends were hungry though, and ordered up fish, shrimp, and chips with guacamole. It was a weekday so the restaurants were hurting for business and the friends felt sorry for the owners. On the weekends this was a popular Mexican destination, but it wasn't well known among the *gringos* so during the work week, customers were scarce.

Dog found herself a spot and dug a well down to the damp sand below. She turned in a circle several times before settling herself comfortably. Truthfully, this was better than the lounge chairs by the pool. She settled in for a snooze and was rudely awakened from her daydream by a cold wet nose sniffing at her tail. She yelped in surprise and jumped up to find herself confronted by a tall, skinny, grayish dog with incredibly bad manners. Dog was confined by her leash so she found it difficult to get out of this lout's way and he seemed to be rather aggressive in his thinking that she was some street strumpet panting for his attentions. Luckily Mom noticed the unwanted attention and shouted at him to get away. He didn't pay much attention and kept coming at Dog, his excitement visible to everyone. Dad gave him a boot, and he slunk away with a growl. The male's attention was quickly diverted to a poor bitch just down the way. She straggled along, teats practically dragging in the sand, her whole appearance a testament to her hard life. She sank into the sand as the aggressive male approached and tucked her tail between her legs in an attempt to rebuff his advances. It didn't stop the male, and despite her protests, he straddled her back and humped away. Dog felt embarrassed by the scene and upset by the crude behaviour of some of her kind.

After a pleasant afternoon spent at Tenacatita, they returned home. They agreed to meet for drinks in the beach bar in Melaque for happy hour. In the meantime, Mom and Dad showered and Dog had her dinner. The guacamole she'd been fed on the beach didn't quite fill her up and she really only ate the tortilla chips to be polite.

Mom said that she wanted to drive to the bar—she was fresh from her shower and didn't want to get all sweaty again walking the several kilometers to the other end of town. She told Dad she would meet him at the camper as she wanted to have a word with the complex owner—despite the hard work of the plumbers, the toilet was still backing up.

When Mom got in the vehicle, she was spluttering with laughter. "Drive" she said, "before the owner sees me".

When they were safely out of sight, she explained. "I complained that the toilet still was not flushing properly, and said that despite Mexican customs and sanitation, North Americans expect to be able to flush toilet paper instead of putting in the garbage. The owner was quite upset about the toilet still being blocked. She asked me if I had seen the plumbers shaking the toilet. I was pretty startled by the question and did say they had removed it. "But did you seem them shake it? Is very important to shake the toilet to make sure nothing stuck!" I had to admit I had not witnessed any toilet shaking and that I was clueless to the plumbing profession here. I wonder if they teach that in the trade schools?" and with that Mom was off into hales of laughter again that had tears streaming down her face. Dad thought she was making up the whole conversation—it was that unbelievable.

Pals

They found a parking spot right near the Bigotes Bar. This was a beach front bar with a great view, and frequented mainly by local Mexicans. Their friends had discovered that the bar offered pitchers of beer for happy hour and drinks were far cheaper than other bars. Mom liked the Melaque Beach drinks which were half strawberry daiquiri and half pina colada, and quite addictive. Dad preferred his margaritas lime flavoured and on the rocks. Dog liked it here because although they were "downtown" she didn't have to be tied up. There was quite a dog clientele here as well and good company. Three-leg Charly was the resident and despite his handicap, he played a mean game of tag. Occasionally he got a little grumpy and snarled, but you had to forgive the guy because it must be tiring trying to jump and run with only three legs. Sometimes the tag games got a little carried away and they found themselves quite a ways down the beach. Dog tried not to forget boundaries and she always came back. The only other rule was not to jump on people or you would find yourself tied to a chair leg pretty quick. But even when you were tied up, this was a fun place. The little boy who was the son of the owner was pretty darned pleased that Dog knew how to behave with small children (at least when Mom was watching) and couldn't stop hugging Dog. He was a cute little guy, even if he hung on a little too tight, and Dog matched his smile grin for grin

Mourning

A few days later, Dog and Dad set out for their daily hike. They didn't get past the pool where everyone was in hushed silence. Something terrible had happened and they immediately returned to the apartment to tell Mom. It was a shocking turn of events—Ben the German Shepherd had gotten sick last night and died! There hadn't even been time to find a doctor for him: apparently his bowels had gotten twisted and he was gone. His Mom was devastated as were his human siblings. His Dad and the boys had found a nice sheltered spot at the corner of the lagoon and buried him. They made a cross and marked his name on it. The grave was covered with stones so that animals couldn't disturb it. Ben's Mom said she didn't want to stay here anymore and wanted to go home.

The afternoon brought a further shock. The man with the Alzheimer's disease had passed away in the night as well. His daughter had known that he would die soon, but it seemed so strange that there would be two deaths in the night. Mom went into town and bought flowers for Ben's Mom and the man's daughter. People slowly gathered by the pool, though the holiday mood was definitely gone. (And to settle the bad news comes in threes, some weeks later a third death would occur when a nice man on an extended vacation would suffer a fatal heart attack.) There was sadness that Ben was gone and that his family should have to suffer another tragedy. There was sorrow expressed about the old man, but it was also said that there must be some relief for his daughter. She hadn't been seen that day but was reportedly downtown making funeral arrangements. Despite being of American citizenship, she had said that it was her father's wish to be buried here in Melaque.

When the funeral took place several days later, it was apparent that the man and his daughter were well loved in the community. Not only had there been a respectful turnout from the snowbird population, but the Mexican locals had donated the grave and grave digging. Mom and Dad didn't go to the funeral (Mom doesn't do well at funerals—she can't stop crying) but did attend the wake in the compound. Typical of wakes, it featured a lot of food and drink and soon took on a party atmosphere. Dog wasn't allowed to wander among the guests and found herself leashed to a nearby palm tree. She didn't take to this too kindly and protested loudly. The bereaved daughter understood that Dog wanted to pay her respects too, and let her off the leash. Dog licked her hand in thanks, and then scurried into the crowd to say hi. Mom caught her eye and didn't look amused; Dog took this as a sign and veered off. She caught sight of Cassan napping on the lawn. She enticed him into a game of tag, but his heart wasn't into it and they never made it past the pool. Instead they lay companionably in the grass, grateful for the warm sun on their bones.

And a Room for Dog

One day, after returning from the early morning pee stop, Dog came into the apartment to find Mom packing. This was usually a sign that they would be heading out on a long road trip again. It turned out though that they were just moving apartments. Dog wasn't very helpful in all the trips up and down the stairs, from one building to the next, and wouldn't carry anything. She also wouldn't stay by herself because she thought it might be a trick to leave her behind. They weren't moving far, just back into the original building they had started out in. This time their apartment was on the third floor and was hugely spacious. There were two extra bedrooms besides Mom and Dad's, with a total of three additional beds so Dog was hopeful about getting a bed to herself. They had an extra bathroom, and two balconies. One balcony looked out into the street, and the other looked onto the beach. The living room and kitchen area was large enough to hold a dance and even the television seemed to be a little less snowy on this side. Dog ran excitedly from room to room—here she could stretch out and no one would trip over her. She knew that the her own bed thing wasn't likely to happen but hey, Mom and Dad would never figure out where she slept after they had gone to bed.

That evening they sat out on the beach side balcony watching the sun set in majestic fashion. As soon as the red ball had sunk into the ocean, they hurried inside. It was absolutely amazing how as soon as the sun set, mosquitoes would swarm out of nowhere and drink freely from any unprotected skin and even through Dog's fur. It was impossible to sit outside during that time, and everyone vanished into his or her house for an hour and a half. After that time, the mosquitoes disappeared again as suddenly and mysteriously as they appeared and it was safe again to take the night air. It was as regular as clockwork.

It became a ritual that they would all watch the sunset then move indoors to have dinner and, if the television reception was passable, watch the BBC world news. The suite had cablevision, but the wires linked, cross-linked, otherwise pirated and massed on the pole downstairs, so badly corroded by the salt air that reception was frequently better left to the imagination.

Sneaking into Bed

After dinner, Dog would be taken for a quick tour of the beach to do her business. She was not let off her leash at these times because she had a habit for sprinting off and playing deaf. This was a perverse game for Dog and her parents; if Dog obeyed commands when off leash at night, she would have greater freedom. Dog, upon sensing freedom immediately sprinted off because she knew that freedom was short lived. So instead, she would walk round and round without peeing, even if lead to the water's edge. She didn't like to uriate while on leash because the leash dragged on her two leg walking trick. Sometimes, out of frustration, she would be let of the leash and she would sprint off. This led to frequent bouts of snarling between Mom and Dad. Dad was of the opinion that she could be trusted to come home when she was good and ready; Mom worried about the dangers in the world—dognapping and getting lost.

Dog did try to behave most of the time. After doing her ablutions, neatly below the tide line where all marks would be washed away, they would return to their street side balcony. There Mom and Dad played dice, or dominoes, and Dog watched the action on the street below. Most nights there was a soccer game happening with the local boys in serious competition. They ranged in age from seven to early teens and took their game very seriously. The 'pitch' was about a half city block bordered on each side by the curb. At one end the goal was marked out by a couple of t-shirts. At the other end, a t-shirt served for one post, and one running shoe served for the other. The matching runner was still on the foot of its owner. Dog watched to see if the shoe was on the kicking foot and determined that it was not. The game was very enthusiastic with much cheering and yelling on both sides. Dog waved her tail in enthusiasm. She would have liked to go down and join in but it was obvious that dogs were excluded from the squad—even Cassan had to content himself with the sidelines. Still, she did her best to demonstrate her interest on the those frequent occasions when she accompanied one of her parents down the stairs to recover the dice that Dad frequently overtossed.

Pig Parts

In the months that they lived in Melaque, Mom and Dad and Dog made many excursions up and down the coast near their town. Wherever they saw a side road leading off towards the seaside, they pull off to explore. Often these roads were no more than overgrown dirt tracks and ten miles to the coast could take an hour of bumping along. Mom joked that if their car broke down they would wind up as a trio of *Katrina* doll skeletons because there was rarely any other traffic. Even the scrawny cattle looked as if it had been years since any human had sustained them.

Sometimes the road led to or past some deserted ruin. They would stop to explore, treading carefully around broken glass and crumbling structures. These were not some ancient civilization's remains but rather the broken dreams of resort developers or the not wealthy anymore. It was amazing how quickly the jungle regained its supremacy and there was something sad about the tennis court just visible under the flowering vines.

Inevitably the track would peter out in the sands of an uninhabited beach. Dog had plenty of room to run. These beaches stretched for miles, broken up only by occasional rocky outcroppings where tiny crabs scurried busily. Dad always made sure to point out these teeming surfaces to Dog and Mom. Dog would have a careful sniff and move on. Mom would peer at the shiny moving surface and say "amazing" and move on.

A lot of these beaches fringed the open ocean and the waves pounded the shore. At the water's edge you could feel the sand being sucked out from under your feet sometimes strongly enough to unbalance you. The presence of a strong undertow discouraged swimming. Instead the uninterrupted beach drew you into long beachcombing walks. They were wild places where you enjoyed the solitude and the feeling that you were the only inhabitants on the planet.

Sometimes they discovered natural swimming holes where rocks further out created a breakwater. Mom and Dad would paddle about happy as toddlers in a wading pool. Dog, ever mindful of her woolly undercoat (thin though it was from the tropics) would disdain all efforts to coax her in for a cooling swim. She was much more content lying in the damp sand at the water's edge, shredding any coconut she unearthed on her explorations. Her only distraction was to chase off the odd seagull that ventured near out of curiosity.

The drive back was usually not as comfortable as the drive in due to salty skin and damp, sandy bathing suits. Dog's long fur took ages to dry even in the hot tropical air, and she managed to cart copious quantities of sand onto her bench seat. The vehicle's windows were wide open and the breeze was soporific. It didn't take long for Dog's eyes to involuntarily close and put her back on the beach, this time in her dreams.

One of their exploratory trips took place on a Saturday morning. Their trek to the beach had taken them through a small village called Arroyo Seco (dry gulch). Dad had waved merrily to a group of men standing outside the village's only store. Mom had wondered at that and asked Dad if he knew any of the people—unlikely as they had never been this way before. Dad replied he did not but they seemed a friendly bunch.

The road, very passable at first, had after the village's limits narrowed to dual tire tracks between a stand of coconut trees. This beach was pretty but had a number of homes strung out along the ocean front. While beaches were considered a public place, they had become accustomed to the wild, seemingly unexplored coasts, and so decided to stay here for no more than a quick look. They retraced their tracks and as they approached the village, Dad declared his thirst. Mom was sceptical about finding a bar of any kind in such a small place but agreed that they could at least stop for some beers at the store.

The same men Dad had waved to were still there. They had organized seating under a blue tarp in the vacant lot next to the store with crates, upturned buckets, and a rough bench providing the furniture. A galvanized tin laundry tub perched on an open fire—liquid bubbling—and one of the men stirred the contents with a long stick. Dad went into the store to buy the beer, and Mom approached the man. She greeted him in Spanish and asked what he was cooking. "Pig" the man answered. "It's almost ready. Come and join us," the man invited as Dad came out of the store. Mom said thank you but no, but the man was insistent in his invitation. He called to his buddies to pass along a beer to the strangers and handed Dad a cold bottle of Dos Equis. Dad, who was apparently in a very social mood what with the waving and all, thanked them and responded positively to the invitation to sit down. The man stirring the cooking pot fished some pieces out of the bubbling oil and placed them on a piece of plank. He proffered the offerings to Mom. "What is it?" she queried. She recognized pork rind, but the other pieces were not as easily identified. "Heart, kidney, liver, stomach," the man explained. "Here, you must have the heart—it is the best part." Mom's face took on a greenish tinge and she tried to decline. She didn't like any animal's organs as a menu item and pig heart boiled in oil ...

Her husband watched in amusement. He had a cast iron stomach though she didn't see him reaching for the titbits. The cook was reassuring her that it was very tasty and didn't seem to be offering the food to anyone else. There was nothing for it but she would have to graciously sample the morsel and hope that a good dollop of hot sauce would help it down the gullet. She simultaneously reached for the offered piece and motioned for her husband's beer.

Having managed to swallow the piece, she thanked the cook and motioned to her husband that it was time to go. There was no getting away from the hospitality however, and she was entreated to sit down and feast some more. Her husband added to the voices, saying in English, "we'll just have a beer—they're really nice guys." She was given a crate of honour, handed her own beer and the plank of cooked pig parts pressed on her again. She managed to decline the food and said mischievously that her husband really enjoyed pork. Actually, with the hot sauce, the morsels were kind of tasty once your mind and stomach accepted the notion that these pieces were edible.

Introductions were made and she mentioned that her husband didn't speak much Spanish but understood a good deal of it. She told of their Canadian origins and how they came to be living in Mexico. The five men explained they all lived in this village and how on Saturdays they had this ritual get-together. The pig had been slaughtered for the village's food and was hanging in some butcher shop, but the organs and tripe made for a nice Saturday afternoon treat. It was customary to cook the innards in boiling oil.

More beer was handed out. It appeared that they wouldn't be heading home immediately so Mom suggested to Dad that Dog be let out of the camper. Dog joined the group and sniffed appreciatively at the scents. Mom would have been very willing to feed the pig parts to Dog but it was apparent that these were gourmet fixings far too good for animals. Dog had to content herself with smells alone.

A village dog ambled by and tried to wander through the group. It too was attracted by the smells of the cooking meat, but knew its place. The local's attention was more on the strange dog in the midst. Dog strained at her leash hoping to be let loose to play. But the local dog wasn't entirely friendly and was shooed out of the circle. Dad was willing to let Dog go explore but Mom would have none of it and tugged at Dog to settle down by her feet.

Dad went into the store and came out with yet more beers that he handed out in reciprocation of the hospitality. The local men didn't want to take them but thirst and insistence prevailed. Dog lay patiently listening to the mixture of Spanish and English. She noticed that the group was getting quite a lot of attention from other villagers passing by and wondered if her Mom had noticed the frowns of the village women. Dog and Mom were the only females in the group and it was obvious from the looks of the others that it was highly unusual for any female to be present at this all male, beer drinking company.

The afternoon progressed, and the topics of conversation ranged from hunting to families and marriage. The men expressed curiosity at Mom's childlessness and risked pitying looks at Dad. Mom explained that Dad had children, just not by her and that she was a wife for his pleasure alone. Mom translated the questions and there was some ribald humour over Mom's wifely duties. In response to Dad's questions, the men explained the local economy and the history of some of the abandoned resorts. Soon the afternoon shadows lengthened. Mom and Dad finally declined yet more beers and said they must be heading home. They had been there for over four hours! A photo was taken and they promised to return soon. As they started up the camper's engine, one of the locals thrust a six pack of beer through Mom's window. "For the drive home," he insisted.

Arroyo Seco gang

Pelicanos

One morning, Dog and Mom were relaxing on the beach facing balcony while Mom had her morning coffee. Out of nowhere came the sound of lowing cattle and a definite ranch smell drifted up. Dog and Mom looked down with interest. On the beach below them, some thirty cows ambled along being guided by a cowboy on horseback. It was quite early in the morning so there weren't any sunbathers on the beach, but the sight was a strange one nonetheless. The cattle had come from town direction and turned down the alley access a few houses down. They appeared to be headed toward Barra but Dog knew that the cowboy was taking them to graze in the freshwater fringes of the lagoon. There the reeds and grasses were tender and green, rare in this dusty party of Mexico, and the cattle definitely looked in need of sustenance. The threat of caimans didn't seem to bother cows or cowboy, and the herd would spend the day munching plants, knee deep in water.

Dad came in with the morning's fresh squeezed orange juice bought across the street at a pittance of a price. He was a bit agitated and reported that Ben's grave had been disturbed, and the cross marker knocked over. "Who would do something like that!" he exclaimed. Mom commented that it was unlikely to be locals, adult or children, as Mexicans are very respectful of death. For that matter, vandalism in any form was rare in Mexico. Dog wanted to put her two cents worth in, but the parents weren't paying any attention. She kept a watch on the cows moving down the beach, surmising correctly that they had probably disturbed the grave in their rush for the green goodies of the lagoon.

Mom and Dad decided that today they would spend sun time at their old haunt at the other end of Melaque. The bay was much calmer there and the waves large but gentle. A person could raise their feet off the sandy bottom and hang suspended in the water as if in a giant cradle. The other added attraction was a table, chairs, and umbrella on the beach with food and beverage service from the adjoining restaurant, Cesar y Charlys. Dog liked that place—their favourite server was sure to provide her with fresh water and the occasional titbit.

They staked out their spot on the beach. Meli, their server friend was quickly by to ask how everyone was. It didn't matter if they had seen each other the day before, there would still be much hand shaking all around and asking after health and family. Meli had been serving them for the last ten years and he was a very amiable man who lived on his own near Melaque while he sent money to support his large family in the mountains of Michoacan. His wife wasn't well enough to travel, and Meli managed to afford a trip home only once a year or so. It was quite a hardship given the importance of family in Mexican culture.

The conversation with Meli took place in Spanish. Even Dad managed the basics, though with Meli they could switch to English. Meli was very amusing that way: He could be very formal and stern with people he didn't know and if certain tourists annoyed him for any reason he would pretend that he didn't understand any English. Although Meli's spoken English was limited, his understanding of the language was quite fluent. Of course Meli also pretended to dislike dogs and would swat away strays. Yet he always made sure that Dog had cold fresh water in her dish and she knew that there was a plastic bucket in the back for the strays as well.

Drinks and lunch were ordered. Dog listened happily to the order of a club sandwich—she would get a share of that. There would also be French fries but Dog wasn't crazy about potatoes. Dad would feed her and then scold her for dropping her food in the sand, though she had learned to wash it off in her water dish. Dog circled in the sand and dug herself a little pit in the cooler, wetter sand below the surface. The only problem with this beach was that her freedom here was severely limited and she had to content herself with snoozing in the shade of the umbrella.

At the water's edge, a local man sorted out his fishing net. It was circular with weights at the bottom edge, and a rope fastening the top. Once he had it carefully untangled, he hefted it in his right hand with the rope looped loosely in his left. He waded waist deep into the water holding the net above his shoulder. The man stood patiently scanning the water surface and then let fly with the net. It arced out and landed in a flat circle on the surface of the water a few feet away and sank out of sight. He pulled the rope taught, closing the net and hauling it back towards him. Once he had it in hand, he waded back to the shore and shook the net out. There were about a dozen tiny fish, no bigger than feeder goldfish, flipping about in the net. It would take many, many more such casts before there was hope of a meal for his family's dinner.

The man continued to fish, tirelessly casting and retrieving. His actions caught the attention of the pelican scout, and soon a flock had moved in to add competition. The pelicans flew into the area overhead in formation tight enough to impress an aerobatics squadron. Once in view of their target, the formation broke up and it was each bird for itself. They would glide on the air current scanning the waters below. When something caught their eye, they would fold their wings tight against their body and stretch their necks downward. They would hit the water with bomb force and would immediately bob back to the surface, raising the bills into the air to help swallow the prey. You could just make out the outline of the fish as it went from deep bill pocket down the gullet.

Dog watched the pelicans with interest. It was obvious that they were having more success with their catch than was the fisherman. Mom had gone in for a swim and was floating on the gentle waves. She must have her eyes closed, thought Dog, because she doesn't seem to have noticed the pelicans. At that moment, one pelican completed its dive with a splash less than two feet away from Mom. Mom was startled, lost her floating position and came up spluttering water. She took a look around and abandoned the water to the fisherman and the birds. With so much action around, it was obvious that there were plenty of little fishes around and Dog knew her Mom wasn't a big fan of fish touching her. Sure enough, here came Mom out of the water, trying to look casual but Dog wasn't fooled for a minute.

When the Cows Come Home

Dog and Mom were strolling along the beach in the direction of downtown Melaque and away from the lagoon. They were admiring the ocean fronts of the houses along the beach. Some had quite elaborate set ups with swimming pools in the back yard, despite being directly on the beach. Most had good security fences keeping the public out, and there were a couple that were patrolled by snarling rottweilers. Dog wasn't sure if they were truly nasty creatures, simply doing their job, or showing their displeasure at being penned in. Either way, she was grateful for the stout fences between them because she was quite certain that mauling would come before socializing. Dog wasn't impressed by their steel-studded collars either—that was so passé—and she much preferred her own hand-woven collar that spelled out her name. Dog demonstrated her superiority and disdain by have a really long pee in front of them. She straightened up and paused. Then, as Cassan had taught her, she plumed her tail straight at the sky, braced her front legs and vigorously kicked back with her hind legs—scrape, other leg scrape, switch legs and scrape. She couldn't quite remember the purpose of this but Cassan sure did look proud and handsome when he did it. She hoped she looked as impressive.

Mom tugged on her leash and said "Come on girl. The cows are coming home and we better warn our visitor". They headed back to the beach fronting their complex where their guest, a relative from home, lay trying to absorb all the sun his one week vacation would allow. Dog listened knowledgeably as Mom cautioned the young man. "You've been out here a while and are starting to get pink, so you better think about coming in. Also, the cows are coming home and you don't want to be on the beach." The young man assured them he would only be a few minutes more, and they left.

Dog and Mom returned to the apartment and joined Dad. They sat in the shade on the balcony with a cool drink and waited. Soon they heard the lowing of the cows as they passed through the neighbouring alley. Barely after the cows had passed, their guest burst through the door.

"I thought you were kidding about the cows! I did see them walking up the beach but thought they'll turn or they'll just go around us. But those cows are crazy! They just go right through you. I had moved my towel up near the wall so I was safe but there was a woman lying in the middle of the beach against one of those little chairs that are all back. The cows just went straight for her, around her on all sides. Her little chair got kicked over and she almost got trampled! Who brings cows on a beach?!"

Mom and Dad laughed. "I did warn you that the cows were coming home … and the cows have been on this beach long before tourists ever were. So shall we go out for lunch?"

San Patricio de Melaque

Melaque is officially named for its patron Saint Patrick and the full name is San Patricio de Melaque. It is unlikely that Saint Patrick ever visited the area so the designation of him as the patron saint is a mystery. Similarly, there are few, if any, Irish in Melaque. Dad was of course an exception, and he took the Saint's Day with all Irish seriousness—a day of partying and drinking. Here in Mexico, where every day seemed a day of partying and drinking, he could hardly wait for the Mexican spin on this holiday.

The morning of March 17th dawned typically sunny with clear skies. Mom started off the day blasting out Irish songs via Van Morrison and the Chieftains on the stereo. Dad chastised her for playing the music too loud to which she commented that the Irish were going to give the Mexicans a taste of their own music—in a manner of speaking. It was very unlikely that anyone would complain about noise levels here.

Mom and Dog took Dad off to brunch at the elegant Maya's restaurant. They had a very fine meal, and Dad made sure to tell everyone that he was Irish and to question them on the meaning of St. Patrick's Day. He was scandalized that the very Catholic Mexicans didn't seem to have the foggiest idea of who St. Patrick was despite their town being named after him. Fortunately there were a few *gringos* about, and they seemed into the celebration. One man even went from table to table decorating patrons with markered on shamrocks, and Dad wore his proudly.

The rest of the day passed peacefully and in the evening they headed for Melaque's town square. If there was to be a celebration, it would happen there. And it was impossible that a city that celebrated nursery school beauty queens with parades would not have some festivities planned for their town's namesake.

They arrived after sunset and discovered the square already abuzz. Carnival rides were set up on the side street a half block away from the square. These were immensely entertaining to watch as Mexican safety standards were well below what was acceptable anywhere else in North America. On the other hand, this did result in more of an adrenaline rush for the participants, including the youngest of children who went whizzing past in the carousel at speeds that would exceed most city limits. Some children clapped in delight, many more screamed their terror, and the parents smiled and pointed. Pointless to try to take pictures—there wasn't high enough speed film available.

Saint Patrick's Day

In the square itself, the piece de resistance was a four-storey tower built with pinwheels affixed to each side. Obviously there would be fireworks! In the bandstand at the centre of the square the community band was warming up its brass. Hopefully the out of tune discordance would disappear when they all played the same song at the same time—well there was always hope.

The people filled the square in greater proportion than on any Sunday. It seemed the entire populace was present and accounted for in their finery. Children ran amongst the adults, and bolted over walls and grassy areas in noisy games of tag featuring fire-crackers. The noise and bustle made Dog shake with nervous tension. She was very grateful when Dad took her back to the camper parked on a back street well away from the spectacle. Normally she didn't like to be left out of things, but it was so blissfully quiet and dark back here that she gratefully sank onto her bench for a snooze.

Dad rejoined Mom on a corner across from the square. Things were heating up and they determined that they had a better vantage point from this spot rather than being in the middle of the fray.

In the square, a man carried a large straw bull. It too was filled with fireworks of some type. He lit one end and screeching rockets came pin wheeling out in all directions. The man did not in fact try to avoid hitting people—quite the opposite and they watched him take aim into clumps of people. Others, armed in a like manner, hit at the crowds at different spots in the square. The piercing whistle of the rockets flying in all unpredictable directions warned seconds before they penetrated the now screaming (and laughing) crowd. Mom and Dad were grateful for their distance and joined their neighbours laughing and pointing.

They bought some cold beers from the store and stood drinking them on the street taking in the chaos. They chased the beers with the sugary *charros*, a donut-like twist sprinkled with cinnamon sold by the street vendors. This was the ultimate in people watching!

The band's discordant sounds played above all the noise—the group hadn't discovered harmony. It didn't discourage a bunch of teenagers who showed off their street dancing moves below the bandstand.

And then they spotted the arms of the pinwheel on the tower beginning to turn. Someone lit the fuses. It could be supposed that the structure was meant to be a giant, rotating sparkler but this was Mexico. Instead half of the pinwheel on one side caught and sparkled as untended. The other half fizzled and added, with bangs, clouds of smoke to the air. The other sides of the pinwheels each behaved in a completely different manner and as the pinwheel turned, the rockets fired off into the sky, into neighbouring buildings, into the crowd in the square.

It was as memorable a St. Patrick's Day celebration as they had every seen and even if the Mexicans weren't sure of who St. Patrick was, by golly they could throw a party.

On the Road Again

The end of St. Patrick's Day signalled that Easter was not far around the corner. The complex's owner was already warning that Easter was a big holiday and she would need all of her rooms. This time there was no pretence of checking for vacancies—they would have to be out well before Good Friday.

Dog and Mom scouted out the other hotels and complexes in town but the answer was the same here. Big crowds were expected for Easter and there weren't any vacancies to be had. The only possibility was the campground just down the street from them. But Mom and Dad agreed that they did not want to camp in the middle of the vacationing Guadalajaran hordes. They looked forward to doing some camping, but this time they would be working their way north.

Dog watched the preparations. Some beach toys were given away to fellow tourists but more to local children. Dog and Mom walked all over Melaque taking photographs of the town, their favourite shopping spots and the people they had made friends with.

Innumerable trips were made from the apartment to the camper with boxes containing pots and pans, bags with clothes, groceries ... And then all of a sudden hugs were exchanged and Dog heard the familiar "Come on ... up up" that signalled the start of the road trip. She looked around for Cassan but he was nowhere to be seen. Ah well.... Good-byes were sad but at least Mom had taken his picture for her.

Juanita and the Wander Home

"Los pistones son malos."

Gringa and her husband stared at the mechanic who had just uttered those words. It sounded like swearing. Comprehension dawned on her husband's face and swear words she clearly understood huffed from his lips. Their Volkswagen, affectionately nicknamed Juanita, had been displaying signs of illness for the past week largely in the form of burps and belches. Now here they were in the dusty courtyard strewn with automotive bits shaded by an enormous tree. This unlikely location served as station to the best mechanic in Melaque.

The news was bad. Juanita had bent pistons and a major engine rebuild was required. Despite the popularity and manufacture of Volkswagen in Mexico, Juanita was water-cooled and of construction totally foreign here. The mechanic shook his head and looked as distressed as they did. Getting parts would be a problem; he would try Guadalajara but might have to import from the United States. The cost? He shrugged at that—there was no answer. Gringa and the Man realized that the cost didn't matter. They had no other way of getting back to Canada with Dog and their effects.

The timing was bad. Friends from Canada had arrived earlier in the week for a surprise visit. The visit started inauspiciously with the plane delayed by a full day resulting in the Man making a futile trip to the airport and the visitors losing a day of their holiday spending it in a hotel in their hometown. The local sights had been exhausted and their small town did not overly impress the man in the couple. He was also the type of man who felt that animals should only be kept if they could earn their keep. Affection and loyalty was not sufficient coin in this man's heart, and Gringa felt added stress from constantly trying to keep Dog out of this man's way. They had been showing the local sights with limited appreciation (who came to Mexico with a professed dislike of relaxing on the beach?), and were hoping to diffuse tension by taking the visitors to Puerto Vallarta. In PV there would be more cosmopolitan attractions and scuba diving expeditions. The loss of Juanita weighed doubly heavily now. She knew her husband would be agitated and sleepless until the mechanical problems were resolved, and his normally infinite patience was at end.

They headed back to their complex and waiting guests. She injected as much optimism in her voice as possible, and laid a comforting hand on his arm. "It will be ok. The mechanic seems like he knows what he's doing and Guadalajara isn't far. We can take money out on Visa … you'll see it will be fine." He didn't answer. As they neared their home, she announced that she needed some groceries for dinner and would veer off to the town centre—be back soon.

Gringa hoofed it instead to the internet café and waited impatiently for a turn at a terminal. She needed to bring home some good news and keep the trip to Puerto Vallarta on track. She logged on to the Alamo Car Rental site and reserved a car for a week's rental to be picked up at Manzanillo Airport the next day. They would have to take a taxi to the airport, an additional unexpected expense but she shuddered at the thought of having to manufacture things of interest for their guests.

She returned to the apartment, quite pleased with herself. She announced the rental plan to all concerned but judged from the look in her husband's eye that maybe this wasn't one hundred percent good news all around. The evil eye grew stronger when she rebuffed the visitors' offer to share the costs of the rental. She found herself defending her logic as she and her husband shared a taxi to the airport to pick up the car.

"They've done a lot for us over the years so I couldn't make them pay. Besides it will do us all good to have a change of scene and maybe while we're in Puerto Vallarta you'll be able to set aside your worries about the camper."

So the rental was picked up and they made their departure for Puerto Vallarta. It was an economy sized sedan and the back seat occupants would have to enjoy Dog's companionship. Gringa immediately gave up her rights to the front passenger seat.

Her husband kept up a travel monologue as they drove along but his voice was becoming a little forced. The visitor in the passenger seat didn't notice—he was deeply immersed in a pocket book the entire three hour journey. If there were sights along the way, he didn't appear in the least bit interested.

In Puerto Vallarta, they made their way to the Posada Lily. They explained to their guests that although modest, the location was fabulous and this was another home away from home. Luckily the innkeeper was able to provide them with two rooms, although their preferred spot on the corner was unavailable. The two couples separated and agreed to meet for drinks after settling in.

The four of them, accompanied by Dog, set out for the bars fronting the beach. The Man reminisced about beers being three for ten pesos in the years gone by, compared to the average of fifteen pesos each charged today. Still they found happy hour with beers in a bucket at three for twenty pesos and considered themselves very fortunate. They had happy conversation and people watched, Dog contentedly guarding their feet. Talk turned to spots for dinner. Gringa and her husband raved about Full O'Bull—a steak house nearby that offered incredible barbecued steaks and stuffed baked potatoes. They made that their destination but found the place boarded up; apparently the Californian owner had had enough of Mexico and closed shop. Gringa and her husband could not get over their bad luck in choosing restaurants with these particular guests (each previous choice had been closed for the evening or the season)—there had to be some kind of curse. In the end, they settled for one of the other restaurants nearby, but the mood was spoiled.

The next morning, the Man, Gringa and Dog drove their guests to the dive shop in central Puerto Vallarta. They wished their visitors happy swimming with the fishes and returned to their favourite beach spot for breakfast. They spent their day swimming, sunning, chatting, reading books. Occasionally their thoughts would drift to their poor Volkswagen and wonder at how her surgery was going. They then made a conscious effort to put it out of their minds as the uncertainty could drive one quickly insane.

They were strolling back to their hotel when they ran into their visitors on the boardwalk. They had, it seemed, finished the dive a bit early and so had resourcefully found their own way back. They went back to the previous day's bar for more happy hour beers and to tell and hear the diving tales.

The female visitor was very enthusiastic about their day. Her husband groused that that diving had not been very good and there wasn't much to see. His spouse countered with the sea-life they had come close to, but he was not to be dissuaded in his opinion that the diving would have been so much better in Manzanillo.

Talk turned towards dinner. Gringa, however, pleaded a headache and said she didn't feel up to dinner. Truthfully, the strain of the past few days was getting to her and she couldn't face an expensive meal that might not be up to standard, or restrictions of places to eat because of Dog's presence. Her husband walked her and Dog back to their room. She apologized for bailing out on him, and wished him a happy evening. She poured herself a drink, swallowed a Tylenol and settled down to read, Dog watching passers-by's from the balcony. Her husband returned some hours later and reported that they had gone to "Brasil", a restaurant featuring all you can eat meat. It had been the male visitor's choice, and of course he had been delighted. The meal cost was two hundred forty pesos per person, plus the cost of drinks. Gringa and her husband rarely paid more than two hundred forty pesos for a meal for the two of them with all drinks included. It had been an expensive evening and Gringa was glad she had stayed home.

The drive back was pleasant and included a stop for *chiles rellenos* at a roadside cantina. The Man thought this was delicious dish with just the right amount of heat. He was amazed that it hadn't crossed his palate before in all their visits to Mexico—he had found himself a new favourite. Their guests equally appreciated the quality and great atmosphere. They stopped at Punta Perula, a seaside village on the Chamela Bay about half way between Puerto Vallarta and Melaque. Here they secured a campsite for fast approaching Easter week, assuming of course that all would be resolved with the Volkswagen.

Back in Melaque, they left their visitors to relax from the journey, and Gringa and the Man set off for the repair garage. They walked quickly and silently, each breathing a prayer for all to be well. Juanita sat unmoved in the same shaded spot, and they caught their breath. The mechanic came out to meet them, with a worried smile. Yes, he had managed to obtain the pistons and the repairs were almost completed. The worried part of the smile came from having to impart the cost, and the news that he needed yet another day to complete the job. Gringa and the Man were very relieved. The repair cost, while high, was still considerably less than it would have cost in the US or Canada. Their only challenge would be to obtain the required thousands of pesos in cash when their banking cards had limits on the amount that could be withdrawn in a day. In the end, they managed by accessing all their accounts and credit cards. Tomorrow they would have Juanita mobile again, just in time to drive their visitors to the airport and say goodbye.

The Man set off at the appointed hour to retrieve Juanita. She started with a full throttled purr, exhibiting no hesitation, and settled into her signature Volkswagen idle. He paid the mechanic, thanked him heartily, and with a much lighter heart put Juanita into gear for the drive home. The ride to the airport would be a good test for the new pistons and the mechanic's handiwork.

At the airport, Gringa and the Man hugged their visitors and hoped that they had enjoyed themselves. Both visitors were enthusiastic in their praises and claimed the best time ever. Oddly, neither party seemed inclined to stretch out the goodbyes over a drink in the bar, and with a last wave, they parted company.

On the Road Again

They arrived in Perula on March 22nd without so much as a backfire fart from Juanita and were directed to the "premium" spot at the Red Snapper campground. Their camping spot was immediately adjacent the restaurant and consequently had the advantage of the restaurant's roof overhang to provide shade, and a cement pad for table and chairs. Next to them on the other side was one other trailer spot without benefit of any kind of shade. In front of the camping spot, several palapas provided cover on the gently sloping beach. There was no one around save for one Mexican family in tents on the other side and out of view. At the moment it was idyllic but Easter was fast approaching and they assumed the seclusion would change significantly. At seventy pesos per night, it was a cheap paradise and would go a long way to nursing their bank accounts back towards health.

The owner came to check that they were comfortably settled and assured them the water truck arrived daily. His assurances were somewhat premature as the water truck did not actually arrive for the next two days, but the owner's wife graciously supplied them with a couple of gallons to tide them over.

The owner, an American by birth, was an interesting man. Short and wiry in stature, he was obviously in his retirement years and had the pruned look of someone who has spent many years in the tropical sun. His wife was Mexican, and yet his conversations were liberally sprinkled with derogatory comments about Mexicans—particularly the youth. To him, they were all escapees from Los Angeles drug gangs, returned briefly to their homeland to flog drugs and stolen goods to support their families. One evening a group of youths gathered on the beach near the restaurant. They built a bonfire and proceeded to party in harmless Mexican fashion. The campground owner waited less than an hour before chasing them off; he was worried the bonfire would send sparks into his palapa roof and create a fire. He professed to be very knowledgeable on the subject of Mexican crime and added that he had been paid very well by certain agencies, if you know what I mean, to "keep an eye on things down here" during the fifties, sixties and seventies. His bluster lost most of its bravado whenever his wife was in earshot, though not completely, and she was surprisingly tolerant about his attitudes. Despite being the owner of the campground, it appeared that the territory was more under his wife's control. He generally spent his time working around their home set back some two hundred feet from the restaurant, only appearing when his wife commanded some boxes or water to be delivered, lifted, shifted, or when beach parties urged his vigilant patrol.

Punta Perula

Gringa, the Man and Dog settled in. They had electrical hook-up and so could read at night without worry about running Juanita's battery down. They even set out the stereo equipment to add Russell Watson's arias to their quiet evenings, though sand or something tended to interfere with the operation of CDs. They stretched out Juanita's awning and borrowed a table and chairs from the restaurant. They could access the washrooms and showers in the restaurant by going to the front of the building and learned to time their ablutions when the restaurant was not at peak service.

Soon company arrived … for Dog. Dolly the boxer made her presence known and became a frequent visitor in search of shade for her very pregnant body.

Judging from Dolly's shape, this was far from the first litter she'd carried in her young life and she was an object of pity. Dolly belonged to the campground owners and felt a right to park wherever she chose. Dog was a little disappointed by Dolly's infrequent desire to play, not realizing how close to giving birth the ungainly dog was. Another presence was a male with Great Dane in his ancestry. He was the picture of hangdog, probably due to his homelessness. He could be a pest towards both Dolly and Dog, and Gringa and the Man tried to discourage him from hanging around.

Their first morning dawned with a high light blue sky with only the faintest skiff of cloud. They looked out to the gentle sea, no big rollers here, and were amazed to see four dolphins swimming parallel to the shore less than fifty feet out, where the water was still only chest deep. Back and forth the dolphins went, either feeding or enticing someone out to play. Gringa hurried but by the time she had her swimsuit on, they were gone and would not be seen that close to shore again.

The Man, Gringa and Dog walked into the village to get their bearings and suss out the place. It was approximately a half mile to the centre with residential streets perpendicular to the main highway all of its length. It indicated a population of three hundred or less. The main drag was long and dusty, although there were sidewalks bordering it in places. Typical of villages, it had a central square fronting the church and pharmacy. The pharmacist doubled as banker and mayor. There were two *tiendas* offering groceries and fresh vegetables, and a beer store where ice could be had. Purchasing ice was tricky because it involved hustling back the half mile to the campsite, carrying the leaking plastic bags in the hot sun. (Juanita was of no help because she was tricked out in camping mode and could not be driven without great disassembling.) They spotted one restaurant and returned later that evening to give it a try.

Taco El Tejamar was located on the ground floor of the owner's house. The living room had simply been converted by pushing the couch to the back wall, and setting four or five plastic tables in a space fully surrounded by tropical houseplants. They were the only customers that evening, but that could have been due to the earliness of the hour. Many seaside resorts closed their restaurants as soon as the sun set to avoid use of electricity and so they timed their evening meal while the sun was still visible. The Tejamar did have electricity though, as evidenced by the television in the corner blaring the evening news. The owner was friendly enough once he realized that he would not have to rely on English. He provided information along with delicious tacos and cold beer. Perula was essentially a fishing village, though tourism became a mainstay during holiday periods and they could expect vast crowds for the Easter celebrations the follow-ing weekend.

By early the following week, people were starting to trickle into town and into the campsite. They now had campsite neighbours in the form a couple with teen-aged daughter and son, towing a trailer that seemed far too tiny to accommodate the four of them. They were nonetheless very trailer proud. It was an affectionate family with "Papi" calling out instructions to the youth as they mounted their dirt bike, or handing over cash for errands and goodies. After the initial smiling "*Buenas Dias*" the campers kept to themselves. Gringa noticed the kids eyeing her wakeboard (a gift from some other BC tourists) and wandered over to offer its use whenever they wanted. This prompted more conversation about who, what and where. They were a family on their annual holiday, in recent years always spent at this campground. Gringa introduced her husband and the conversation continued in a mix of English and Spanish and gesturing. Papi explained that they were very fortunate to own a trailer. In Mexico it is illegal for Mexican citi-zens to own a trailer or camper with kitchen facilities in it (out of fear of the pop-ulace homesteading in inappropriate places) and Papi showed that their trailer was indeed sleeping space alone. Gringa and the Man reciprocated with a tour of Juanita's features that led to very wistful sighs from Papi for the travels that could be undertaken in such luxury!

In the days leading up to Good Friday, the beach became increasingly busier and so too patronage of the restaurant. Gringa found their "prime" spot all of a sudden to be less than prime. The restaurant's menu was predominantly fish and seafood. Gringa was allergic to both and found the smell of frying fish skin espe-cially nauseating. Fumes would waft over the wall constantly from lunch to din-ner-time; their prime spot was immediately adjacent the open air/windowless kitchen, and Gringa would be forced to retreat to the beach in search of breath-able air. In addition, the opening bars of "Don't Worry, Be Happy" and "Take me to the River" would sing out with annoying frequency. They finally tracked down the source to a couple of novelty fish parked on the restaurant's counter—said fish breaking into song whenever any person moved within the motion-sensing field. After a couple of days of this Gringa and her husband were ready to break in to drown the fish, or at the very least steal the batteries but they wondered if the fish might not be some security detection system?

As the Easter weekend approached, Gringa walked into town and noticed signs of the upcoming festivities. Easter is reputedly the most sacred and impor-tant of holidays in Mexico, even more so than Christmas. On Palm Sunday, the ladies of any community gather near the church to weave palm leaves in fantastically detailed crucifixes and other shapes. There are no Easter bunnies on display and the holiday retains its holy meaning. The town squares do evidence the more prosaic festivities with roving amusement parks, and trailers filled with novelties and sweets. The travelling amusement park was setting up, and around the square were countless trailers selling *dulces* (a variety of Mexican candy and sweets) and assorted novelties. She bought some fudge for her husband, and some other varieties of sweets for Papi and family. After lending the wake board to the children, Papi was anxious to reciprocate the kindness in every way possible—just the evening before when Gringa had gone to find out the word for dice (she needed to buy some), he had immediately sent his son on the dirt bike to buy a quantity for Gringa and her husband. The dice were very unique and their lack of uniform shape made the games very interesting, but they treasured them for the kindness with which they were presented. She also bought sweets for the campground missus who had promised to make *chiles rellenos* when the vegetable truck next delivered the appropriate peppers.

Cash was running low but Gringa had it on the campground owner's authority that the pharmacist did money exchange. There are no banks or ATMs in Perula and the nearest would mean a drive back to Melaque. Gringa approached the pharmacist with the request to exchange some US dollars—he looked down his nose at her and quoted an exchange rate far from favourable. Still, needs must, and Gringa accepted the terms for just the amount to tide them over to next week. She was not impressed with the pharmacist's customer service demeanour. She learned later that the man was also the town mayor and that would, of course, explain the puffed up self importance.

On Good Friday, Gringa walked into town to see how the festivities were progressing. She had just turned the corner onto the main street when she spotted a congregation making its way in her direction. At the head of the group was a man dressed as Jesus Christ, labouring under the weight of a large wooden cross. The crown of thorns was represented with a crown of cedar boughs and while likely less painful, it was certainly itchy enough to sustain the pained expression on his face—no acting there.

A crowd followed the "Savior", including a lady with a bible and a man carrying a microphone with portable speaker. The procession stopped near a shaded tree where a clothed table with flowers was set up. The lady with the bible loudly led the group in prayer, and the procession moved on. Gringa figured out it was an enactment of the Stations of the Cross. She trotted ahead of the group to be able to photograph them. They turned the corner onto the street leading to a church on a low hill. Gringa was amused when the "Savior" walked past one of the "Stations" and was hailed back by the man with the microphone—something along the lines of "Hey Jesus come back!" Gringa was curious to see how the procession would end—what happens with the crucifixion? But at the end of their journey, the group made its way into the church, and although Gringa waited a while, it was obvious that mass would keep the congregation in place for some time yet, and so she made her way back to the campsite.

Easter at Punta Perula

After Easter and as the following weekend neared, Gringa telephoned the *pensione* in Puerta Vallarta. She was advised that there were rooms available midweek but the weekend was booked. They decided to up stakes and head north before the weekend crowds descended.

At the Posada Lily, they were given a room fronting the main street and told with some form of Mexican logic that they could keep the room as long as they liked ... however, if they wanted the room just for the weekend, it was not available. They told the innkeeper that they would let him know their plans as soon as they were finalized. In the end, the lure of Puerto Vallarta was strong and they booked themselves in for a total of six days. It was very hard to leave Puerto Vallarta without knowing how long it would be before they were able to return. And while they didn't have a timetable to adhere to for leaving Mexico, the car permit was due to expire mid-month. It was a crapshoot as to how bureaucratic the government would be about an expired permit. They reasoned that staying in Puerto Vallarta a few days longer would give them the opportunity to visit the necessary government offices to obtain an extension.

The days were spent visiting favourite spots, intensified with the need to store nostalgia for a lifetime. Each drink or meal served on the beach brought sighs of appreciation and comments like "I'm going to miss this ..." In the evenings, they set out to have dinners at their favourite restaurants, though tourism season was winding down and many places were already closed. There were fewer people on the streets, and even the time-share purveyors were winding down in pitch. They spent time at Andeles with their favourite bartender. He and Gringa exchanged shirts—she gained one of his old Andeles branded shirts; she passed off a firefighter's t-shirt which he said would be a guaranteed chick magnet. At home the NHL playoffs were getting into full swing, and to the Man's delight they managed to find a sports bar, run by a Canadian, that showed their home team in action.

The Man took Gringa for dinner one night at the Brasil Restaurant, so touted by the friends who had visited. Dog wasn't allowed in and although she tried her best to charm the doormen, she wound up having to wait for mum and dad in the camper. The charm wasn't wasted however, because for every night after that the doormen insisted that Dog be brought by for a treat or two—whole tinfoil packets of steak, chicken, sausage. The restaurant charged for the all you can eat menu, and consequently more than one tourist (Gringa included) wound up with large uneaten portions on her plate. Although a good deal of the left over food undoubtedly went home with the cook and wait staff, Dog certainly ate well for the days they spent in Puerto Vallarta.

They tried to figure out which government department was responsible for car permits, and the manager of the Internet café suggested the Minister of Finance. The Man and Gringa were set to make the pilgrimage on Monday but the café owner cautioned about multi-hour waits. Not knowing whether this was even the right department, Gringa and her husband decided on a policy of asking for forgiveness instead and skipped the bureaucratic visit.

April 7th they finally bid farewell to Puerto Vallarta. Juanita had not exhibited any ill effects from her surgery, but the Man was determined to be gentle. All drives were to be short, and so they made their next stop a short distance away in

Sayulita. Before leaving town, they stopped at one of giant grocery stores to stock up on camping supplies. The grocery stores offered everything from clothing to computers, but Gringa's favourites lay in the bakery department. They purchased coffee, vegetables, some baked goods, beer and pop, and at the last minute decided on a cooked barbecue chicken for their supper.

They telephoned their friends from Perula, Papi and his family, to arrange a drop-in visit as their home was on the way to Sayulita. Papi's wife sounded very welcoming and provided directions to the house in Las Juntas just near the Nayarit state border. They had promised to contact the family when they arrived in Puerto Vallarta, and wanted to give the boogie board as a gift to the teenagers.

Papi's house was a modest duplex with living quarters upstairs. It seemed that Papi was quite well off, and his wife, although somewhat shy, was proud of her home. Papi chastised them for not having called earlier—it had been his plan to meet the Man and Gringa for a full day fiesta at one of Puerto Vallarta's beaches. Gringa apologized and explained that their plans had not been concrete though she was privately glad that the visit was more on their timetable than Papi's. Had the beach fiesta taken place she and her husband would likely still be in Puerto Vallarta and nursing severe hangovers to boot!

Email addresses and street addresses were exchanged, and the usual exhortations to visit expressed. Papi presented the Man with a bottle of fine aged tequila, and Papi's wife presented Gringa with a potpourri sachet. The boogie board was presented to the teenagers, despite protestations by Papi that it was too valuable a gift.

Final hugs were exchanged and the family escorted the Canadians to their vehicle parked in the street outside the house. The Man opened the side door to allow Dog a chance to express her greetings and was dismayed to find the barbecue chicken laid out for Dog's obvious pleasure. He scooped up the remains and tucked them out of sight, saving the scolding until they were away from their Mexican hosts.

Sayulita

Dog hopped out of the camper in Sayulita, anxious to have a good sniff around and relieve her body of some of the chicken she'd stolen. She felt mildly guilty but hey, warm barbecued chicken sending aromas from the handy bag was just too much temptation. The campsite they were parked in appealed to her—lots of grass and lovely landscaped hedges and flowers. The campground ran from the administration building at the end of a quiet street down to the beach. Beach-side there was an intriguing looking house available for rent, but according to Mom, it was expensive. Two storey houses with attractive verandas right on the beach, fabulous views of the small bay and flat sandy beach—Dog could picture them living there. But camping would be fun. The only drawback Dog could see was that there was a strict leash policy and it would be tough to get a good run in.

Gringa and the Man set the camper up—up went the pop top, down came the chairs from the roof rack, out came the box of cooking utensils. Ten minutes and Juanita was transformed from vehicle to home. They had passed through Sayulita on a previous trip and were anxious to take a closer look. The campground was very well tended and not terribly expensive at one hundred twenty pesos per night. This time of year it was only about a third full, which added to its charm.

They set out for a reconnoitre walk. The road leading to the beach separated the two halves of the campground. The other side held a large building which housed bathrooms, showers and laundry facilities. Another building housed a ping pong table and a lounge area. There were more rv sites, but these were grouped closely together and didn't have a nice grassy area, so they considered themselves fortunate in their chosen location.

The town itself was a triangle nestled between the highway, a hillside and the bay. All the roads were of the pounded dirt variety though here and there a stub of sidewalk adjoined. The hillside held some interesting looking houses, no doubt American owned and American priced. Sayulita was becoming one of the trendy "found" places of Mexico. They hoped that it wouldn't lose its culture altogether.

In the village depths, the streets held a mixture of modest homes, dusty grocery shops, empty lots, and the oddly placed, out of the way, restaurant. The air had a pervasive equine heaviness to it, and one had to watch one's step for the more physical reminders of horse back riding tours headquartered in one of the sparse lots. At the triangle point closest to the beach two stores catered to the shopping tourist, but overall the village exuded a dusty sleepiness. The people in the street were neither cold nor welcoming; rather they seemed to look through tourists as if by ignoring the presence they could go back to being undiscovered.

Back at the campground, they noticed campers had settled into the site next to theirs. To Dog's delight, the group included a six week old, fluffy puppy. The seven year old *seniorita* who claimed ownership identified the bouncing ball of fur as Candy. She quickly scooped the squirming pup away from whatever captured its curiosity. Dog stretched with belly as close to the ground as possible and whimpered to be allowed to play with this moving toy. Candy pranced fearlessly close and barked, enticing Dog into some form of game, rules undetermined. Dog had never seen anything so small and active before, who could babble in her language. She jumped up to take up the chase. "Dog! Gentle!" her mum's words startled her back. Mum needn't have worried—Candy was quick to find shelter in tight spots when needed, and darted out to torment Dog in this strange game of tag that circled the picnic table. Dog's grin reached from ear to ear and she wondered how she could get one of these amazing playthings for herself. She tried whining in her most pitiful voice when Candy's owner took her back to her own site.

The Man and his wife settled themselves comfortably, sitting in their director chairs with feet propped up on the picnic bench, cocktails near to hand.

They watched as a large tour bus pulled into the compound. It disgorged a group of ten or so who set about relieving the roof rack of its load of tents and kayaks. The side of the bus indicated an eco-adventure tour. Sayulita was a favourite stop on a two week tour, and provided the tourists with kayaking and surfing opportunities. With the camp set up, the group took itself off into town for dinner. Gringa and the Man watched in amusement as Candy, left unsupervised, wriggled her way into one of the tents and came out prancing with a climber's headlight proudly carried between her teeth. They liberated the object and reattached the puppy to her leash in her own campsite.

They didn't spend much time in Sayulita. Gringa found herself in a strange frame of mind. On the one hand now that they were Canada bound, she was anxious to get back, decide where they were going to settle, and have a home again. On the other hand, it was difficult to think of not waking up to sunshine, tropical breezes and freshly squeezed orange juice. They were determined to not race back, and to savour every moment of the journey.

They left Sayulita and did the four hundred fifty-six kilometer drive to Mazatlan in one day. Dog found herself heaving as they negotiated the tricky twists and turns of the first part of the trip. Mom popped a motion sickness tablet down her throat and Dog went to sleep just as they reached the flat divided highway.

They pulled in to the Mar Rosa campsite in downtown Mazatlan around four o'clock in the afternoon. The Man was well pleased with the Volkswagen's performance—not a hint of overheating or backfire. It seemed their engine woes were over.

Although it was not quite the middle of April, the campsite was almost deserted. There were only four other units in residence and everyone appreciated the ability to stretch out. The manager said it had been a good year with almost full capacity and that Canadians had greatly outnumbered Americans. The Americans apparently still felt unsafe travelling after the horrors of the previous year's 9/11 terrorist attacks.

One of the neighbouring campers came over to their site the next afternoon to enquire about Spanish speaking abilities. Their dog was in some kind of distress from a sore in its mouth and wouldn't eat. The couple had located a veterinary clinic but felt uncomfortable about not being able to communicate clearly. The Man immediately volunteered Gringa's service. Gringa saw the woman's anxiety and good naturedly agreed to tag along on the vet visit. She pocketed her Spanish/English dictionary and crossed her fingers. At the vet's she was able to translate the couple's story and the dog's medical history. The normally yappy breed was docile and pathetic. After a brief examination, the vet came back and spoke in lightening fast sentences. Gringa nodded her head sagely as he went on. In fact she was only picking up on about every third word, but felt she had the gist of the problem. "Bad teeth is what he said, and they'll have to pull one/some", she translated. They were told that they could come back in the morning to retrieve the dog. Gringa was amazed that these Americans didn't even ask what the procedure would cost. But then she reasoned, what difference would it make to know the price when you knew you would have to have the required procedure for your beloved family member no matter what the cost.

The couple thanked her profusely for accompanying them. They felt they could handle matters from here and assured her that Gringa needn't bother coming with them in the morning. Gringa said, "OK, but let me know if you change your mind, because it's no big deal." She went back to their campsite and reported on the trip. "Now I speak dog dentistry too" she laughed, but then admitted that the Spanish had been way to fast for her to consider herself at all fluent.

Next morning Gringa set off down the main drag on a shopping expedition. Their anniversary was in July, and although it was only April she couldn't let the lure of Mexican silver pass her by. She had in mind to buy her husband a dressy belt with silver buckle, and she had seen a promising jewellery shop here on their previous visit. She found the ideal buckle set. It was weighed to determine the price and Gringa splurged. She justified the cost by planning the gift for their anniversary. She wondered if she would have the fortitude to keep the gift hidden for all those months.

Next door to the silver shop was a leather store. There were hundreds of belts to choose from, but in typical Mexican fashion, none were the right width to fit the belt buckle. The shop owner rescued the situation by suggesting a custom made belt. "*Si senora,* we can cut to size and have the belt ready in an hour. It will not cost much more." Gringa was delighted as even at the inflated price, leather in Mexico was a fraction of the cost in America or Canada, and of course she could easily kill an hour shopping.

Well satisfied, Gringa returned to the campsite. Her husband didn't question the Cheshire Cat grin, and seemed satisfied with her explanation of being very pleased with the sandals she'd bought.

Trials and Tribulations

Los Alamos lies fifty kilometers off the *autopista*. Guidebooks tout it as a picturesque mountain town being lovingly restored by artsy *norte americanos* from its silver mining days of splendour to a picturesque and quaint tourist destination. At the moment, the Man could care less about sightseeing or anything quaint. He scrambled under the Volkswagen's back end for the fifth time and felt sick to the pit of his stomach. The coolant reservoir was empty and refills simply gushed out the bottom of the engine.

They had travelled quite a distance that day—over five hundred kilometers—but the route had been straight and flat with constant speeds on the toll highway. They had left the *autopista* at Navajoa and managed to come within two kilometers of Los Alamos when Juanita had, suddenly and violently, overheated and shut down. He had refilled the coolant and given her engine a half hour rest break but as soon as the key was turned the heat indicator swung out of sight. Finally he had taken the chance and managed to coast into this campsite at the edge of town. He suspected a cracked engine head and was desperately worried that this might prove the end of the road.

His wife had set out as soon as the vehicle was parked in a camping spot. She was determined to find help but he had his doubts about mechanical solutions to be found in this sleepy town far off the beaten path.

Gringa was resolute. She would find a mechanic to come to the campsite to look at the problem. Then, if it wasn't a simple fix, they would get a tow back to Navajoa. The campsite they were in was very attractive with lots of shady trees so they would be comfortable until the solution could be found. The complex had a hotel attached to it, and oddly, a water bottling plant. She would start her search at the office. Good thing she spoke Spanish car.

There was no response to her knock on the office door so she made her way toward the sound of rushing water. Large five gallon water jugs were being filled from a hose and loaded onto a truck. She cast a quick thought to whether that water was actually purified or just coming from a tap, and then attracted the attention of one of the work men.

She explained their predicament and pointed out the VW in the camp lot below. A per night camping fee was agreed to, and he offered the information that there was a mechanic just down the road heading into town. She thanked him and headed off. Sidewalks bordered the road leading into town. The height of the sidewalk varied from curb level to six or seven stairs high, giving testament to the rains that must flood the region. She crossed a bridge over a dry gulch and found herself looking towards a leafy avenue and square a few blocks away. The town certainly looked promising and she noted the location of the food shops, liquor store, and butcher with refrigerated meat cases. She hoped that their vehicle problems would be quickly resolved so that her husband could enjoy the town.

Another block on and she spotted high metal gates painted white and spread wide to reveal the automotive yard. "*Hola*," she approached the man working below a hoisted vehicle. "*puede usted ayudarme, per favor?*" She launched into a quick description of the problem. Her Spanish wasn't really that fluent when it came to speaking about unknown car problems but in her experience she found that she managed to get her point across if she talked fast and didn't think too much about the words she was using—sort of a subconscious stream of automotive terms in Spanish. The mechanic zeroed in on one term and shook his head. He did not work on Volkswagens. He turned back to his work, the conversation and Gringa dismissed.

Gringa would not be deterred. "Is there another garage? Another mechanic?" she persisted. Los Alamos had a population of ten thousand. Surely there would be more than one garage … The man reluctantly lifted his head from under the hood, his irritation obvious. He directed her back the way she had come, and a further half kilometer out of town from the campsite—there was a man there who worked Volkswagens.

Gringa hoofed it back the way she'd come. It was hot and she was sweaty but felt on the path to victory. At the directed corner, all there was a wooden stall selling candies and newspapers. She asked for directions to the mechanic and walked the four blocks *a la direcha* and one more, again to the right. She arrived at another outdoor mechanic station. This one was even more primitive, with strewn car parts and a manual block and tackle. Eventually she got the attention of one of the men working there and launched into her tale. This man heard her out with scepticism on his face. He apologized and said he didn't think he could help. "My father used to repair Volkswagens but he is retired now. You could, maybe, ask him for advice." To Gringa's bemusement, she was directed back to the stall selling the candies and newspapers.

Eventually, Gringa returned to the campsite. She was hot, foot worn, and thirsty. She related her tale to her husband, but in his distress over the vehicle he saw no humour in the Mexican go-around. "Look," she said, "this old guy used to be a mechanic who worked on VWs. He's going to come by later and have a look. Then we'll at least know what could possibly be wrong, and we'll take it from there."

"I already know what's wrong" her husband growled. "There's a crack clearly visible that the coolant is running straight out of. We're f***ed."

Gringa, unable to sit about without an action plan, headed to the campsite office. She spoke to another man and negotiated a telephone call. It was established that there was a large VW dealership in Navajoa, back fifty kilometers at the highway junction. They would reopen on Monday. She thanked the campsite owner and returned to their site. She asked her husband if he wanted to accompany her to town for dinner and drink supplies. Once again, she set off on her own. She picked up steaks at a butcher that amazingly had Canadian grain-fed Alberta beef in his cooler. She preferred the locally grown Sonoran beef (some of the best in the world) but felt pleasantly nostalgic at simply having seen the Canadian product. The butcher explained that the large local American and Canadian population had a preference for beef products from their own countries, despite the expense. She walked further into town and picked up beer, wine, and a bag of ice. Then heavily laden, she limped back intent on cheering up her husband.

The elderly gentleman wandered into their campsite around supper time. He didn't even bother to look at the engine but simply pronounced that they would need a tow. He would arrange for the tow truck driver for Monday morning. The cost was an astounding fifteen hundred pesos but was non-negotiable. Gringa and the Man knew they were being taken advantage of but were in no position to argue. Gringa found it particularly ironic to learn that the retired mechanic was the brother of the campsite owner, and the tow truck driver was another relative. All three would without doubt share the fifteen hundred pesos. She just wished that the Mexicans had been a little more forthcoming with the information and saved her the blisters accumulated that day.

On Sunday, they managed to set aside their vehicle problems for the day, and set out to enjoy the sights of Los Alamos. They climbed the curved streets to the main square and admired the large church. The streets were lined with high white-washed walls, with flowering shrubs hanging over in colourful profusion. The occasional gate provided a glimpse of fantastic courtyards and well maintained homes. There was an appropriate Sunday morning quiet with even the usual stray dogs off somewhere taking a Sabbath rest. The town was extremely clean, and the North American dollars spent on renovations clearly evident.

Los Alamos

They wandered through some art galleries and upscale souvenir shops. They learned that Los Alamos was the home and only location of the famous Mexican jumping bean—and, creepily, that the beans jumped as bugs incubating inside hatched and came to life. They opted to not add bug infested beans to their souvenirs though the grandchildren would be engrossed rather than just grossed.

They walked back to the lower square and found the local Mexicans in Sunday parade under the beautiful large shade trees. A market offered fresh produce, cereal goods, and cheap clothing. They stocked up on more ice and returned to while away the afternoon at their campsite.

Monday morning the tow truck driver arrived, amazingly, promptly at nine o'clock. He would not consider a reduction in the tow charge and in a very un-Mexican way, was not hesitant in holding firm on the price, and demanding payment up front. The Man helped him secure the VW to the tow truck, and it was decided that the Man and Dog would ride in Juanita and Gringa would ride with the tow truck driver. No pesky safety rules here.

Gringa struck up a conversation with the driver. She made the usual polite enquires about wife and children and was surprised with the responding tale of woe. The driver's wife had died of a brain tumour only several months previously and he was still learning to cope with two young, motherless children. There were, of course, aunts and cousins to lend assistance but the grief in the man's voice was evident. Gringa felt better about the fifteen hundred peso tow bill.

About half way to Navajoa, they were waved to a stop by an army patrol. The driver was questioned intensively, and the soldiers asked to see the interior of the VW. They were unsurprised by it containing passengers and were charmed by Dog. The search was cursory and involved only a couple of cupboards being flipped open.

The vehicle ahead of them was experiencing more intensive scrutiny. The truck with its flat deck piled high with stones was being laboriously unloaded, boulder by boulder, by the driver and his helper under the watchful eyes of the armed soldiers. The tow truck driver explained they were searching for drugs.

Just after ten in the morning, Juanita was pulled into the back courtyard of the shiny, and obviously new, Volkswagen dealership in Navajoa. Gringa and the Man went in to discuss their automotive difficulties while the tow truck driver unclamped the VW and sped off.

The dealership manager came forward and said they could not repair this type of Volkswagen. Gringa told him point blank that he didn't have any option because the vehicle was incapable of going anywhere and a tow over the border, several hundred kilometers distant, was out of the question. The manager insisted they didn't know how to work on these types of engines. "But you're a dealership with full service," Gringa exclaimed. "Don't you have computers and manuals that you can look repairs up? *Computatdor? Manuel?*" she enquired putting a Spanish spin to the word manual. The dealership manager looked confused but led them around back to where the vehicle was. He spoke in rapid fire and a mechanic shrugged. They both turned to Gringa expectantly. Gringa and the Man were confused; some obvious miscommunication going on here. And then it dawned on Gringa; the mechanic's name was Manuel and he and the manager were wondering why Gringa had such faith in him being able to fix the vehicle. New negotiations took place. It was agreed that they would leave the mechanics to look over the vehicle while she and her husband located a hotel. They would come back just after lunch to check on progress.

Just one block away, off the main road, they found a very pleasant motel complete with large swimming pool and patio area. Rates were a reasonable three hundred fifty pesos per night, rooms were available, and Dog was welcome. The pool had a fancy waterfall at one end, and the patio area had barbecues available for guests' use. The rooms had televisions with cable, and there was even a schedule of televised NHL playoff hockey games. Gringa beamed at her husband. Things were definitely looking up.

Hotel in Navajoa

At one o'clock, they walked back to the dealership. The place was very quiet and deserted though the gates to the rear compound stood open. They walked back and saw that Juanita had been moved. Even more promisingly, her engine compartment was open, and a mechanic's legs stuck out from below. They walked closer, calling '*Hola*', with no response. The Man looked down into the engine and to the ground below. Manuel was fast asleep with this head nestled against the wheel. This was too "Faulty Towers" to be believed.

In all, they spent one day shy of a full week in Navajoa. Their days fell into a routine. Get up and wander over to the VW store to get misinformation on progress. Return to the hotel for breakfast, walk around town, return after lunch to the VW store for more misinformation and disappointment that the repairs would take yet another day, hang out by the pool, barbecue dinner, watch television, sleep, and repeat.

Navajoa is a small city with a plain Jane appearance. It was built as an urban centre to serve the needs of the surrounding rural areas and had no particular cultural or visual redeeming features. Gringa was amused by a street sign that said "*No Reelecion*" and took pictures to send back to fellow Clerks in Canada. The market filled up a morning's wandering and offered up some cheap belts. The local Ley grocery store kept them stocked with cold breakfasts and barbecue victuals. They met a couple of nice travelling men one night at the pool-side who shared their tequila. The businessmen confirmed that the tow job should not have cost more than five hundred pesos, and that they would have had better luck in Ciudad Obregon some thirty kilometers away.

Manuel established that the problem with the VW lay in a cracked head. The mechanics felt that this could be repaired without replacing the engine and the time delays resulted from machining down parts and locating the appropriate seals. A trip to a part store thirty kilometers away ended with the man sent having to stay overnight, and that delay had Gringa snapping rudely about having to wait while a fellow serviced his girlfriend instead of their car.

On another day, Juanita was pronounced fit and ready for the test drive. They waited with baited breath while Manuel filled the coolant reservoir and turned over the engine. Hope sank when the coolant immediately dripped to the ground below.

Finally, on the Saturday, they were told that the VW would be ready to travel at noon. After all the "*mas tardes*" they were afraid to believe that the problems would finally be over. They arrived a little before noon and just as Manuel pulled in from the test drive. He jumped out of the vehicle, all smiles, and walked around to the back. He patted the VW's hatch, and scratched a benedicting cross into the dust on the rear window. Now came the worry about the bill—an estimate had been provided in the roughest of forms. The bill came to three thousand five hundred eighty-one pesos and seemed entirely reasonable. Anything would have seemed reasonable to them so long as it meant escape. One final difficulty arose when the cashier refused the Man's Visa Gold Card saying that the Mexican banks would not accept foreign credit cards. This final stupidity had Gringa and her husband apoplectic with frustration and demanding the Manager's attention. "How do all the tourists manage to spend their money?" Gringa fumed to the cashier. In the end, the manager himself ran the Visa slip over to the bank across the street, and they were finally away.

There were no fond backward glances at the Navajoa city limits, and they both seemed anxious now to put Mexico behind them.

The High Spots of the North

They didn't travel far—it didn't seem right to tax Juanita so soon from her sick bed—only a couple of hours further to San Carlos. The guidebooks had much to tout about San Carlos in its location on the Sea of Cortez but the first glance was a strip mall of a town leading down to a fancy marina. Peak tourist season was behind them and the town had an abandoned air. They let Dog wander along the beach, a rocky kind with an abundance of seashells to testify to a rough tide. After the fine sands they were used to, this beach seemed worthy only of beachcombing and not bathing; perhaps in the morning.

They settled into a trailer park. This one was over ninety percent unoccupied and resembled an empty drive-in theatre, only occasionally punctuated by small-ish trees. The screen end presented a vista of the mountains with the moon climbing the edge. It was hard to imagine spending any great lengths of time here, but some of the rigs still in place showed that many people settled here for the long haul. They parked themselves at a distance from any neighbours, and set about dusting away Navajoa from the camper's interior.

Gringa decided they needed some supplies and offered to find a shop. The clerk at the check-in had said the grocery store was only a quarter kilometer away and Gringa felt that was a reasonable walk. After hiking for what seemed like miles instead, she finally came upon the grocery store and thought ruefully about the walk back carrying ice et al. She decided just on the minimum for dinner and breakfast, although the ice was a must. She would cross the street and head back hoping for a taxi, bus, or even a hitchhiked ride. The ten year old bag boy at the grocery store insisted on helping her with the purchases and answered that "*sí*" there was a bus. He then insisted on waiting with her so that he could impor- tantly tell the driver her destination.

In the morning, Gringa made several trips to the Administration office look- ing for American quarters necessary to work the laundry facilities. The Adminis- tration office had a sign stating morning hours started at eight thirty am, and by eleven am and her fifth trip, Gringa was pretty steamed when the administration teenager finally put in an appearance. He shrugged at the mention of the time of day and seemed even less apologetic for not being able to supply any change.

(One would think that after six months in the country such often expressed attitudes would have mellowed Gringa somewhat, but she found herself quickly re-acclimating to North American expectations.) She was very grateful when a fellow traveller, with Alaska licence plates, offered her the change she needed.

San Carlos campground

By noon they were on the road again, this time heading north to Hermesillo, capital of the State of Sonora. It was Sunday and a short drive would allow them time to check in to the chosen hotel, have a sight seeing tour of the capital, and settle down in the comfort of their room in time to watch the hockey play-offs on satellite cable.

They passed a Tecate factory and factory store on their approach to downtown. The Man wanted to stop to drop off empties and restock his beer supply but his wife convinced him they should locate the hotel and check in first. It was not quite one o'clock and there was plenty of time. They had a coupon showing very modern rooms in a hotel described as a historic piece of Hermosillo and she was anxious to be sure that they would get a room without a prior reservation.

They located the hotel and were pleased to see that it had a car park. The building looked historically non-descript unless one was envisioning some fine piece of architecture from the Stalin era. The surrounding area, too, was rather run down and might have seen its heyday a half century ago. Still, the lobby of the hotel was reasonably modern and the desk clerk assuring about room availability and cable television. They finished signing the register and Gringa inquired about the nearest store to buy beer.

"Sorry *senora*, they are all closed because it is Sunday. In Hermosillo, you cannot buy liquor after 2:00 in the afternoon on a Sunday."

"But this is Mexico!" Gringa spluttered unbelievingly. She glanced at her husband whose face was taking on a stony countenance. Pictures of the Tecate factory flashed in her mind. "Don't worry" she muttered, "we'll find you some beer."

They walked up a crooked ramp leading to the building that housed their room. The rooms were arrayed around an inner courtyard with absolutely no access to blue sky or fresh air anywhere. They took the stairs to their floor and passed a number of rooms, all with curtains pulled tight against peeping toms passing by. Their door opened into an old fashioned room with double beds and décor from the forties or garish fifties. They didn't bother pulling back the curtains. Historic indeed! The only thing indicating history of any sort was the fact that all of the corridors on all of the floors were sloped and uneven—but maybe that was shoddy workmanship and not time-worn history at all? At least the television worked and the schedule did indeed indicate the desired hockey game.

They set out on their beer quest thinking that they would retrace their steps to the Tecate factory store. First they stopped at a gas station with a convenience store. Stacks of cases of beer lined one end and the cooler was full of refrigerated beverages. Gringa pulled a six pack out barely glancing at the yellow tape and moved to the cash register. The clerk apologetically said they could not sell beer as it was after two pm.

The found the Tecate factory closed.

The Man was looking mightily pissed off as they turned around and headed back to the hotel. "Stop right here!" Gringa called out. She had spotted a cantina and it was obviously open. "Wait here," she called and hopped out. She circled to the front door and pushed into a small square building with all of its windows blacked out. Inside, the low-ceilinged room was full … of men … and the jukebox was deafening. Still, in Gringa's mind everything in the place came to a silent halt as she set foot in. Obviously not a place with a steady tourist trade. She determinedly headed to the bar and asked the elderly *patrone* if she could purchase six cold beers to go. The woman regarded her suspiciously and said no. Gringa persisted, swearing that she was a tourist and would tell no one where she managed to buy beer. She offered to pay whatever price the bartendress wanted, but still the answer was no. Gringa turned to find her husband at her elbow. He looked around and suggested quietly that she forget it and they get out of there. Images of news headlines about slain tourist bodies found dumped in a seedy part of town flashed through their minds. Still, Gringa was determined to redeem herself for refusing to stop to buy beer when it was available. "Go get the backpack," she asked her husband. When he brought it to her, Gringa pushed the empty backpack towards the bartendress. "Please *senora*," she pleaded in Spanish, "it's very important." The bartendress took a look at the Man and back to Gringa.

"One hundred twenty pesos and you tell no one," she muttered as she shoved a six pack of Tecate into the backpack.

Gringa paid her, thanked her profusely and grabbed backpack and husband in a haste to be out of there. The price was six times the beer's value, it was her husband's least favourite brand but it was beer on a Sunday in Hermosillo.

They stowed the beer in their cooler back in the hotel room, and set off for a quick view of the sights before the hockey game started. The fashionable part of Hermosillo's downtown was only a few blocks away. Typically, the cathedral flanked the central square where the Mexicans paraded in their Sunday church clothes but it was early for the proper promenade and not many people were about. Sonora was an agriculturally important state, and so it seemed fitting that there would be pigs rooting about under a tree in front of the cathedral. Otherwise, the city looked dusty and self important with little to recommend it for sight seeing.

Hermosillo square

Back in their room, the Man got comfortable on the bed with pillow supporting head and back in supreme television watching mode. He had a cold beer in his hand and readied himself for the game. He flipped to ESPN 2 and desultorily watched the end of the baseball game—baseball was a time wasting sport in his mind. The game ended and the announcer promised the quick turn now to the NBA basketball playoff game. "What!" exclaimed the Man. He quickly flipped through the channels to ESPN 1 but there was the same basketball game. He ran through all the channels and checked the guide again. The guide said hockey, the television showed basketball. He was ballistic, but there was nothing for it—basketball had won over hockey in the Mexican programming decision.

Gringa suggested they might as well go out for dinner, and offered a suggestion of a promising-sounding Mexican buffet restaurant. They drove there, after getting lost a few times, to find a place full of Mexicans with undisciplined children, and a menu with inflated prices. Definitely not what he was in the mood for. Gringa checked the guidebook and found an alternate restaurant. She offered directions, but badly, and they found themselves pulling off the freeway a couple of times. Her husband's mood was not improving. They finally found themselves in a hopeful looking neighbourhood and Gringa spotted the steakhouse she had picked out. "There!" she cried, and her husband spun the wheel to turn. Brakes screeched and horns blared—he had unwittingly run a red light and they were lucky not to have been in an accident. Now the chance of a happy meal seemed light years beyond them. She hoped desperately that a proper cocktail (could they make martinis?) and a decent meal would put the Man in a better mood.

The steakhouse offered a passable martini, although the Man thinking again on the near accident, decided to stick with beer. The steak was delicious—a real steak and not some deflated cow's ear—and the meal did make him feel somewhat better, particularly when his wife paid. They returned to the hotel without mishap and the sports news had a line telling him his team had lost 3–1. It was good to turn out the lights on this frustrating day.

Run for the Border

In the morning they made the final run for the border. Truth be told, Gringa was ready to put Mexico behind her—at least for a while. The Man was more nostalgic and annoyed Gringa with his utterances of "saying good-bye to Mexico forever" and "we'll never come this way again". Most unlikely, and certainly Gringa was not ready to put future vacations away forever. Right now it seemed more pressing to get back to Canada and find a place to live, get her consulting business fledgling, reacquaint with their household effects.

They arrived in Nogales mid-morning and without mishap. Nogales was supposed to be a sleepy border crossing without much traffic. In reality it was a fair sized town with a disproportionate number of auto part shops of giant box store variety. They visited one in the hopes of scoring a musical horn for Juanita. The Man had visions of announcing his daily arrival home to the tune of "Tequila", or of sneaking up on Asian drivers in Vancouver with a blast of the "Mexican Hat Dance." They were mightily disappointed to learn that the "*klaxons*" were illegal. According to the sales clerk, they were illegal all over Mexico—this fellow had obviously never ventured out of his home state.

The line up to the border crossing was a sight to behold. Twelve lanes across at minimum, it resembled a huge drive-in theatre parking lot with all the participants creeping along in a fog of exhaust. To the one side, big rigs were directed into a giant drive-through box equipped with x-ray equipment.

It didn't take long, less than an hour, and they were approaching US customs. After an absence of more than six months and with a Canadian's natural guilt at any goods brought in legally or over limit, Gringa was prepared to let her husband do all the talking. She hoped he wouldn't be too chatty. The border guard had long since gotten over 9/11. "Any food products?"

"No."

"Dog looks bored … Going home?"

"Yes."

And they were into the United States. They had lived in Mexico six months and eight days.

Tuscon

They found a familiar Motel 6 with an empty lot next door that had Dog so excited chasing gophers that her business went unattended. Gringa tromped next door to a grocery store and stocked up on a barbecue chicken and salads for dinner and treated her husband to Guinness and Grolsch beer. It seemed strange to be back in the States and the lack of Mexican voices was disconcerting.

Next morning, they moved on to Phoenix. Gringa re-acclimated with a trip to the mall. A short power shopping stint loaded her up with foot lotion, running shoes, and a new outfit for the planned trip to Las Vegas; she would look fine in her gold silk pants and silk black sweater. Next they located a vet and Dog restocked with anti-flea/anti-tick medication.

The hockey game was not on television—a good thing because the Canucks lost. Gringa took the Man back to the mall to buy some dress pants so that he would look equally as fine in Las Vegas. Juanita's cooling light came on inexplicably in the parking lot and set up new worries. Over Chinese food in a nearby restaurant, Gringa tried to ease her husband's mind; at least they were in the land of VW dealerships and parts ready at hand.

In the morning the Man phoned one of the local VW repair shops. A phone diagnosis indicated a new thermostat might be required but none were in stock. More phone calls located and reserved the part in Las Vegas. They would just keep close watch on the coolant level until then.

Gringa and Dog in the meantime were outside watching some snooty King Charles Spaniels being exercised. They were living the room next door. The owners seemed a bit humourless but then they had travelled over a thousand miles to breed their bitch. Of course the show dogs were not allowed to associate with Dog.

Juanita's coolant level was checked and the bags loaded. The cooling light remained dark and they set off for the short one hundred sixty kilometer drive to Dead Horse Ranch State Park. This proved to be a green little oasis in the desert, close to the mountains. The pamphlet informed this was a historic area of the Verde Valley and warned of rattlesnakes and scorpions. Gringa offered to set up camp while the Man and Dog ventured off for a walk. On their return, the Man admitted that Dog had startled a two foot snake though he insisted it wasn't a rattler. Gringa was grateful there was a good size step up into the camper and couldn't imagine tenting in a place like this. They say you have to be especially careful about snakes and scorpions in April and May, and when daytime highs are above eighty-two degrees Fahrenheit—Great! It's April and Arizona was in a heat wave!

Late afternoon they built a fire and readied steaks for cooking. A chatty retired couple in the site across the way engaged them in conversation. Their motor-home was thirty-eight feet long with two slide-out rooms. The owner from Wisconsin proudly pointed out all the electronic gear and stowage space. They kept up the conversation until the cooking fire coals were almost out. Despite that, Man, Gringa and Dog shared a good t-bone for dinner. The fire was restoked and mellow music on the Juanita's tape player played softly. They enjoyed orange brandy and the desert stars until midnight.

Las Vegas

They decided to head out in the morning with the intention of getting closer to Vegas for Friday.

Reading Beauty and the Beast

A little Texan girl came by to play with Dog while camp was dismantled and the dishes and chairs stowed on Juanita's roof. The four year old kept up a steady stream of dialogue regarding her love for dogs and cats. When Dog refused to play, the girl trotted off to her campsite and returned with a book in hand. She plunked herself on a log next to Dog and read *Beauty and the Beast* to her less than attentive audience.

Their drive took them up a winding, mountainous road through Jerome—a historic and charming town carved into the mountainside. An hour later, the road flattened out and they picked up speed. They commented on the number of motorcycles sharing the road, mostly Harleys. A stop at a gas station provided the information of some large motorcycle get together in Laughlin.

They stopped at the Hoover Dam and marvelled at the modern look considering it was built in the 1930s. It still looked futuristic. Gringa could tell that her husband was itching to take the available tour but the day was quite warm and it would be unfair to leave Dog in the camper.

They crossed over the dam and enjoyed the mountain scenery along the Colorado River. Eventually they pulled into a campground by Lake Mead. Las Vegas was only thirty miles away but they decided to camp so that they could eat up most of their perishables.

After dinner they played dice games and settled up the scores from games played over the last several months. The Man was quite disgusted to find himself owing his wife $120.00 US, and claimed the points system was rigged to favour games she was good at. Gringa argued that stakes had been agreed to long ago. She was looking forward to having play money for the casinos.

They were in Las Vegas by ten am the next day. They missed a turn-off and wound up approaching the Strip from the north in a backwards way. They had picked up a discount coupon book and drove around looking for the Klondike Motel—$29.95/night plus free dinner and breakfast seemed a deal too good to be true. And it was: for one thing they arrived on a Friday and all cheap deals were for Sunday to Thursday only. One motel had a big sign outside advertising rooms for $19.99 but the desk clerk said "It's a busy weekend and we don't have many rooms left so we're charging ninety dollars." Gringa commented that the motels certainly don't jump up in class to match the increase in rates. In the end, they wound up back at the Klondike, even if the rates were higher than advertised. This motel looked a bit seedy on the outside but had comfortable enough rooms with 40s vintage furniture. It also featured a short-sheeted king size bed. Still, it was accessible and was on the Strip just across from the Luxor.

They found Dog a nice place to stay at the Animal Inn reasonably close by. Her room rate was $18.50 per day and included play time.

Next on the agenda was the VW shop for the thermostat. The shop proved to be well out in the boonies and they felt they were half way back to Mexico by the time they located it. The outfit would do well in Mexico as well (it had that flavour) and was run by a long-haired, over aged hippy type. He sold them the thermostat but said there was really no need to install it. Either he was too busy or he didn't know how. Juanita had been behaving in the last while, so the Man took the hippy's advice.

Back in Las Vegas, they joined the throngs of tourists gawping at the hotels. They are fantastic—everything from pyramids to castles, pirate ships to New York skyline, Paris, Venice and the Roman forum. They decided that their favourite was the Venetian with its two Guggenheim museums, and entrance portico and lobby with ceilings that could have been painted by Michelangelo. The shopping arcade replicated Venice complete with canal and singing gondoliers. The walkway opened to a square where period costumed staff entertained with lutes, juggling, and opera. Most amazing was the ceiling painted like a sky, with lights changing the look to simulate the passing of the daylight hours. One would never guess that you were not outdoors.

The casinos were mind-bogglingly big, bright, and noisy. The first slots they played cashed out eighty dollars in quarters to the Man but those triumphs were short lived and their buckets were soon empty again. It was easy to understand how the casinos could offer free drinks as the odds were definitely against you. Drinks were not all that readily available either as some times the waitresses ignored you. The Man caught on that the servers were quick to serve those who were playing. He fed a five dollar bill into a slot machine and asked his wife to let him know when a server was in the vicinity. At her signal, he hit the "cash out" button and the machine discharged his five dollars in quarters. At the clinking sound of the "pay out" the server immediately came over and offered a drink. Now that the Man had an action plan for a steady supply of import beer, he was ready to take Vegas on.

Gringa had often fantasized about attending a show in Las Vegas. She pictured sitting at a cute table for two, stage side, and enjoying cocktails along with the finest entertainment. They dithered about whether to see Rich Little or Robin Williams but settled for a dinner show recommended by the Tourist Bureau—"Fielding West's Magic Tricks and Naked Chicks". It was affordable and came with a steak and lobster dinner.

They had a cocktail in their room as they dressed for the great evening out. Gringa even dusted on some makeup—something completely foreign after all these months in Mexico. She complimented her husband on his classy looks and they set out for the Flamingo Hotel.

The Flamingo, though a well known name, had passed its glory days at least two decades ago. It had a very small casino in the lobby, with mostly slots and tellingly, these were predominanntly the nickel variety. Nothing high end here. They presented their tickets for the show and were directed to the restaurant for dinner. Gringa was very disappointed that one dream was obviously going down the tubes. Her disappointment was soon lost to humour. She and her very well dressed husband found themselves in a brightly lit luncheonette surrounded by fellow show-goers dressed in their finest jeans, shorts, and t-shirts. So much for glamour! Dinner was indeed steak and lobster although the meal had a more fast-food than gourmet dining feel to it—maybe it was the little plastic packets of salad dressing.

After dinner they were herded into the theatre. It was intimate (ok, small) and had the little tables. Unfortunately you had to go out to the casino bar to fetch your own drinks. Fielding West took the stage with his two showgirls. Gringa commented that their boob jobs had not gone well—the breasts were of an unlikely size and so perky they seemed to point in the wrong direction. Her husband commented he didn't see anything wrong with them. In the end, the show was a very amusing blend of ribald humour and cheesy magic tricks and they left feeling well entertained. The Man even scored a t-shirt as a memento though his wife doubted she would be seen anywhere in public with him wearing it.

They wandered through the Bellagio Casino on their way back to the motel. Gringa felt twenty dollars burning a hole in her pocket and wanted to play roulette. At a five dollar minimum bet, she would probably just manage one drink. Her husband left her and came back twenty minutes later to find his wife with a tumbler full of Bailey's beside her and her eyes sparkling with excitement. She won another betting round, then lost one and wisely decided to cash in. She had translated her twenty dollars into one hundred twenty (back to where she started) and was flushed with victory (and Bailey's!).

They headed back to their motel. Gringa had the full gambler's haze on and insisted on trying her hand at blackjack. The blackjack tables at the big casinos were intimidating but their local allowed you to bet as little as fifty cents at a time. The Man grumbled that it was well past bedtime. Gringa played a few hands but found that even in this casual atmosphere, their dealer could be snarly about little things like lifting your cards for a peek. And so they called it a night.

Death Valley—Some Make It
And Some Don't

The next morning they packed up and headed to the hotel restaurant for a complimentary breakfast of bacon and eggs. The eggs were runny, barely cooked—Gringa was constantly amazed by cooks' abilities to ruin simple fried eggs—and the Man complained that he received ham instead of bacon. Gringa said "That's Canadian back bacon." to which the Man vigorously retorted that he could tell the difference between ham and bacon, and this was not bacon. Gringa thought about making a bet but felt the pickings were too easy. She would simply point out back bacon the next time there were in a grocery story.

They collected Dog at the Animal Inn. Dog was beside herself with joy to see that she hadn't been permanently abandoned. The caregivers reported that Dog had behaved well though had ignored her food. The Man and Gringa realized that Dog hadn't been separated from them for more than a few hours in the entire trip so some anxiety at the boarding kennel was to be expected. Besides, she seemed none the worse though with her skinny body meals were important. Dog happily bounced onto her seat in the camper and settled down for a snooze.

They drove through the desert and arrived at Furnace Creek in Death Valley. The campground was at one hundred eighty feet below sea level. The campsite offered some straggly trees for shade, but the rest of Death Valley's landscape was bare and harsh. The borax salted earth undulated in interesting dunes and one could easily picture themselves as on the moon.

Once camp was set up, the Man announced he was going to go to the Tourist Information Centre for maps and information on a possible route to Yosemite. Gringa said she needed to catch up on her diary. Dog, who had seemed listless on the drive, was sleeping in the shade of a tree and showed no interest in going for a walk, so the Man set off on his own.

Gringa looked up from her writing and was startled by a coyote crossing the road fifty feet away from her. Her first thought was that Dog had slipped her lead but a look over her shoulder confirmed that Dog was still sound asleep. She got her camera and snapped some photos of the coyote ignoring her at one hundred paces and Dog ignoring her at ten.

The Man returned and reported that the information centre was very interesting and informative. Unfortunately though, Yosemite's roads remained inaccessible until June and so that route was out. Gringa told her story of the surprise coyote visit, although the coyote had by now moved off. Dog, however, hadn't moved a muscle and they were starting to get a little concerned.

There wasn't much else to do in this campsite, so Gringa took herself off to visit the Tourist Info Centre. She browsed through the exhibits and the shop and bought a heat activated t-shirt that changed from white to pastel steer skulls and the motto "Death Valley—some make it, some don't".

That evening, Dog refused to eat anything, and more worryingly, refused to drink water. She staggered and had to be helped into the camper, unable to jump the short step. Then she started shivering and vomiting. Gringa and the Man were seriously worried; Dog was obviously very ill but they were miles from any town and it was late. They covered Dog to help stop the shivering but were unable to coax any water down her throat. All through the night, they woke repeatedly and checked on Dog, fearing the worst. Gringa felt very guilty about her t-shirt and prayed it wasn't prophetic.

In the morning they headed off at first light. Dog had survived the night but was still wobbly and refusing food and drink. They needed a vet and the nearest town was Ridgecrest on the other side of Death Valley.

Gringa spotted a veterinary's office as they entered the town. She jumped out of the camper and ran ahead, calling for her husband to carry Dog in. She rushed to the counter and breathlessly said to the woman "We're travelling and our dog is very, very sick. We need to see a vet right away."

The woman behind the counter looked at her. "Do you have an appointment?"

Gringa was stupefied. She repeated her message as her husband came in with Dog walking on a leash.

"I can give you an appointment for this afternoon but it will cost you extra," the woman came out with.

Gringa could not believe her ears. She asked if there was another vet in town. Unbelievably, the woman confirmed that there was but would not give directions on how to get there, saying instead "But you don't have an appointment there either …"

Gringa grabbed her husband's arm and slammed through the door before the woman could finish the sentence.

They found the other vet's office a number of blocks away, and again Gringa was out of the camper ahead of the Man and Dog. She rushed up to the receptionist and again ran through her breathless spiel about Dog being very ill.

This receptionist looked at her and said "I can give you an appointment for this afternoon ..."

Gringa lost it. "What is the matter with you people in this town? What is it about emergency that you don't understand? My dog is sick and we need to see a vet NOW!"

Of course, at that moment the Man came in with Dog happily wagging her tail. For some reason, she liked going to the vet and treated it as a fun experience. She didn't look particularly sick either which made Gringa look churlish.

Gringa explained what had been happening and the receptionist countered that by offering an appointment in the afternoon she was simply giving them a way to avoid paying an emergency call fee. Gringa politely, again, explained that they were travelling and did not have hours to spend waiting for an appointment.

The vet examined Dog and wondered aloud whether it might be the parvo virus. Gringa didn't feel that was possible because Dog's vaccinations were all up to date. The vet suggested that some lab tests might need to be run, and Dog hospitalized at least overnight. The prospective bill was adding up over a thousand dollars with no sign of a diagnosis.

"Isn't it possible that dogs get flu?" Gringa wondered. She also asked whether Dog could not be simply hydrated by injection rather than running a lot of expensive tests looking for the unknown.

The vet took a bag of saline solution and injected the liquid under the skin around Dog's ruff. Minutes after the solution was completely transferred, Dog felt herself perk up.

Gringa and the Man decided that they would purchase a supply of the intravenous bags and needles and treat Dog along the way. If she didn't improve, the Vet said she would telephone a prescription for an antibiotic into any pharmacy they requested. They paid the bill, already over two hundred dollars, and set out. As soon as Dog climbed back in the camper, she headed for her water dish and had a big long drink. Thirst satisfied, she settled on her bench for a snooze.

By now it was early afternoon and there didn't seem much point in making a long trek. The map showed a state park on the edge of the Mojave Desert just over thirty miles away. They decided to try for a campsite there, hoping that the early arrival would provide a better choice of first come, first served sites.

Red Rock Canyon State Park offered no frills campsites tucked up against hoodoos. The park was very barren, but beautiful with the strange rock formations. Adding their tired physical and mental state, the whole atmosphere took on a surreal lunar feel. With their customary efficiency, they had Juanita's roof popped and camp assembled. The Man enticed Gringa and Dog for a walk before the sun set. They managed a half mile loop before it became obvious that Dog was completely out of energy so they returned to their site. Dog managed a couple of sips of water, but turned her nose away from any offer of food. They still had a couple of logs in the camper from their stay in Death Valley and the Man created a small campfire out of a few sticks. The meagre fire was welcome because as the sun disappeared behind the rock formations, the air grew noticeably colder. Soon they were all shivering and took refuge in Juanita's warmth.

Camping in Red Rock Canyon

The next morning, Dog was as listless as ever, refusing both food and water. The Man confidently connected an IV bag to a fresh needle and injected at Dog's ruff. Gringa commented on his dexterity and praised Dog for not even flinching. She held the plastic pouch aloft to speed the fluids and the bag was empty within about ten minutes. Thus revived, Dog immediately headed to her water dish for an energetic slurp. The Man checked Juanita's coolant levels and topped her reservoir off, and they set off.

As they drove along, Gringa kept glancing back at Dog. A pattern soon emerged; as the fluids were absorbed and used up by Dog's body, she became listless and stopped drinking. Inject her with fluids and she would rush to her water bowl, though food was still problematic. At noon they stopped at a gas station and reboosted Dog's fluids through the IV injection, and Juanita's fluids through additional coolant and gas. Gringa decided that it might be best if they put Dog on the antibiotics in addition to the fluids. They were heading for Paso de Robles and could phone the vet for a prescription from a pharmacy there.

The road wound over some hills and down to a flat plain. Soon vineyards appeared and the countryside grew more verdant. This was countryside lush and beautiful with magnificent oaks (the "*Robles*") standing guard over vines and over fields of wildflowers. Gringa tried to take some photos, but they were travelling at highway speed and there weren't any convenient pullouts.

They reached their destination town and pulled into a mall with a Walmart. Gringa ran in to the pharmacy and asked for their telephone number so that she could have a prescription called in. Then she got on the pay phone to the vet's office back in Ridgecrest and asked that the prescription be called in right away. She cursed herself for lack of foresight—should have taken the prescription when they were there.

After about an hour she returned to the pharmacy to pick up the prescription.

"Oh," the assistant exclaimed, "we got the prescription call but didn't realize you were in the store waiting for it." Gringa huffed, and said "Remember me? I asked you an hour ago for the phone number so that I could have the prescription called in from out of town? I explained we were travelling through so where did you think I would be?"

Nothing for it, she would have to wait though the assistant promised that they would have it ready in another half hour. Gringa found her husband sitting patiently near the entrance. She recognized the martyred shopper look. She explained the hang up and suggested that they pick up some warmer clothes, in the former of sweats, while they waited.

After the half hour, she returned to the long line up at the pharmacy. The assistant advised that the pharmacist wanted a word …

"We're just completing the prescription now. I'm sorry it's taken so long, but we didn't have pills in the strength prescribed and the only other option was to give you liquid. Instead, we're just finishing cutting all the tablets in half."

Gringa was stupefied. "You do realize this is for a dog?"

"Yes, the prescription does specify K-9."

"And you don't think it might have been actually easier to get a dog to swallow a liquid rather than shove a pill down its throat?" Gringa queried.

"Well, but these are chewable and they're grape flavoured." came the reply.

Gringa paid for the prescription and returned to her husband, shaking her head in absolute disgust at weird logic.

The Man had not been idle during the interminable wait. He had the appalling news for Gringa that any campgrounds in the area charged well over forty dollars a night, and even at that choices were slim. Gringa pleaded for a motel. She felt beyond stressed and was not in the mood for another cold night of camping. The Man looked at her tear-filled eyes and recognized desperation. He headed off to the pay phone and came back announcing that he'd booked them into a bed and breakfast in near-by Cambria and that the B&B welcomed dogs.

When they checked in the Cambria Shores Inn, they found that the owners' claims that they welcomed dogs more than people was believable. After receiving a key to their room and an invitation to come back later for a welcoming wine and cheese reception, they were handed a basket of goodies for Dog. It contained *Bark Magazine*, a towel for drying off after a beach run, dog cookies, a mat to place food dishes on, and a blanket to sleep on that matched the décor in the room. Dog showed a complete lack of interest in cookies or magazine, being in need of a liquid fix. The Man obliged, and Gringa forced Dog to swallow an antibiotic. Dog showed no appreciation for the grape flavour, and as for chewable—spat the pill out on the first try.

Later, despite the blustery cold wind, they took a bottle of wine and some cheese out to the Adirondack chairs on the front lawn. They cuddled up in blankets thoughtfully provided by the hotel management and enjoyed a calming view of the sun setting into the Pacific.

They ventured back into the picturesque town of Cambria, all new-age California coupled with English village charm, and found an appealing restaurant. They were more than pleased to be allowed to sit on a weather-protected and heated patio with Dog by their side. Gringa ordered prime rib and was happy to see that Dog shared a few morsels.

Blood Too Thin even for California

Next morning, after a lovely brunch of muffins and fruit left hanging in a basket on a specially designed hook outside their door, they checked out and set off. Dog refused food again, and spat out the antibiotic tablets twice before the Man managed to massage them down her throat. Dog was still refusing to drink water unless she had been infused first. They were starting to run low on the IV packs and worried that Dog didn't seem to be getting better.

They pointed Juanita along the coast road, heading north toward Carmel. It was a windy, overcast day, but occasionally the sun would pop out to illuminate the fields of wild California poppies growing in such profusion. The road was narrow and winding but the scenery was spectacular. If it was this beautiful here, they could only imagine the delights of the more famed Oregon coast. They stopped to admire the coastline and let Dog run free but Dog only took a disinterested pee and walked reluctantly along with them.

Gringa took pictures of the poppies and the backdrop of an old ruined abbey before they continued on. About midway to Carmel they had to stop for gas and were shocked at the three dollars a gallon price. The Man said the prices were bound to be higher on this difficult and remote road. Gringa felt it was more a matter of gouging.

They arrived in Carmel and were charmed by the village. The residential streets were tree lined and each house a very upscale cottage. They walked down to the beach—very fine powdered white sand overhung with twisted arbutus trees. They could see famed Pebble Beach Golf Course on the point and promised themselves a closer look. Dog was let off leash for a run, but for one short burst she wasn't remotely interested in playing games and was leery of checking out the local canine action. They wandered back to towards Juanita and decided to look for a place to stay. The money in this town was abundant and readily apparent. It dawned on them that despite the number of restaurants and high end stores, there was a complete absence of neon which gave the place a very restful aspect. Gringa would have liked to spend more time poking through the shops and galleries but her husband was worried about parking tickets and Dog just wanted to sleep.

California poppies

They stopped in at a visitor information booth to get the low down on affordable accommodations. The guide was extremely enthusiastic about all the listings on offer but his enthusiasm was suspicious when they realized that he was quite confused about the exact location of most of the listings. Still, they located and checked in at the El Adobe Motel in neighbouring Monterrey—a smallish room but with a king-size bed. Nearby was an organic superstore, a Mecca for health conscious Californians. It was bigger than most Safeways and everything within was organic or homeopathic. Gringa splurged on a can of organic dog food and hoped the gourmet treat would tempt Dog out of her lethargy.

Back in the room, they hydrated Dog again. Gringa offered up the four dollar a can dog food but Dog took one sniff and turned away. Gringa persisted and scooped some of the dog food in her fingers trying to coax Dog to consume something. Dog felt she was going to heave at the smell of the food but looked in her mistress' eyes and gently took a small lick to appease her. She didn't want to hurt Mom's feelings, but food just did not taste good and all she wanted was to nap in peace.

They went out for dinner, skipping the touristy spots. They had visited Fisherman's Wharf and Cannery Row earlier in the day and been disappointed. The place just had some large restaurants, not much to see and certainly nothing to evoke Steinbeck. Now instead they drove into an older section of Monterrey and found a promising looking Mom-and-Pop-shop type of Japanese restaurant. The Man feasted on sashimi. He particularly enjoyed it because it was sushi without fear. There had been lots of occasions for sushi and sashimi in Manzanillo but somehow, in Mexico eating raw fish always held its subtle element of danger—heat, raw fish, questionable water ... Gringa enjoyed the variety of a bento box and ate all with gusto.

The next morning, after showers and hydrating Dog, they decided to tour Pebble Beach before heading off for San Francisco. Juanita's fluid levels were dutifully checked and her coolant and oil topped before they set off.

The Pebble Beach peninsula was home to several golf courses with mansions in between. It was a very private area and the riff-raff were kept out by charging an entrance fee of seven dollars just to make the seventeen mile drive. They pulled in at Pebble Beach and wandered around. Green fees here were three hundred fifty for eighteen holes—midweek. The par three course was "only" one hundred fifty dollars. They bought a golf ball for the Man's golfing-nut son and Gringa splurged on a Pebble Beach sweatshirt to flaunt on the courses back in Canada (though she didn't dare tell her husband what it cost.) There was something awe-inspiring about being in this famed location and they felt like they had made a holy pilgrimage. At the same time, they both commented on the poor shape the course was in, with patchy fairways instead of the expected lush green.

They left the coast and made the hour's drive to San Francisco. Juanita and the Man found driving here a challenge. The hills were tricky to manoeuvre and Juanita wasn't known for her power. Despite the hills and the volume of traffic, no one seemed inclined to slow down—so much for laid back Californians. After some frustrating motoring, and more frustrating search for affordable accommodation that welcomed dogs, they found a motel on Lombard, near the Presidio. So far San Francisco's welcome was windy, cold, expensive, and anything but romantic.

They settled in to their room and tried force-feeding Dog. Dog wasn't having any part of it though she stood patiently still while the IV needle was again poked into her ruff. Gringa decided that she was going to stop with the antibiotics.

"They're obviously not doing any good and it's a major struggle to get them down her throat," she said to her husband.

They headed to North Beach in search of dinner for themselves. The guide magazines hyped North Beach as the trendy place to be and promised all kinds of funky restaurants. Parking, however, was a nightmare. On street parking was a cutthroat business particularly when coupled with the hills and the traffic. Around Fishermen's Wharf large signs proclaimed free three hour parking but small print revealed this was only when validated after a meal in a particular over-priced, tourist-trap restaurant. In North Beach they circled several blocks only to be beaten out for a parking spot just as they pulled up. The Man was feeling claustrophobic and tense and in the end gave in to Gringa's pleading to pull into a parking lot. Even the parking lots were no picnic as they were small and over-crowded, with the greedy attendants squeezing every inch of space into service whether vehicles got dinged or not. By the time the Man shut off Juanita's engine and handed over ten dollars he was sweating profusely despite the cold.

They wandered around North Beach in wind and rain, finding little charming about the atmosphere. They picked out an Italian restaurant at random. Gringa enjoyed its atmosphere but the Man groused about the paper placemats and glass of crayons on the table. "I'm not five years old for Christ sake," and would not appreciate his wife's comment that the paper and crayons were to stimulate brain-storming during business lunches. And she had to agree that the food was not great either.

They returned to their neighbourhood and took Dog for a walk in the grassy areas around the Presidio. For forty-five minutes they paraded and coaxed but Dog did not so much as sprinkle two drops of pee. The antibiotics and small por-tions she'd been eating had left her constipated as well and she just wanted to get home to bed. They returned to their room bone-chilled. The room was heated but their thinned blood had succumbed to San Francisco's damp. The final romance was taken out of the romantic city when Gringa crawled under the cov-ers fully dressed in a sweat suit. They drifted off in a fitful sleep. The Man's sleep was even more fitful given the Dog chose to wake him at one thirty in the morn-ing to go out and finally have a pee.

The new day dawned bright and sunny. They set off to play tourist starting at Union Square. Parking continued to be a nightmare but they finally found a spot well away from the square in seedier part of town. The locals hailed them with "Yo bro" and "what's going down my man" and gestures that left the Man quite nervous about leaving Dog to guard the vehicle. He walked his wife as far as Union Square and then decided to head back to retrieve the vehicle even before the hour was up on the meter. He would take Dog to the park and meet his wife at Fisherman's Wharf in time for lunch.

Gringa, in the meanwhile, set off for a shopping 'fix'. She wandered through Neiman Marcus and marvelled that anyone would pay seven hundred dollars for a simple black cardigan. She played a game with herself, imagining that price was no object and found that she still wasn't tempted by any 'purchases'. Feeling somewhat deflated, she jumped on a cable car to head to Fisherman's Wharf. The last stop was a considerable distance from where she was to meet her husband and with time running short, she hailed a pedi-cab to take her the last eight blocks. The trip cost ten dollars and left her grumpy.

They had lunch at one of the tourist spots to take advantage of the parking bonus. The Man had traditional fish and chips, while Gringa settled for some onion rings—she was allergic to fish. After the meal, they checked on Dog, sleeping peacefully on Juanita's back bench, and left her for a round trip cable car ride. Gringa commented that she felt San Francisco was overrated as a city, but agreed that it might be strain over Dog's health and their limited funds that coloured her view.

In the evening, they decided to give North Beach another try. This time the trip went smoother as they returned directly to the previous night's parking lot. They had a drink in a crowded Irish bar, and then wandered around people watching. They couldn't decide on a restaurant and so settled on a pizza to go. In the pizza shop, an outlandishly dressed couple in their mid thirties came in to collect their to-go order. The man had huge, oversized eyeglasses that served to highlight his severely bucked teeth, while his companion had actual feathers stuck in her blue, fake-feathered hair. This couple picked up their pizza and then settled in at a nearby table to eat. The restaurant owner didn't seem too thrilled with this clientele and they weren't even offered napkins. Gringa and her husband collected their own pizza and returned to the hotel for dinner.

They hydrated Dog again, and Gringa fed her a couple of fingerfulls of dog food. Dog was not getting any better and they worried that another trip to the vet might be required. Dog had now gone five days with almost no food and her already skinny body was beginning to look emaciated.

Sunny Wine Country and Gourmet Sonoma Food

They crossed the Golden Gate Bridge and found themselves bathed in warm sunlight. As they headed through the wine country, the day warmed up enough for them to feel comfortable in just t-shirts. That alone was enough to brighten their spirits, as was the sight of Dog slurping water this morning without having been hydrated first.

They stopped in Sonoma, and parked in the main square. Gringa eyed all the enticing shops and said "OK, I have to check these out. I'll be back in an hour," and left her husband and Dog. When she returned, she found her husband sitting with the camper's side door open, sharing a picnic with Dog.

"A man came out of that restaurant" he explained pointing to a black door in front of the camper. "It's some kind of supper club. Anyway, he said he thought our dog looked hungry. I explained to him that she has been ill and not wanting food. He went in and came back out with a big sack of food. Look—a whole roast pork, prosciutto ham, a whole roasted and deboned chicken. And believe it or not, Dog made a liar out of me and gobbled roast pork in front of the man as if she had never seen food before! As for the rest, it's mighty gourmet stuff here and Dog can share!"

They were delighted with this turn of events, not the food itself but Dog's appetite. Dog was obviously feeling better! Gringa led her husband and Dog to a nearby Irish pub to celebrate. They sat outside with Dog at their feet. Gringa was even more delighted to find the bar offered Strongbow Cider—a treat she had not had since leaving Canada. Sitting in the sunshine, enjoying good Irish food and drink, they found the strain of the last week slipping away.

At length, they tore themselves away and drove another thirty miles to Sugarloaf Ridge State Park. Here they camped under towering trees fringing an alpine meadow. A river near their campsite was home to a chorus of noisy frogs. Despite it being early in the camping season, the park was quite busy. They collected firewood and sat at the campfire watching impromptu soccer games in the field. The air cooled considerably as the sun set, but both Gringa and the Man felt suddenly so stress free, they sat by the fire well after dark.

The Redwoods and Dog Rebounds

By the next morning, Dog had fully recovered. She poked her wet nose into Dad's face at the crack of dawn, anxious to be let out for a pee and to explore those noisy frogs. After her morning ablutions, she attacked the shared bacon and egg breakfast with gusto. As quickly as she had become sick, so too she recovered; the diagnosis of the illness would remain forever a mystery.

They broke camp and travelled north through more wine country. After about four hours they came to Humboldt State Redwoods Park. The State Park road paralleled the highway and was called the Avenue of Giants. Enormous stately redwoods towered on either side of the road giving credence to the name. They toured several of the campsites and found them eerily dark and shadowed by the massive trees. Some sunlight barely managed to filter to the ground but the over-all aspect was gloomy and the Man commented that it would be cold camping there. They chose instead the Albee campsite situated on an old homestead and orchard.

They set up camp intent to stay a couple of days to give themselves a break from travelling. They headed into nearby Eureka to do laundry and stock up on food. Gringa took herself off for a ten dollar haircut and then bemoaned the sad results. She also stopped in a pet store and bought their husky a coat. It would help keep some of the wind out and wouldn't look quite as silly as Dog wrapped up in blankets and her husband's jean jacket.

Dog was noticeably friskier now and they played a game of monkey in the middle, tossing a ball between them. The leash was restricting Dog, so Gringa removed it thinking Dog would stay nearby so long as the ball game was on. That lasted about two minutes: Dog suddenly perked up her head and took off. She accelerated at a speed most automakers would rave about, in pursuit of a deer some five hundred yards distant. She caught up with the deer just as it sprang over an old, overgrown hedge. The hedge was no deterrent to Dog either and she disappeared from sight.

Cold camping

The Man went running after Dog, whistling and calling while Gringa headed in an angled direction to hopefully cut off the path. Dog was no where to be seen and was still not responding to their calls a half hour later. Gringa and the Man rendezvoused in a thicket of ancient fruit trees and discussed strategy; Gringa would return to the campsite and the Man would continue the search.

Finally, almost an hour later, Gringa spied Dog well collared and being lead back by her husband.

"I was calling and calling her but couldn't find her," her husband panted. "Then all of a sudden she was right by my side in all this thick scrub. She brushed against me and I almost had a heart attack thinking it was some wild creature, she was that quiet."

Dog stayed on a leash thereafter. As the sun set, the temperature grew steadily cooler. They sat as close to the fire as possible, almost in it, desperately seeking warmth. Dog's new coat was several sizes too big but she had the sash wrapped around her belly keeping it in place. Despite the coat, she shivered continuously and looked a very abject picture of a snow dog.

Home

Over the next couple of days, they travelled the rest of the route back to Canada. They pointed Juanita along the Oregon coast even though it was less direct. The coast road led through small towns and some wild bays, and they occasionally stopped to explore. Gringa found the famed Oregon coast wasn't as colourful as the California coast, and wasn't as wild or rugged as the British Columbia coast. Obviously the Oregonians were very good at marketing even though the product wasn't up to competition elsewhere!

They crossed into Washington State at Astoria. There were several Tall Ships in the bay and they felt as if these had been sent especially to welcome them back. They stopped for one last night at a familiar Motel 6 in Washington and felt the circle was complete.

Finally, on May 11th, they presented themselves at the Canadian border.

"Anything to declare?"

"Nothing much, just the usual touristy stuff well under the limit," Gringa blithely replied.

"Did you do any improvements to your vehicle?" the border guard asked. "If you made improvements to your vehicle you have to pay duty."

The Man turned pale. "What qualifies as an improvement? We had to have the pistons replaced ..." He was thinking that this was a final irony. Just as he was feeling relief at Juanita having successfully brought them home, here came one last whopping bill.

"Well I'd say that having the pistons replaced would be called a necessary repair and not an improvement," said the border guard. "You couldn't very well drive without pistons could you. You didn't have air conditioning or anything like that put in?"

The Man flashed back in his mind to all the dusty repair places and the various parts—the rocker arm in the depths of the Taxco desert, the bent pistons in Melaque, the head gasket in Alamos and Navajoa, the thermostat in the Nevada desert (still uninstalled).

Tall Ships in Astoria

"No, no improvements."

"Have a nice day," said the border guard. And they were home. Still homeless, but home.

Epilogue

Juanita continued to present problems off and on during the following summer. She would mysteriously sputter to a stop and refuse to start. A mechanic found pieces of silicone clogging her gas lines.

Finally, on a trip between British Columbia and Alberta, she overheated one last time. Luckily this happened in Kamloops near a VW repair place familiar with Juanita's conniptions. In the end, Juanita had a complete engine replacement and she has faithfully carried the family on further journeys. Just to keep things interesting, she still has the occasionally choking fit to remind the Man that she needs a new gas tank installed. The family has no plans whatsoever to part with her, and the Man is confident that Juanita could easily carry them on his dream trip to the tip of South America and back. Gringa is a bit leery.

Dog has never again exhibited the illness that plagued her through the trip back through the United States. She still does not recognize chewable tablets, but other than the occasional deworming pill, these have been unnecessary. She is a robust fifty pounds and still fast as lightening. She has also never differentiated between Mexico beaches and their long driveway and loves to weave her dolphin-like run now in front of cars—very unnerving for guests.

Gringa and the Man remain happily married and are always looking for the next adventure.

978-0-595-44274-4
0-595-44274-9

Printed in the United States
78920LV00004B/190-219

9 780595 442744